Buckskin & Broadcloth

Buckskin & Broadcloth

A Celebration of

E. Pauline Johnson

Tekahionwake

1861-1913

Sheila M.F. Johnston

Canadian Cataloguing in Publication Data

Johnston, Sheila M. F.
Buckskin & broadcloth: a celebration of E. Pauline Johnson-Tekahionwake 1861-1913

Includes bibliographical references and index.
ISBN 1-896219-20-9

1. Johnson, E. Pauline (Emily Pauline), 1861-1913.
2. Poets, Canadian (English) - 19th century - Biography.
3. Mohawk Indians - Canada - Biography. I. Title.
II. Title: Buckskin and broadcloth.

PS8469.0283Z72 1997 C811.4 C97-931195-0
PR9199.2.J63B82 1997

Natural Heritage Books

Published by Natural Heritage/Natural History Inc.
P.O. Box 95, Station O,
Toronto, Ontario M4A 2M8

Design: Derek Chung Tiam Fook
Editor: Rosemary Tanner
Printed and bound in Canada by Hignell Printing Limited, Winnipeg, Manitoba

Natural Heritage/Natural History Inc. acknowledges the support received for its publishing program from the Canada
Council Block Grant Program. We also acknowledge with gratitude the assistance of the Association for the Export of
Canadian Books, Ottawa.

Le Conseil des Arts | The Canada Council
DU Canada | for the arts
DEPUIS 1957 | SINCE 1957

Emily Pauline Johnson

Tekahionwake

1861-1913

When asked when she was first con-
scious of the wish to write,
Pauline would answer:
"I do not know – unless it was always."

Table of Contents

I dedicate this book to

my husband Simon Johnston;

to my parents E. Madeline and Eric D. Ferguson;

and to the spirit of Emily Pauline Johnson - Tekahionwake

whose example of tenacity and forbearance was invaluable in my completing this project.

E. Pauline Johnson, Christmas, 1897, aged 18.

Introduction

By Sheila M. F. Johnston

*M*uch was written about Pauline Johnson - Tekahionwake during her lifetime. Much has been written about this extraordinary Mohawk poet-performer since her death in 1913. Most of it has been interpretive and subjective. I believe the time has arrived for Pauline to regain her own voice. She left us enough of herself that if we listen closely, we can hear what she has been saying all along.

In researching Pauline Johnson's life over the past seven years I have often wondered-what would it have been like to have spent an afternoon in her company during the last years of her life? Would she show me her collection of clippings from years on tour? Would she allow me to read correspondence she had cherished? Would she pull out snapshots of friends and family members? And would she let me read the poems she left out of her so-called collected work, *Flint and Feather*?

I believe Pauline Johnson would have created an album had she been spared a painful death from breast cancer at the age of 51. *Buckskin & Broadcloth* is that album, as I envision it. This is not an interpretive biography. The narrative I have written aids the reader in enjoying this showcase of her life and work. The excerpts from her short stories, the recounting of interviews, the anecdotes written by her sister, all are woven together to bring her story to life.

Pauline Johnson should enjoy prominence and wide recognition in two fields: literature and theatre. Canadian writers should acknowledge the standards she set in poetry and prose. Canadian performers owe her a debt for having blazed a trail across the stages of this country, before the advent of the tour bus or aeroplane.

She was a natural, passionate, stirring, sincere and comedic performer. She made her audiences laugh, cry and reflect. She was a trouper, a barnstormer, a vagabond, an itinerant player. She was a pioneer of Canadian theatre and she single-handedly invented the concept of "Canadian content."

I celebrate Pauline Johnson because she spoke for women. She lived in an era when social values and practices were personified by Queen Victoria, and exploited by the "stronger sex." Members of the so-called "weaker sex" were discouraged from expressing themselves creatively. Housework, child care, personal diary jottings, singing in choirs, and needlework were the accepted creative outlets of Victorian women.

Pauline did not accept her society's boundaries. She had the talent, as well as the need, to express herself. She started with her pen. Later, with a firm voice and a natural dramatic flare, she unbridled her performing talents across Canada, in England, and throughout the United States. Geographical boundaries could not hold her either.

It was as though the pen in her hand, and the audience at her feet, were the keys that unlocked the shackles that her gender and her era's values imposed upon her.

As the daughter of a Mohawk chief and the granddaughter of a Mohawk warrior, she cherished her Native roots and spoke eloquently and articulately on behalf of the First Nations of North America. She eschewed the required sycophancy and politesse regarding her heritage in a predominantly white society.

She proudly, unabashedly and defiantly celebrated her Nativeness by performing her poetry, much of it dealing with Native issues, in buckskin with pride, dignity and integrity.

She spoke from her heart about Canada, just as the country was beginning to take its place in the Twentieth Century. She gave the national personality a much needed shot in the arm. She introduced her audiences in the East to her audiences in the West, and vice versa, by relating stories and personal experiences gained from her constant travelling back and forth across a country which she loved passionately.

Pauline accomplished all of this, plus the publication of three volumes of poetry and three volumes of prose, before movies captured people's attention and imagination. The movies undid much of her work, by introducing audiences around the world to a stereotypical, narrow and wildly inaccurate interpretation of the North American Native. Her aims and North America's popular culture of the Twentieth Century clashed.

Pauline Johnson said: "My aim, my pride, my joy is to sing the praises of my own people." Sing their praises she did, and in so doing, touched people of red skin, white, yellow, brown, or any variation thereof. I hope this book will help Pauline Johnson achieve her aim.

Preface
by Alexandr Vaschenko

E. Pauline Johnson (Tekahionwake) is a phenomenon defying any preconceived ideas, and breaking set boundaries between countries and continents, and above all, between human hearts.

Today is the time when she chooses to re-establish her power and significance, not only as a prominent figure in Canadian literature, but as a world classic.

I had no doubts about this even before. During my first visit to Canada, with a group of writers, as part of our tour we had one day's visit to the City of Vancouver, British Columbia. We arrived late the day before, the protocol being to be present next morning for an official meeting at the City Hall at 10:00 a.m.

Yet, three hours before, the rising sun had found me doing my first priority-my pilgrimage journey on foot to Stanley Park; a visit to Pauline Johnson's resting place. For the City of Vancouver long ago had come into reality for me through Pauline Johnson's magic lines, and thus, once and for all, it was *her* city.

Never shall I forget that quiet morning as I went by the seashore, beyond ships in the distance, beyond time, on a date with one who was once most alive in this beautiful city.

It seems that this person, whom the people knew by crowds, then forgot and regarded as marginal, proved to be central in regard to the universal values, and, therefore, will always call for a celebration.

Pauline Johnson's personality and creative heritage extends important lessons, for they bring joy and life-affirmation with the integrity and fire, equal to herself.

Contemplating this phenomenon, we are forced to redefine the notions of smallness and greatness. At the period of historical crossroads for her Native People, she brought before the public and claimed their oldest traditions, in order to communicate the uttermost truth: all cultures are brothers, just as their bearers should be, in life and beyond death. In her dream of universal peace, she voices her far-off Iroquois ancestor, the legendary Peacemaker.

Her message she brings to us through the wisdom of Native Canadian culture. Yes, she was a romantic; but as a true romantic she had a gift of seeing right to the core of her culture, and expressing it. She acted as a mediator and an advocate between cultures; and she dared to be the first in everything she did.

The chain of miraculous and wonderful events shaping her "shooting star" career, then her literary destiny, continues to this day. One of them is the making of this book.

Indeed, as if in keeping with the tradition of marvellous storytellers who joined in the personality of Pauline Johnson and produced her writing, two creative people of today, Sheila M.F. Johnston, an Anglo-Canadian, and Raymond R. Skye, a Native Canadian, created the "Pauline Project" partnership for the sake of preserving and celebrating Pauline Johnson's name and heritage. They have travelled her paths all over the country and beyond, found many forgotten and lost relics, and made many exciting discoveries. This book is a tribute of deep love, and a result of meticulous analysis; truly, a life-time achievement.

The study of Pauline's biography through rare photographs, original illustrations, and newly discovered poems and letters-all join in to disclose the great significance of Pauline Johnson's contribution to world culture.

This book is unique, and it is multi-faceted: scholars, students, Pauline Johnson's fans, as well as average readers, will use it with equal profit. It is an important reflection of Canadian culture, through literature, history and personality; the solid foundation of which Canadians can be really proud.

It is my firm belief that the readers of various backgrounds, by means of this book, will better understand the essence of Pauline Johnson's complex phenomenon. Because her lively spirit serves as a remedy for all hearts.

Alexandr Vaschenko
Moscow Russia

Alexandr Vaschenko, friend of Sheila Johnston and Raymond Skye, at Chiefswood (birthplace of Pauline Johnson, Six Nations Reserve, Brant County, Ontario). He is holding the book of Miss Johnson's prose and poetry that he translated into Russian and published in Russia. It was a bestseller.

Acknowledgments

The scope of this book demanded that I contact, and correspond with, many people across Canada, and in England and the United States. These people included family members, friends, academics, librarians and archivists, as well as people who wrote to me to express their passion for Pauline. The following acknowledgments attempt to be complete. If, inadvertently, I have neglected to mention anyone whose help I sought and received, I am most apologetic.

I owe a huge debt of gratitude to the late Evelyn H.C. Johnson, Pauline's sister, who, before she died, dictated her memoirs so that we could learn about her family's history. I used these remembrances liberally.

My friend, Marcus Van Steen of Brantford, is the author of the 1965 book *Pauline Johnson: Her Life and Work*, and I thank him for giving me his Pauline papers.

My "Pauline Project" partner, Raymond R. Skye, has been of great assistance to me, over such a long period of time. Many's the time he and I have stood before an audience and related the story of Pauline Johnson's life. He was instrumental in teaching me how to correctly pronounce Pauline's native name, Tekahionwake. His wife Wilma Skye and daughter Shawnee Skye have also been of great assistance to me.

I received nothing but support from friends like Charlene Embling and Mary Price. Support also came from my niece Erica Ferguson and my brother Peter Ferguson who acted as proofreaders. My dear parents, Eric and Madeline Ferguson, did double duty as research assistants and proofreaders. Of course my husband, Simon Johnston, has helped me over the rough bits. My husband's siblings who reside in Ontario, William Johnston and Jacqueline Johnston, have been unerring in their support for my work; his sister Valerie Hofer in Vancouver was of great help to me when I conducted research and fulfilled public speaking engagements in Vancouver; and his brother Peter Johnston, who lives in England, helped me track down Pauline's 1894 London address. Thanks to you all.

I enjoy on-going correspondence with three special women who share my passion for Pauline: Phyllis McNinch of Grimsby, Ontario; Isabel Duncan of Vancouver, B.C.; and Helene Marynick of Brantford. I thank them for the encouragement which their letters have given me over the years. I value their friendship highly.

Three friends from the Six Nations agreed to help me when I most needed it: Paula Whitlow, who curates Chiefswood Museum on Six Nations; Sheila Staats; and George Beaver. Tom Hill and his staff at the Woodland Cultural Centre in Brantford lent me their time and expertise. Jeff Burnham and his wife Linda offered me their support and encouragement on numerous occasions. Others from the Six Nations Community who have been helpful include Jake Thomas, Mrs. Florence Hill, Tim Johnson, Scott Smith, Mona Staats, Don Monture, Ron and Belva Monture, Ron and Catherine Roberts, and Eva Williams. I would like to acknowledge members of the Chiefswood Museum Restoration Committee, with whom I had the pleasure of working during the 1980s. I wish the Chiefswood Museum Board of Trustees nothing but success.

Sue Twist formerly of the Brant County Museum in Brantford was always forthcoming with her time and never turned me down when I asked for access to materials in the Brant Historical Society collection. Wayne Hunter, with his vast knowledge of the history of Brantford, was invaluable to me. Thanks also to Jamie Legacy of Brantford.

Brian Wood at the Bell Homestead assisted me in tracking down the rare photograph of Sir Alexander Graham Bell for this book. Marion MacDonald of Simcoe and the late Ralph Miller of Marburg, Ontario, made rare photographs of Pauline available to me. I corresponded with Rev. Louis McRaye, the son of the late Walter McRaye (Pauline's performing and business partner), and I gratefully thank him for forwarding family photographs to me and entrusting them to my care.

Sincere thanks to Keith Jones of Simcoe, Ontario, and to Dr. John Hall of Port Dover, Ontario. At McMaster University in Hamilton, Ontario, I was assisted over many years by Renu Barrett and Charlotte A. Stewart while researching The William Ready Division of Archives and Research Collections. Without their help and their sincere interest in my work, I could not have done this project nor produced this book.

I would like to sincerely thank the staff at the following institutions: the Archives of Ontario; the Harriet Irving Library at the University of New Brunswick; the Provincial Archives of New Brunswick; the City of Vancouver Museum; the Manitoba Provincial Archives; the National Archives of Canada; the Province of British Columbia Archives and Records Service; the Glenbow Museum in Calgary; the Hamilton Public Library; the Brantford General Hospital; the Brantford Public Library; Trent University in Peterborough, Ontario; the Saskatchewan Archives Board; Queen's University Archives; the Provincial Archives of Newfoundland and Labrador; Archives nationales du Quebec; the Vancouver Public Library; the Provincial Archives of Alberta; the Archives of the Diocese of New Westminster, B.C.; and the Ethnology Department of the Royal Ontario Museum.

Others whom I called upon include Suzanne O'Halloran of Midland, Ontario; Don Stewart of Vancouver; Donald B. Smith of the University of Calgary; the staff of Huronia Museum in Midland; Linda Wikene Johnson of British Columbia; the staff at Pauline Johnson Collegiate in Brantford; Library of Congress in Washington, USA; the Bell Canada Telephone Historical Collection; Keltie and Bruce Law of Hamilton, Ontario; Mr. William Patterson of St. Mark's Anglican Church in Barriefield, Ontario; the Steinway Company of London, England; Greg Hancock of Toronto; A. LaVonne Brown Ruoff, Professor Emerita of English, University of Illinois at Chicago; and Al Bowen of Vancouver, B.C.

Care has been taken to receive permission to use the sources, both literary and photographic, in this book. Any inadvertent oversights will be rectified in any future editions.

Sheila M. F. Johnston

Poems in *Buckskin and Broadcloth*

*T*his book contains poems that can be found in Pauline's book, *Flint and Feather*, as well as poems that are not found in that volume, poems which, for the purposes of this book, are referred to as "uncollected." A list of these uncollected poems follows, but first, a word.

Flint and Feather was first published in 1912, just months before Pauline's death in 1913. She was a very active participant in selecting poems for her book.

The third edition (1914) of *Flint and Feather* referred to the book as "*collected* verse," while the fifth edition (1917) is subtitled "The *Complete* Poems."

I believe that Pauline never intended *Flint and Feather* to represent her "complete" nor her "collected" works. The fact that I have gathered together 44 of her "uncollected" poems for this book underlines that belief.

Despite the availability of these 44 uncollected poems, some of Pauline's poems are elusive. They have yet to be found.

In this book, each uncollected poem is identified by a double border.

Sheila M. F. Johnston

Uncollected Poems
(in the order in which they appear)

My Little Jean
The Firs
Rover
At the Ferry
The Re-interment of Red Jacket
Brant: A Memorial Ode
The Rift
A Request
Temptation (originally Misguided)
Unguessed
What the Soldier Said
Fortune's Favors
The Lumberman's Christmas (at one time entitled A Backwoods Christmas)
Rondeau
In April
In the Shadows (My Version)
The Laying of the Cornerstone
Song
Evergreens
Two Women
The Death Cry
Held by the Enemy
Keepsakes
Rondeau: The Skater
The Portage
Depths
Winnipeg at Sunset
The Prairie
His Majesty, the West Wind
Kicking-Horse River
Curtain
The White and the Green
The Good Old N.P.
The C.H.W. (also known as Heidelberg)
Rondeau: Morrow-Land

Aftermath
His Majesty the King
October in Canada
Made-in-Canada
Traverse Bay
To Floretta Maracle
Reclaimed Lands
La Crosse
To Walter McRaye

Flint and Feather Poems
(in the order in which they appear)

In the Shadows
A Cry from an Indian Wife
The Song My Paddle Sings
A Prodigal
Autumn's Orchestra (excerpted)
The Trail to Lillooet
Good-Bye
"And He Said 'Fight On'"

The Great Peace of The Six Nations Iroquois Confederacy
by Raymond R. Skye

The founding of the Iroquois Confederacy almost 2000 years ago came about through the efforts of a person called the *Peacemaker*. At that time, the league consisted of Five Nations: the Mohawk, Oneida, Onondaga, Cayuga and Seneca. These Five Nations allied together with the guidance of the Peacemaker to form what is known as "The Great Peace of the Iroquois Confederacy." It is also referred to as "The Great Law."

This Great Peace brought back the unity and spirituality that most of the Iroquois people had lost. A divine message of peace, given to the Peacemaker from the Creator, gave him the power to eliminate the warring taking place among the Iroquois Nations. Once established, the Great Peace became a new order of political and social existence for the Iroquois people. Peace and harmony once again returned to the land.

The Peacemaker formed a Grand Council of fifty chiefs to administer all the laws of the Great Peace. With the help of the women who were clan mothers, political and social order was maintained.

A great white pine was chosen by the Peacemaker to symbolically represent the Great Laws of Peace and the unity of the Five Nations. He told his people that the roots of this tree would extend out to other Nations who also desired peace. The branches signified shelter, protection and security. All weapons of war were buried beneath this tree, never to be taken up against one another. With these weapons were also buried all the hostilities that perpetuate war.

The eagle, said the Peacemaker, shall be placed at the top of the tree of peace. His eyes will watch for any danger that might approach the Confederacy and cause harm to the Great Law. If anything threatens the Great Peace and the people, he will scream a warning. He will be your strength and the vigilant guardian of the *Great Peace of the League of the Iroquois Confederacy*.

The Great Peace of the League of the Iroquois Confederacy still exists today. With the adoption of the Tuscarora Nation in approximately 1712, they became the Six Nations of the Iroquois Confederacy.

CHAPTER 1

Ancestry

1758-1854

This telling of Pauline Johnson's story begins in 1758 with the birth of her paternal great-grandfather, Jacob. He was born into the Six Nations Confederacy. His mother was a Mohawk and the identity of his father has been lost in history.

Soon after the boy's birth, their mother took Jacob and his sister from their home in the Mohawk River valley, in what is now New York state, to a festival on the Niagara Peninsula. During the festivities Jacob was baptized into the Christian faith. Besides the name "Tekahionwake" (which Pauline and her sister translated as "double wampum" and which those who speak fluent Mohawk translate as "two rivers flowing side by side") he received the name "Johnson," when Sir William Johnson, superintendent of Indian Affairs for the northern district of the American colonies, stepped forward and offered his own surname to the baby boy. It was thereafter accepted that Sir William Johnson was godfather to both Jacob and his sister.

In 1784, during the aftermath of the American Revolution, nearly 2,000 members of the Six Nations migrated north to settle along the banks of the Grand River, in the heart of what is now southwestern Ontario, Canada. The 680,000 acres, purchased from the Mississauga Nation by Governor Sir Frederick Haldimand, was granted by the British Crown to the Six Nations. It comprised a strip of land six miles on each side of the river, a river which winds 298 kilometres from its source at Dundalk, Ontario, to its mouth at Port Maitland on Lake Erie.

The land was received by the Six Nations through the efforts of the Mohawk warrior Captain Joseph Brant. Brant, or Thayendanegea, was born in 1742. He was the brother of Molly Brant, wife of Sir William Johnson. Captain Brant was the surrogate godfather to Jacob and Mary

Sir William Johnson, 1715-1774. Trader, Indian agent, soldier, and Superintendent of Indian Affairs (appointed in 1756) in the Mohawk River valley, New York. He gave his surname to Pauline Johnson's great-grandfather, Jacob Johnson-Tekahionwake. Sir William was known thereafter as Jacob Johnson's godfather.
(National Archives of Canada, C-005197)

Johnson, at Sir William's request.

Jacob Johnson was one of those who moved north and settled on the newly designated Six Nations territory. One of his sons, born at the Johnson settlement near Cainsville (near present-day Brantford) in December of 1792, was named John Johnson. The boy's Mohawk name was Sakayanwaraton, meaning "disappearing mist." He was known as Smoke, and he was Pauline Johnson's grandfather.

As a young man, Smoke Johnson travelled to Montreal with Captain Joseph Brant. Later he was recruited by Sir Isaac Brock to fight in the War of 1812. Warrior Smoke Johnson fought at the battles of Lundy's Lane and Stoney Creek, and was at the Battle of Queenston Heights when Brock fell and died in October of 1812. Warrior Johnson is credited as the man who started the fire that burned Buffalo, New York, on December 30 of 1813. Johnson was awarded a silver medal by Edward, the Prince of Wales. The decoration was given "in recognition of your loyalty in battling for your own people even as your ancestors battled for the British Crown."[1]

Upon his return to the Six Nations territory, Smoke Johnson married Helen Martin, daughter of Catherine Martin and her second husband, George Martin (Onhyeateh). Helen's mother, Catherine (Rollston) Martin, was a white woman of Dutch descent, who, after the age of 13 was raised by a Mohawk family.

Smoke and Helen Johnson built a home overlooking the Grand River and they had a family of seven children. On October 10, 1816, their son George Henry Martin Johnson was born at Bow Park, near Brantford, Upper Canada. He was christened "George" for King George, "Henry" for his uncle Chief Henry Martin, and "Martin" after his mother's maiden name. George H.M. Johnson was Pauline Johnson's father.

After the War of 1812 the British government, acting through the Indian Department, made an unprecedented request of the Six Nations Council. Would the Six Nations make Warrior Smoke Johnson a chief? Not only had John Smoke Johnson demonstrated his patriotism to the Crown during the recent war, but he spoke English. He could act as an intermediary between the Six Nations and the British. After much deliberation the Council made Smoke Johnson a Pine Tree Chief. His title would not be inherited by any of his descendants. Chief Smoke Johnson was not one of the fifty hereditary chiefs because his ancestors were not descended from one of the founding families of the Six Nations Confederacy. His wife Helen, on the other hand, was descended from a founding family.

Chief Smoke Johnson's talent for oratory earned him the nickname "the Mohawk Warbler." He was soon named Speaker of the Six Nations Council, a post he held for 40 years. Pauline Johnson believed that she inherited her talent for recitation directly from her eloquent grandfather.

The Chief's duties on the reserve included relaying the death cry up and down the Grand River. Wampum strings were delivered to him by

A photograph of Pauline's grandfather, Chief John Smoke Johnson, at an advanced age. He was the son of Jacob Johnson, the father of George Johnson, and the grandfather of Pauline Johnson. When she was dying in Vancouver in 1912/13, Pauline remarked to friends that she would never forgive herself for not finding out more of the wealth of her grandfather's knowledge.
(Brant Historical Society #418/P60)

runners who wished to relay the string's message to the Speaker. On Sundays he went to the Mohawk Chapel, and in the Mohawk language he read the Ten Commandments. He was an important man on the reserve, widely respected and well liked.

His son George was educated in Brantford. He had a good ear for languages, and while his first language was Mohawk, George picked up English and French, as well as vocabulary from the other languages on the reserve: Cayuga, Oneida, Onondaga, Seneca and Tuscarora.

As a young man, in 1837, George Johnson went to Kingston as a dispatch rider during the Rebellion, under the leadership of Sir Allan MacNab. When he returned to the Reserve he was hired by the new Anglican missionary, the Reverend Adam Elliot, who in 1838 became the Church of England's missionary to the Grand River Indians, and who wished George Johnson to translate services from English into Mohawk. Mr. Elliot and his family were to have a profound effect on the young Mohawk. In 1840 George Johnson was formally appointed interpreter for the Anglican mission on his reserve.

Adam Elliot was a tall Scot, a young clergyman from Picton, Ontario. During a visit to Bytown (later Ottawa, Ontario), he stayed with the Reverend and Mrs. Mary Rogers. Mrs. Rogers' sister, Eliza Howells, was visiting from her home in Pennsylvania. Mr. Elliot was attracted to Eliza, and when she returned to her father's home in the United States the young minister followed her and proposed marriage. Eliza accepted his overture, married him, and they had four children.

The Elliots were posted to the Six Nations territory where they lived in the Tuscarora Parsonage. George Johnson moved into the parsonage in order to better carry out his duties for the minister and the Church.

In 1843 the Elliot household expanded to include Eliza's younger sister, Emily Howells. Emily came to the parsonage to keep her sister company and to help her raise her small children. Emily Howells was to be Pauline Johnson's mother.

Emily was born in Bristol, England on January 21, 1824, the youngest of thirteen children born to Henry Howells and Mary (Best) Howells. Henry Howells was a member of the Society of Friends, the Quakers. Mary Best was not a member of the Society. By marrying outside the Society, Mr. Howells was forced to leave the Quakers. His wife died in 1828, four years after the birth of Emily. One year later Henry remarried and emigrated to the United States with his new wife and his children. The family settled in Ohio, where Mr. Howells, an abolitionist, worked in the underground railway. He taught his children to pray for, and to pity, Indians and black slaves.

At the age of 21 Emily left the family home and moved to Kingston, Upper Canada, into the home of her eldest sister, Mary Rogers. From there she moved to her sister Eliza's home on the reserve. George Johnson and Emily Howells did not marry until a decade after their first meeting. During that time George suffered from a severe case of typhoid fever. Adam Elliot, fearing that George would succumb to the disease, asked his sister-in-law to nurse the young man back to health. This Emily did, showing a natural flair for nursing.

George Johnson proposed marriage to Emily Howells on June 21, 1848. She accepted, but there was no announcement and they entered into what was to become a long, secret engagement. Meanwhile George's mother, Helen, followed the Mohawk practice of selecting a woman for her son to marry. Conflict was inevitable.

Before the question of George's marriage arose, however, another grave matter demanded attention, the replacement on the Six Nations Council of Helen's late brother, George's uncle, Chief Henry Martin.

One of the associates of Hiawatha had been a Mohawk chief who had the name Teyonhahkewea, or "double life." He had been one of the great chiefs who sat on the first federal council of the Confederacy. His name had descended to his successors, last carried by Chief Henry Martin.

Helen Johnson was the matron of her family and it was her duty as clanmother to select her brother's successor. She chose her son, George Henry Martin Johnson. The Six Nations Council confirmed George's appointment, but soon thereafter the chiefs tried to reject the appointment, since by this time George Johnson was in the employ of the Canadian government, acting as official interpreter on the Reserve. The chiefs feared that young Chief Johnson was in a position of conflict of interest.

George Johnson had a powerful position on the Reserve. His official duties included assisting the Reserve's superintendent, a white man; interpreting between the superintendent of the Reserve and the Six Nations Council; interpreting at court when Six Nations witnesses were called to testify; attending the semi-annual distribution of annuities which accrued to the Six Nations from the sale of their lands; and executing both the laws enacted by the council and the regulations of the Canadian government. In essence, George Johnson was the Reserve's chief executive officer.

Not only did the Six Nations Council fear a conflict of interest, but they were uneasy about the fact that George's father, Chief Smoke Johnson, also sat on the council. The Six Nations were matrilineal and descent was traced through the mother. A son never succeeded his father on council as a son was liable to vote the way his father had before him. In order to insure the independence of the Six Nations Council, only the nephew or cousin of a chief succeeded him. Having a father and son on the council at the same time was unprecedented.

For these two reasons the chiefs wanted Helen Johnson to select a replacement for George. She refused to do so. Her argument, made before the whole Council, was that they could depose a chief for something he had done, but they were about to depose her son for something they feared he would do. She refused to appoint another candidate. The Mohawks would have one less than their usual nine representatives. It was a standoff. Helen Johnson won.

Chief Smoke Johnson, a Pine Tree Chief for life, and Chief George Johnson, an Hereditary Chief, sat on the Six Nations Council throughout the 1860s, 70s and early 80s. With his appointment as chief, George Johnson donned a traditional buckskin outfit which he wore with great pride. His outfit was adapted to meet his personal taste. He adorned it with various accessories which appealed to his flare for dressing impressively and his love of pomp and ceremony.

In 1849 George and Emily wanted to marry. George's rejection of his mother's choice of a wife led to an estrangement between mother and son. With George's marriage to Emily, his cousins and nephews could not carry on the hereditary chieftainship, as they would have done if he had married within his Nation, and if his intended Mohawk wife had become matron of the family. The Indian community did not approve of George marrying a white woman because of the women's role in chief selection. Not only that, she would acquire Indian status and the right to a portion of her band's annuities and other benefits. Before wedding plans could be made, however, Emily's sister Eliza died of consumption. Soon after, three of Eliza's four children died. An extended period of mourning ensued.

George and Emily finally wed on August 27 of 1853, but not before they had cleared one last hurdle. Emily wanted her brother-in-law, the Reverend Mr. Rogers, to perform the ceremony, and she travelled to her sister's Kingston, Ontario home for that purpose. Mr. Rogers, realizing that his young sister-in-law was engaged to a Mohawk, not only refused to perform the ceremony, but turned Emily out of his house. She found refuge with her friend, Jane Harvey, who helped Emily rearrange the wedding plans.

On the wedding day Chief George Johnson arrived in Kingston and learned of the change in plans. He and Emily exchanged vows in St. Mark's Anglican Church in Barriefield, a small village near Kingston. With her marriage, Emily Susannah Howells Johnson legally became an Indian. Any children she bore would be Mohawks. Eleven months after the wedding Emily gave birth to Henry Beverly Johnson. After Bev came Eliza, Allen and, in March of 1861, Pauline.

The Six Nations
by E. Pauline Johnson

There are few historical events recorded in America that are more interesting than that touching the consolidation of the "Five Nations" into one vast confederation, under the statesmanship of Hiawatha, nearly four centuries ago.

In following up the history of this people we find them, subsequent to their alliance, engaged in all the early colonial wars. French and English colonists alike feared, yet pandered to, this great war-like nation, who at one time ruled the land from the Atlantic sea-board to the Mississippi, and from North Carolina to the great lakes and river St. Lawrence.

That the remnant of this all-powerful people who once dictated terms to every white and red race on the continent, is, in the present day, a law abiding, peaceful, semi-agricultural nation, occupying a great portion of our own county, and the adjoining one of Haldimand, is telling evidence of the Nineteenth century march of advancement, and the possibilities of all intelligent races that are given opportunities of absorbing what is best in their sister-nations, whether it be art, habit or handicraft.

The English and the Iroquois, as we know them in the county of Brant, have made a brotherly exchange of many things, within the last few decades, which happily bodes more good to both nations than those erstwhile interchanges of musket shots and tomahawks.

The Canadians have adopted the Iroquois use of Indian corn as an almost national food. The Iroquois national game of lacrosse has been Canadianized, and although thirty years ago it was absolutely unknown among the whites, it is to-day known the world over as Canada's national sport.

Snow shoeing, tobogganing, canoeing, all are adaptations from the red man, who in his turn has adjusted himself to civilized habits and customs, profiting by their excellencies and, let us trust, learning as little harm as possible from their imperfections.

It has been a long but astonishingly rapid leap from the wigwam, and the council fire of a century ago, to the neat little, well-ordered, governmental building, known as the "Six

Nations Council House," at Ohsweken, yet through all that time with its changes in the Imperial parliament, its strange happenings in Canadian politics, the Iroquois nation have held their system of government intact. It stands to-day, as it stood in the days of Hiawatha, unshaken, unadulterated, unaltered, a living monument to the magnificent states-manship of the man who conceived it, and carried it, and culminated it before ever the white man had entered the depths of America's forest lands.

The Indian reserve on the Grand River has dwindled from what was the first Imperial grant, that is, the lands that lay for six miles in depth on each side of the river from its source to its mouth, to a tract comprising but fifty-two thousand acres, the greater portion of which is under cultivation, for unlike western tribes the Iroquois have shown a great aptitude for agriculture, as those who have visited their annual industrial exhibition in the spacious agricultural building at the village of Ohsweken will readily testify.

The little village of Ohsweken is of much interest to the visitor, being as it is the seat of the Six Nations' government, where the local "parliament" is held, and the affairs of the nation discussed and disposed of by the lineal descendants of Hiawatha's "Fifty-two Noble families," who comprised the first great council of the confederation.

The present council house was erected in 1863 and since that time has been in constant usage. Prior to that year various buildings were used in various localities. At one time the council house was at the now village of Middleport, and in yet earlier times some assert it was one of the ancient, and now-desolated buildings on Tutela Heights.

In addition to the Ohsweken council house, there are two others devoted to the exclusive use of the Pagan Indians, one for the Cayugas, the other for the Onondagas.

These latter buildings are called "Long Houses," and are in reality the places of worship of these two conservative old tribes, where they hold their various religious dances and festivals throughout the year, worshipping in the exquis-ite beauty of "Pagan" faith, and simple belief in the "Great Spirit," that wondrous, peaceful, large-hearted God of the unchristianized Indian, that God that they believe no sin can really estrange them from, whose love and favor is theirs, it matters not how unworthy they may be, that God that is pleased with the simple dances and feasts of his red children, who har-bors no ill-thought or feeling towards them, and who has for souls and bodies after death, whether they be bad or good, limitless reaches of happy hunting grounds, and through all eter-nity the happy atmosphere known only where an everlasting "Peace-Pipe" is in daily use between God and man.

But in early times the dances of the domesticated Iroquois were not always the out-come of religious zeal and good-fellowship with the Great Spirit; for America knew no greater terror than when a band of eight or ten thousand Iroquois warriors chose to don their war paint, and set forth conquering and to conquer; their fierce visages, and half-naked bodies, decorated with the ominous streaks of black and red, meaning "Blood and Death," always the war colours of the Mohawks.

For miles across the country could their terrible war cries be heard, and the hated Huron crouched fearfully in his wigwam beside the Georgian Bay, and the faithful Jesuit father crossed himself to no purpose, when the Iroquois roused with a just ire, impassioned by a taunt, marched northward, and in one fell battle exterminated Jesuit and Huron, leaving the little Christian hamlet a desolation, and dancing a triumphant war dance on the hills that overlook Penetanguishene.

No, it is not a fiction. The ancestors of those calm-eyed Indian men, of those low-voiced, gentle-faced women, who on market days throng our busy little streets, were some of the bravest, most intrepid and valiant warriors known to the history of the world; men who defended their country and the "ashes of their fathers" against the inroads of a great all-conquering race; men who fought, and bled, and died to hold the western continent against an incoming eastern power, as England's sons would battle and fall to-day, were their own mother country threatened with a power that would eventually annihilate, subject-then alas! absorb their blood, their traditions, their nation, until naught promises to remain save a memory.[2]

Catherine Rollston's Adoption by the Mohawks
by Evelyn Johnson

During the earlier days of the American Revolution, when the colonists were endeavoring to enlist the sympathy and aid of the powerful Six Nations there occurred, what is generally known as Cresap's War, the several terrible massacres provoked by the "wanton cruelty," of a subaltern officer of that name, and the retaliatory massacres and reprisals of the Mohawks (1770s).

...At the close of one of the battles, the Mohawks in searching the homes of the German or Dutch settlers came to one house from which all the family had fled, and there they found alone a young girl of thirteen-Catherine Rollston...The Mohawks took the young girl captive and brought her with them upon their return to their homes on the Mohawk River. She was adopted by the family of Teyonhahkewea ("double life") one of the great chiefs of the Confederacy, whose title he inherited from a compeer of Hiawatha.

...Catherine Rollston was brought up as an Indian, acquired the Mohawk language and customs and was given the Mohawk name by which she was known "Wan-o-wen-re-teh," English meaning, "throwing over the head," as a ball, a stone, etc.

...When she was a young woman of marriageable age...her marriage was arranged for her by the good old Indian custom of the mothers of the groom and the bride agreeing to the alliance...This engagement of Catherine Rollston Wan-o-wen-re-teh and George Martin Onh-yea-teh, therefore was understood.[3]

The Story of Queen Anne's Silver
by Evelyn Johnson

The family of Teyonhahkewea was appointed by the Mohawks as the custodians of the pipe of peace, and the silver communion service presented to the nation by Queen Anne.

These precious possessions were guarded as jealously by the Indians as life itself, and were for a time in true Indian fashion, buried for safe-keeping at Niagara during those troublesome times.

When, therefore, the Mohawks in loyalty to the Crown, turned their backs upon their old-time hunting grounds and despoiled homes in the beautiful valley of the Mohawk River, and turned their faces towards the setting sun of the Canadas, a problem presented itself as to ways and means of conveying the treasured silver in safety to their new home on the river Ouse, or Grand River, in Upper Canada.

Catherine Rollston-Martin solved the problem. She took a number of pieces of clothing, together with a quantity of rags, and wrapping therein the pipe and communion service, together with the wealth of Indian silver brooches, she made all into a bundle, in appearance a bundle of rags, and taking a Gas-ha-ha, an Indian custom-belt for the chest or forehead, she bound the bundle upon her back and was ready for the trail.

The march to Niagara was a long and lonely one. The Indians were accompanied by British soldiers who hurried them forward...the weight of the silver together with the long and arduous march bore heavily upon this loyal and determined woman. She felt such weariness that her step lagged somewhat, and a soldier urged her forward with his bayonet, which he thrust into the bundle on her back with an admonition for her to hurry. No doubt the soldier considered the bundle contained but rags, as it appeared, but the point of the bayonet struck one of the pieces of silver.[4]

The Martin Settlement
by Evelyn Johnson

All the Six Nations know of the Martin Settlement founded by George Martin Onh-

yea-teh and his wife Catherine Rollston Wan-o-wen-re-teh...It is estimated that Martin built his house about 1783-84, shortly after the Mohawks removed to the Grand River...on a high bluff commanding a magnificent view up and down the Grand River, about two miles southeast of Cainsville.

Here were born the family of children whose descendants include names of national celebrity among whom are the late Chief George H.M. Johnson and Miss E. Pauline Johnson.

...From this house was distributed the government presents to the Six Nations, previous to the time that their own monies were available...To receive these presents crowds of Indians assembled from every part of the forest, from Lake Ontario, where Brant resided, to the lands stretching far below Dunnville towards the mouth of the river and for miles towards its source. The presents consisted of powder, lead for bullets, knives, tomahawks, blankets, beads, paint for personal adornment, clothing and other articles.

At these gatherings great games were played; feasts were made; the woods and river abounding in game and fish. George Martin's hospitable home stood with wide flung door, an invitation to any and all of the vast throng.[5]

George Martin's Temper
by Evelyn Johnson

Old George Martin was noted for his fierce temper. One day three chiefs called upon him...in reference to a claim of land. When they had presented the claim, George Martin became so incensed and exasperated that he ordered them out of his house. As they did not immediately comply he seized his tomahawk, which hung upon the wall, threatening dire chastisement upon the offenders.

At the same moment, his wife, Catherine seized him about the waist, exclaiming, "George! George!" and urging the three men to depart.

Chief (George Henry Martin) Johnson, then a little boy, and who happened to be at his grandparents-terrified by the uproar-sought refuge under a bed which stood in one corner of the room, and from which point of vantage, he was a trembling witness of the scene.

His grandfather struggled to free himself from his wife's hold, who "hung on to her self-appointed task," "a great fat Dutch woman," to use Chief G.H.M. Johnson's words, as he saw her at that time, "holding on to her husband," brandishing his tomahawk as he drew nearer the three chiefs, who filed out of the door in haste.

George Martin, burying his tomahawk in the side of the doorpost, just as the last man removed his hand. The men fled around the house across the fields and were presently lost to view, but they never returned to renew the claim.[6]

Pauline's Grandfather Howells

by E. Pauline Johnson

Like most transplanted Englishmen, [Mr. Howells*] cut himself completely off from the land of his fathers; his interests and his friends henceforth were all in the country of his

adoption, and he chose Ohio as a site for his new home. He was a man of vast peculiarities, prejudices and extreme ideas-a man of contradictions so glaring that even his own children never understood him. He was a very narrow religionist, of the type that say many prayers and quote much Scripture, but he beat his children-both boys and girls-so severely that outsiders were at times compelled to interfere. For years those unfortunate children carried the scars left on their backs by the thongs of cat-o'-nine-tails when he punished them for some slight misdemeanor. They were all terrified of him, all obeyed him like soldiers, but none escaped his severity.[7]

Pauline's maternal grandfather. On the back of this portrait is written, by Pauline's mother: "My father, H. Howells. Photograph received by me Emily S. Johnson from my sister Mrs. Marie McCandlish April 20th, 1875, and copied from an ivory miniature which was given to my mother Mary Best, August or September 1805, Bristol England, by my father, aged 21 years.
(Brant Historical Society #553)

Mary Best Howells, first wife of H. Howells, and maternal grandmother of Pauline. Her youngest child, Emily, was only four years old when Mary Howells died.
(Brant Historical Society #535)

*In Pauline's story, *My Mother*, she substituted the name Mr. Bestman for her maternal grandfather's name, Mr. Howells. For the purposes of this book, "Mr. Howells" is used.

Emily and Her Sister Eliza
by Douglas R. Reville

In the early part of the last century an English family, Howells by name, came out to this continent and settled in the State of Ohio, the father was a Quaker and was married four times having many children. There were two of the sisters by his first wife who in the matter of age and temperament were particularly suited to each other and both possessed free and happy natures which made the stern discipline of those days exceedingly hard to bear. It is therefore very easy to imagine the relief with which Emily, the younger, followed the fortunes of Eliza the elder, when the latter met and married a young Church of England clergyman, Rev. Mr. Elliot, and came with him to a life of missionary work on the Six Nations Reserve.[8]

My Mother
by E. Pauline Johnson

Emily* was abnormally sensitive, prone to melancholy or extreme jollity, and, according to her own statement, was high tempered; but I can never recollect having seen her more than "irritated" or "annoyed." She had conquered her temper very early in life-completely subdued it. Early, too, in our infancy she looked for those traits in us, expected them,

*In Pauline's story *My Mother* she substituted the name of Lydia for her mother's name.
For the purposes of this story, "Emily" is used.

recognized them and grappled with them.[9]

Emily Travels from Ohio to the Six Nations
by E. Pauline Johnson

A stage coach conveyed her from her home in Ohio to Erie, Pennsylvania, where she went aboard a sailing vessel bound for Buffalo. There she crossed the Niagara River, and at Chippewa, on the Canadian side again took a stage coach for the village of Brantford, sixty miles west. At this place she remained overnight and the following day [Rev. Elliot's] own conveyance arrived to fetch her to the Indian Reserve, ten miles to the south-east.

In after years little Emily used to tell that during that entire drive she thought she was going through an English avenue leading to some great estate, for the trees crowded up close to the roadways on either side, giant forest trees-gnarled oaks, singing firs, jaunty maples, graceful elms-all stretching their branches overhead. But the "avenue" seemed endless.[10]

Emily Meets Her Future Husband
by E. Pauline Johnson

She had never seen an Indian, consequently was trying to reform her ideas regarding

*In Pauline's story, My Mother, she substituted the name of Mr. Evans for her uncle, the Reverend Adam Elliot. For the purposes of this book, "Rev. Elliot" is used.

them. She had not expected to see anything like this self-poised, scrupulously-dressed, fine-featured, dark stripling. She thought all Indians wore savage-looking clothes, had fierce eyes and stern, set mouths. This boy's eyes were narrow and shrewd, but warm and kindly, his lips were like a Cupid's bow, his hands were narrower, smaller, than her own, but the firmness of those slim fingers, the power in those small palms, as he had helped her from the carriage, remained with her through all the years to come.

That evening at supper she noted his table deportment; it was correct in every detail. He ate leisurely, silently, gracefully; his knife and fork never clattered, his elbows never were in evidence, he made use of the right plates, spoons, forks, knives; he bore an ease, an unconsciousness of manner, that amazed her.[11]

Chief George H.M. Johnson
by E. Pauline Johnson

A man revered, respected, looked up to by a vast nation, a man of sterling worth, of considerable wealth as riches were counted in those days, a man polished in the usages and etiquette of Emily's own people, who conducted himself with faultless grace, who would have shone brilliantly in any drawing-room

(and who in after years was the guest of honor at many a great reception by the governors of the land), a man young, stalwart, handsome, with an aristocratic lineage that bred him a native gentleman, with a grand old title that had come down to him through six hundred years of honor in warfare and the high places of his people.[12]

Emily Becomes Aware of a Different Side of George Johnson
by E. Pauline Johnson

Emily never forgot the first time she saw him robed in the full costume of his office. Hitherto she had regarded him through all her comings and goings as her playmate, friend and boon companion; he had been to her something that had never before entered her life-he had brought warmth, kindness, fellowship and a peculiar confidential humanity that had been entirely lacking in the chill English home of her childhood. But this day, as he stood beside his veteran father, ready to take his place among the chiefs of the Grand Council, she saw revealed another phase of his life and character; she saw that he was destined to be a man among men, and for the first time she realized that her boy companion had gone a little beyond her, perhaps a little above her. They were a strange pair as they stood somewhat apart, unconscious of the picture they made. She, a gentle-born, fair English girl of twenty, her simple blue muslin frock vying with her eyes in color. He, tawny skinned, lithe, straight as an arrow, the royal blood of gener-

George H.M. Johnson, received by Emily Howells in November of 1847. Noted on the back: "Engaged to George Henry Martin Johnson June 21, 1848."
(Brant Historical Society #567)

ations of chiefs and warriors pulsing through his arteries, his clinging buckskin tunic and leggings fringed and embroidered with countless quills, and endless stitches of colored moosehair. From his small, neat moccasins to his jet black hair tipped with an eagle plume he was every inch a man, a gentleman, a warrior.

But he was approaching her with the same ease with which he wore his ordinary "white" clothes-garments, whether buckskin or broadcloth, seemed to make but slight impression on him.[13]

Emily and George Reveal Their Engagement
by E. Pauline Johnson

Reverend Elliot was almost beside himself with joyousness when the young people rather shyly confessed their engagement to him. He was deeply attached to his wife's young sister, and George had been more to him than many a man's son ever is. Seemingly cold and undemonstrative, this reserved Scotch [sic] missionary had given all his heart and life to the Indians, and this one boy was the apple of his eye. Farsighted and cautious, he saw endless trouble shadowing the young lovers-opposition to the marriage from both sides of the house. He could easily see Emily's family smarting under the seeming disgrace of her marriage to an Indian; he could see George's family indignant and hurt to the core at his marriage with a white girl; he could see how impossible it would be for Emily's people to ever understand the fierce resentment of the Indian par-

ents that the family title could never continue under the family name. He could see how little George's people would ever understand the "white" prejudice against them. But the good man kept his own counsel, determining only that when the war did break out, he would stand shoulder to shoulder with these young lovers and be their friend and helper when even their own blood and kin should cut them off.[14]

Emily and George Johnson Agree on Their Marriage Roles
by E. Pauline Johnson

And Emily, with her glad and still girlish heart, gloried in her husband's achievements and in the recognition accorded him by the great world beyond the Indian Reserve, beyond the wilderness, beyond the threshold of their own home. In only one thing were their lives at all separated. She took no part in his public life. She hated the glare of the fierce light that beat upon prominent lives, the unrest of fame, the disquiet of public careers.

"No," she would answer when oftentimes he begged her to accompany him and share his success and honours, "no, I was homeless so long that 'home' is now my ambition. My babies need me here, and you need me here when you return, far more than you need me on platform or parade. Go forth and fight the enemy, storm the battlements and win the laurels, but let me keep the garrison-here at home, with our babies all about me and a welcome to our warrior husband and father when he returns from war."

Then he would laugh and coax again, but always with the same result. Every day, whether he went forth to the Indian Council across the river, or when more urgent duties called him to the Capital, she always stood at the highest window waving her handkerchief until he was out of sight, and that dainty flag lent strength to his purpose and courage to his heart, for he knew the home citadel was there awaiting his return.[15]

A proud Chief George Johnson with his arm protectively around Emily Johnson.
They pose for a formal portrait, probably taken at the time of their wedding, in 1853.
She holds the family's treasured tomahawk-peace pipe.
(Royal Ontario Museum 77ETH 128 922.1.103)

Illegal Timber Traffic Depletes Six Nations Forests and George Johnson's Health
by E. Pauline Johnson

Evils had begun to creep into his forest world. The black and subtle evil of the white man's firewater had commenced to touch with its poisonous finger the lives and lodges of his beloved people. The curse began to spread, until it grew into a menace to the community. It was the same old story: the white man had come with the Bible in one hand, the bottle in the other. George had striven...to overcome the dread scourge...The entire plan of the white liquor dealer's campaign was simply an effort to exchange a quart of bad whiskey for a cord of first-class firewood, or timber, which could be hauled off the Indian Reserve and sold in the nearby town markets for five or six dollars; thus a hundred dollars' worth of bad whiskey, if judiciously traded, would net the white dealer a thousand dollars cash. And the traffic went on, to the depletion of the Indian forests and the degradation of the Indian souls.

Then the Canadian government appointed young [George Johnson*] special forest warden, gave him a "V.R." hammer, with which he was to stamp each and every stick of timber he could catch being hauled off the Reserve by white men; licensed him to carry firearms for self-protection, and told him to "go ahead."

He "went ahead." Night after night he lay,

*In Pauline's story, *My Mother*, she substituted the name of George Mansion for her father. For the purposes of this book, "George Johnson" is used.

concealing himself in the marshes, the forests, the trails, the concessions lines, the river road, the Queen's highway, seizing all the timber he could, destroying all the whiskey, turning the white liquor traders off Indian lands, and fighting as only a young, earnest and inspired man can fight. These hours and conditions began to tell on his physique. The marshes breathed their miasma into his blood-the dreaded fever had him in its claws.[16]

Emily Nurses George
by E. Pauline Johnson

Emily was a born nurse. She knew little of thermometers, of charts, or technical terms, but her ability and instincts in the sickroom were unerring; and when her husband succumbed to a raging fever, love lent her hands an inspiration and her brain a clarity that would have shamed many a professional nurse.

For hours, days, weeks, she waited, tended, watched, administered, labored and loved beside the sick man's bed. She neither slept nor ate enough to carry her through the ordeal, but love lent her strength, and she battled and fought for his life as only an adoring woman can. Her wonderful devotion was the common talk of the country...She never left the sickroom save when her baby needed her. But it all seemed so useless, so in vain, when one dark morning the doctor said, "We had better send for his father and mother."

Poor Emily! Her heart was nearly breaking. She hurriedly told the doctor the cause that had kept them away so long, adding, "Is it so bad as that? Oh, doctor, must I send for them? They don't want to come." Before the good man could reply, there was a muffled knock at the door. Then Milly's old wrinkled face peered in, and Milly's voice said whisperingly, "His people-they here."

"Whose people? Who are here?" almost gasped Emily. "His father and his mother," answered the old woman. "They downstairs."

For a brief moment there was silence. Emily could not trust herself to speak, but ill as he was, George's quick Indian ear had caught Milly's words. He murmured, "Mother! mother! Oh, my mother!"

"Bring her, quickly, quickly!" said Emily to the doctor.

It seemed to the careworn girl that a lifetime followed before the door opened noiselessly, and there entered a slender little old Indian woman, in beaded leggings, moccasins, "short skirt," and a blue "broadcloth" folded about her shoulders. She glanced swiftly at the bed, but with the heroism of her race went first towards Emily, laid her cheek silently beside the white girl's, then looked directly into her eyes.

"Emily!" whispered George, "Emily!" At the word both women moved swiftly to his side. "Emily," he repeated, "my mother cannot speak the English, but her cheek to yours means that you are her blood relation."

The effort of speech almost cost him a swoon, but his mother's cheek was now against his own, and the sweet, dulcet Mohawk language of his boyhood returned to his tongue; he was speaking it to his mother, speaking it lovingly, rapidly. Yet, although Emily never understood a word, she did not feel an outsider, for the old mother's hand held her own, and she knew that at last the gulf was bridged.

...But many and many a happy day within each year found Emily and her husband's mother sitting together, hour upon hour, needle in hand, sewing and harmonizing-the best friends in all the world. It mattered not that George's mother could not speak one word of English, or that Emily never mastered but a half-dozen words of Mohawk. These two were friends in the sweetest sense of the word, and their lives swept forward in a unison of sympathy that was dear to the heart of the man who held them as the two most precious beings in all the world.[17]

Helen Johnson
by E. Pauline Johnson

Chief George Johnson's mother, small and silent through long habit and custom, had acquired a certain masterful dignity of her own, for within her slender brown fingers she held a power that no man of her nation could wrest from her. She was "Chief Matron" of her entire blood relations, and commanded the enviable position of being the one and only person, man or woman, who could appoint a chief to fill the vacancy of one of the great Mohawk law-makers whose seat in Council had been left vacant when the voice of the Great Spirit called him to the happy hunting grounds.[18]

In this photograph, taken in the 1860s, Chief George H.M. Johnson is pictured (seated to the left, identifiable by his unique feathered hat). He was a lacrosse enthusiast and on the reverse of this photo Emily Johnson has written: "Lacrosse game, the nation game of Canada-These Indians played at Toronto under the direction of the Chief and led the Torontonians-A few days ago the Chief got a letter from the Mayor of Troy with an offer of (an amount in British pounds)-and all expenses free. The Chief accepted it and will go with his Indians."
(Brant Historical Society #246)

CHAPTER 2

Chiefswood Days
1854- 1884

*E*mily Pauline Johnson was born just before noon on March 10, 1861 at Chiefswood, the Johnson family home. The house still stands, located less than 10 kilometres from the community of Ohsweken on the Six Nations Reserve in Brant County, Ontario, and approximately 20 kilometres from the city of Brantford.

To celebrate the birth of her fourth child, Emily Johnson planted a walnut tree between the house and the gate. The baby was given the name "Emily" after her mother, and "Pauline" after Pauline Borghese, Duchess de Guastalla, Napoleon Bonaparte's sister. Pauline's father's pet name for his youngest child was "Mary."

As a child Pauline suffered from colds, bronchitis and earaches. She also suffered from erysipelas, caused by a bacterium similar to that which causes strep throat.

Pauline's mother lived by and actively promoted the virtues of self control and moderation. To her four children, Bev, Eliza (known as Eva), Allen and Pauline, she stressed the importance of aristocratic bearing and was suspicious of social intimacies. Hence her children were self-disciplined and subdued. Pauline's vivacious personality could not be completely repressed, however. The true nature of the youngest Johnson child was one of passion and joie de vivre.

The Johnson household of six also included a Native nursemaid, a cook and a stableman. A governess was retained from time to time to tutor the children at home. Pauline roamed around the grounds of Chiefswood and as she grew older she ventured farther afield by canoe, on snowshoes, on foot and on the family's pony.

As her father's companion she learned lessons of the trail and woods. She listened as he related stories of Napoleon's great battles. She heard thrilling tales of Hiawatha and Tecumseh and she listened as he read her the popular Canadian novel *Wacousta*, written in 1832 by Major John Richardson.

From her grandfather, Chief Smoke Johnson, she learned her family's history and the history of her people, the Mohawks. When Bev and Eva were away at school

Pauline Johnson in 1864, when she was three years old. Her serious gaze into the camera belies her personality, which was chatty, funny and mischievous.
(Brant Historical Society #1679)

in London, Ontario, Pauline and Allen kept one another company. Pauline used the upstairs hall bedroom, occupied by Bev when he was home from school, as her writing room. She spent days composing poems.

According to the biographical notes in *The Legends of Vancouver* (1911), notes presumably either written or at the least approved by Pauline; "Her education was neither extensive nor elaborate. It embraced neither high school nor college. A nursery governess for two years at home, three years at an Indian day school half a mile from her home, and two years in the Central School of the city of Brantford, was the extent of her educational training. But besides this, she acquired a wide and general knowledge, having been through childhood and early girlhood a great reader, especially of poetry. Before she was twelve years old she had read Scott, Longfellow, Byron, Shakespeare, and such books as Addison's *Spectator*, Foster's Essays, and Owen Meredith's writings."[1] Pauline found all this material in the well-stocked library at Chiefswood.

Pauline's sister, Eva, left detailed memoirs from which we learn details of life at Chiefswood in the 1860s, 1870s and 1880s. George Johnson would go from room to room, ringing a brass bell to awaken the household in the morning. Some days he took the train to Brantford, where he interpreted at the Court House or at the Indian Office. On other mornings he walked to the Six Nations Council House in Ohsweken.

Emily Johnson received copies of *Godey's Ladies' Book*, the leading woman's magazine of the period, from which she dispensed sensible household tips to her daughters.

The Grand River flowed past the front of the house. On summer nights, the family saw lights in canoes and along both banks, indicating where people had settled to fish. They saw scows loaded with lumber going from Caledonia upriver to Brantford. Young men canoed across the river and congregated on the grassy flats near the home, where they played lacrosse and ball until dusk.

During the 1866 Fenian Raid, the sound of the guns at Ridgeway, Ontario, was audible at Chiefswood. While Emily prepared bandages for the wounded, Chief George recruited men to send to the action. Before his men left the Middleport train station, word was received that their services would not be required, and Chief George sent the men home.

Members of Britain's royal family visited Brantford, and sometimes took a trip to the Six Nations Reserve. Chief George Johnson was in attendance during these occasions as he was a prominent representative of the people of the Reserve. In 1860 the Prince of Wales; in 1869 Prince Arthur; in August of 1874 the Governor-General of Canada and his wife, Lord and Lady Dufferin; and in 1879 Princess Louise and the Marquis of Lorne visited the reserve. It is unlikely, however, that their strict schedules allowed these dignitaries the leisure time to visit the pastoral riverside estate of Chief and Mrs. George Johnson.

While she attended Central School in Brantford, in the mid 1870s, Pauline boarded with Mrs. E.G. Dew on Colborne Street. She invited Mrs. Dew and some other friends to Chiefswood on one occasion, where the guests witnessed a war dance after tea. There was a dramatic recital from the life of Pocohontas, in which Pauline took the part of the heroine. Her interest in the dramatic arts was well developed by this time.

At school Pauline met Jean Morton, who became her closest friend. The two remained friends for life. In the 1890s Jean married Douglas Reville, a journalist from Brantford.

Douglas gives this insight into the young Pauline Johnson: "To know her best was during one of her many canoeing trips in which she loved to indulge, for she was a past mistress in the art of manipulating that frail craft. The most turbulent rapids had no terror for her."[2]

In 1877 or 1878 Pauline left Central School and returned home to Chiefswood. There were picnics with friends, canoeing on the river, games of chess and checkers, horseback riding in the summer, archery, tobogganing in the winter, and opportunities to entertain visiting family members and many friends.

In 1881 Pauline and a group of friends went to Camp Knock-About in the Muskoka district. She would holiday for weeks with friends in Goderich, in London and in Wingham. Through the years she made frequent trips to Paris, Ontario, to stay with her cousin, Kate Howells.

All this time Pauline was writing-both poetry and prose. Sometimes at the end of her prose pieces she signed using a pen name: Margaret Rox or Katherine Roulston. The latter name was a variation of her Dutch great-grandmother's name. At times she coyly used "The Pasha" to identify some of her musings. Pauline was thrilled when, in January of 1884, her poem, "To Jean" (also known as "My Little Jean"), was published in the prestigious periodical *Gems of Poetry*.

Shortly after this triumph, on February 12, 1884, Chief George Johnson attended a reception at Grace Church in Brantford, then rode to Chiefswood through a persistent winter rain. He developed a severe cold, which turned into erysipelas. On February 19, with his aged father and his beloved wife at his side, Chief George Henry Martin Johnson died at home after a week-long illness. He was 68.

On two occasions during his life, Chief George Johnson had been assaulted by people determined to remove him so they could continue with money-making schemes on the Six Nations Reserve. It was widely believed that these violent events led to the breakdown of his health, and ultimately to his death. The first assault was on January 21, 1865 at 5:30 p.m. at Middleport, Ont.; the second was on October 11, 1873, at 2:00 a.m..

The first attack, which occurred when Pauline Johnson was only three years old, came as a result of Chief George Johnson's efforts to halt the removal of valuable timber from the reserve in exchange for liquor. John Mills, one of two assailants, battered the Chief's head, using a lead plumb attached to a heavy elastic. It took months for Chief Johnson to recover. In the meantime, Mills was sent to the Kingston Penitentiary for five years. This attack had been preceded by threats: "threatening and anonymous letters had more than once been received by her husband," wrote Pauline many years later in her autobiographical essay, 'My Mother,' "letters that said he would be *put out of the way* unless he stopped interfering in the liquor trade."[3] There were threats that Chiefswood would be burned down in the dead of night, and threats that Chief Johnson's horses and cattle would be maimed.

The 1873 attack, coming when Pauline was 12, was because of Chief Johnson's continued efforts to rid the reserve of liquor traders. This time there were six assailants. They broke his fingers, beat him, and shot him with his own revolver. The bullet passed through his clothing, but did not enter his body. Emily's expert nursing skills assisted him in recuperating, but he never regained his former robust health.

This second attack on the popular Chief aroused indignation, and as the ethnologist Horatio Hale recounts: "all classes, whites and

Indians alike, shared in the sentiment and in the determination to crush the mischief. Before this blaze of public wrath the vile conspiracy shrivelled at once, as if smitten by lightening. The malefactors were hunted down, and expiated their crime either in prison or by flight and self-banishment."[4]

Emily Johnson was consumed with grief at the death of her husband and she could not attend the funeral service at the Mohawk Chapel. A private service was held at Chiefswood, which Emily overheard, confined to her upstairs bedroom, as she mourned the passing of her beloved George.

A few months after his death a posthumous gift from Chief George to his Emily arrived at Chiefswood. It was a portrait of Lord Horatio Nelson, the great British naval leader. The gentle, mutual teasing the Johnsons had enjoyed throughout their 30-year marriage, "was Nelson or Napoleon the better man?", culminated in one last tender gesture from George to his wife.

The three Johnson women lived at Chiefswood for only eight months after the death of Chief George. The estate was leased to a farmer for an eight-year period for $250 a year. This provided part of the income for the Johnson women.

Some more came from portions of the salaries earned by Bev and Allen. Both men were employed in the insurance business, Bev in Montreal and Allen in Hamilton. As well, there was an annuity for Emily, prepared by her late husband, and a small income of her own.

Eva's memoirs include this passage: "The last I saw of Chiefswood, my old home from which everyone had gone a few months after father's death and where we would no longer dwell, was the house, dark, lonely and forsaken, the November moonlight casting weird shadows on its lightless panes."[5]

The three Johnson women moved into Brantford where they took a semi-detached, yellow-brick home at 7 Napoleon Street. Much later the street was renamed Dufferin Avenue. The Johnson's home stands to this day.

In the months following their father's death, Eva and Pauline travelled with other Six Nations representatives to Buffalo, New York. They were part of a delegation which participated in a ceremony to re-entomb the late Seneca orator, Red Jacket. The re-entombment became necessary when Red Jacket's resting place was disturbed by the construction of new buildings. Pauline submitted a poem for the occasion, "The Re-interment of Red Jacket," which was published in the report of the Buffalo Historical Society. It must have been a great disappointment to Pauline that her father had not lived to see this poem in print.

Chiefswood: Its Early History

According to Eva Johnson, her father had always admired the home of a family named Lovejoy. Their home was near Cainsville (now part of Brantford) and Chief Johnson modelled his plan after the Lovejoy estate. More than one plan for Chief's Wood (or Chiefswood as it is commonly known) was drafted, presumably by Chief George Johnson. He would show each draft to Emily, and the final draft for the building bears George's signature, dated 1856.

The plans followed a Gothic-Italianate design complete with high ceilings and heavy interior details. The approximate square footage of the two floors is 2100 sq. ft. Chief George Johnson purchased the land in October of 1853,

Chiefswood, the riverside home of Chief George Johnson, Emily Johnson and their four children, Bev, Eva, Allen and Pauline, as it looked in the 1870s. This etching shows the front of the dwelling (the side facing the Grand River). Emily is leaning against the lower door frame, while one of her daughters is leaning against the upper door frame. *(from the collection of the author)*

a few months after his and Emily's wedding. Ethnologist and friend of the Johnson family, Horatio Hale, recounts that "a fortunate venture, into which a mercantile friend had persuaded [Chief George Johnson], had yielded a good profit and put him in funds."[6] Chief Johnson's purchase bought him 200 acres of land fronting the Grand River.

Today Chiefswood still stands. The historic site comprises four acres, between Highway #54 and south to the Grand River. "As both lookouts were attractive, father had the house built so that a view could be obtained in both directions," wrote Eva Johnson in her memoirs. "The front of the house faced the Grand River, while the back of the house overlooked the road from Brantford to Caledonia." Eva writes that this back door was never opened. "It was very cold in this vestibule and we called it the cellar and used it as such. The other vestibule (facing the river) was filled with vines and flowers."[7]

Using trees from his land, Chief Johnson's house was constructed of three-inch lumber, the walnut planks being laid one on top of the other. They were secured with wooden pegs. The finish was stucco, or "rough cast." In time the finish mellowed and weathered to a beautiful cream colour, prompting Eva to refer to their home as "the white house on the hill."

Chiefswood was ready for occupancy by December of 1856. By then George and Emily were already the proud parents of Bev and Eva. Extending from the eastern wall of the house was a shed-roofed, single-storey summer kitchen wing, which, when covered by overgrown vines, appeared to be part of the shrubbery. Besides the stately home with its clean lines, its symmetrical arrangements of French doors and large windows, its hipped roof and five chimneys, the Johnson estate included a cowbarn, a horse stable, an ice house (in which to store ice taken from the Grand River in winter), a tenant's house, a wood shed, a garden, a grape arbour, an orchard, a melon patch, and a well for watering purposes. There was also a tree with a swing, a croquet set on the lawn, and a space for other outdoor games.

George and Emily Johnson loved birds and Chiefswood was a sanctuary for all types, including whippoorwills, wild pigeons, wild ducks, domesticated ducks and some peacocks. Between the Grand River and the home's front door there was a tow path, picnic flats complete with tables and benches, a ravine, a spring, a pond and a hill with trees. At the base of the trees grew wild strawberries and raspberries, lilies, wild columbine, violets, blood root, wild anemone and tiger lilies.

Is it any wonder that, according to Eva: "All the year round guests came to the hospitable country house-men and women of culture, of learning, of artistic tastes, of congenial habits. Scientists, authors, artists, all made their pilgrimages to this unique household, where refinement and much luxury, and always a glad welcome from the Chief and his English wife, made their visits long remembered." She adds: "Chiefswood was in those days one of the showplaces of Ontario. A letter addressed 'Chiefswood' alone and posted up the lake to us would be delivered, as has been done, so well known was our home."[8]

More than 140 years after Chiefswood was completed, it still stands as a testament to the varied accomplishments of each member of the celebrated Johnson family who inhabited it for 24 glorious years, between 1856 and 1884.

He Who Has the Great Mansion
by Horatio Hale

The Chief, who had a natural taste and talent for architecture, erected on his farm one of the finest dwellings in the country. A white stuccoed building, of two lofty storeys and a spacious and imposing front, rose, elegant and stately, upon a terraced eminence overlooking the Grand River, in the midst of a parklike grove, in which almost every variety of the native woods was represented. The house, it may be added, obtained for its possessor the Indian personal name by which he was best known-that of Onwanonsyshon – *he who has the great mansion.*[9]

Pride of Race and Heritage
by E. Pauline Johnson

Their loves were identical. They loved nature-the trees, best of all, and the river, and the birds. They loved the Anglican Church, they loved the British flag, they loved Queen Victoria...They loved music, pictures and dainty china, with which George (Johnson) filled his beautiful home. They loved books and animals, but most of all, these two loved the Indian people, loved their legends, their habits, their customs-loved the people themselves. Small wonder, then, that their children should be born with pride of race and heritage, and should face the world with that peculiar, unconquerable courage that only a fighting ancestry can give.[10]

a wagon-box full, and the butternuts at 50 cents per bag.[11]

Chiefswood's Arbour

Hamilton Spectator, February 1878

The Committee appointed by the Arts and Agriculture Association for the purpose of examining the various nut-bearing trees found growing on the property of G.H.M. Johnson, Esq., Chief of Six Nations Indians, begs to report:

That this lovely native park is situated on the east bank of the Grand River, in the Township of Onondaga. The land rises from the river to the commodious dwelling of the Chief in three broad and beautiful natural terraces of some seventy feet or more in height. That the various kinds of nut-bearing trees enumerated below, were found growing and bearing in equal luxuriance on each of the terraces. Your Committee were [sic] informed, by the Chief and his very intelligent and communicative son, that there were growing on their estate some 800 walnut, 300 butternut, and about 200 hickory trees of various kinds. Many of these trees were noble specimens, especially the walnuts. One upon the terrace below, and almost in front of the house, was really a majestic tree, with a large massive globular head of some 120 feet in circumference. The lower branches nearly touching the ground, and the head rising to at least 40 feet in height, and every branch drooping with its load of large fruit, some specimens measuring eight inches in diameter. Your Committee were informed by the worthy Chief that he sold, or, we might say, gave away, the walnuts at $2 for

A Welcome Visitor in Society

by Horatio Hale

The chief was often sent by his people as a delegate to bring their needs and occasionally their remonstrances, to the attention of the government. If not in all cases successful in such missions, his appearance and address always secured him attention and respect. Governors and statesmen received him with courtesy and interest. At Government House, and everywhere in society, he was a welcome visitor. At public entertainments, his fine Napoleonic figure and face, set off by the Indian costume which on such occasions he frequently assumed, made him a center of attraction which his quiet dignity of manner and a happy style of conversation, combining good sense with humor, and made more piquant by a half foreign accent, was well calculated to enhance. At home he was the most genial and kindly of men. The attractions of the place and of the household brought many visitors, who all came away delighted with a reception in which Indian hospitality had combined with English courtesy and refinement to make the guests feel themselves pleasantly at home.[12]

Henry Beverly Johnson, 1854-1894

On July 18, 1854, Bev Johnson was born at the Tuscarora Parsonage on the Six Nations Reserve, Upper Canada. He was the first of four children born to Chief George and Emily Johnson. His father wanted him christened Napoleon Bonaparte because of the great love the Chief had for the French leader. The boy, however, was named "Henry" after his Godfather Henry Racey of Brantford, and "Beverly" after Captain Beverly who was stationed in Toronto and who, after the Rebellion of 1837, sent Chief George Johnson a sword in appreciation of the Chief's patriotic work. Bev's nickname was "Boney," so in a way his father got his wish. When he was a teenager, friends gave him another nickname, "Hell" Johnson, presumably because he enjoyed raising some.

Bev was educated first at the Mohawk Institute near Brantford, and later at Hellmuth College in London, Ontario. He was an accomplished amateur musician. When he was 10, a friend of his father's gave Bev an ebony flute with silver keys and mountings. While at college Bev swept all prizes for music. His collection of sheet music for piano included pieces by Chopin and Gilbert & Sullivan, among other composers. Bev was a natural athlete and at college he won a gold medal for running and another medal for lacrosse. He grew to be a very handsome man and his sister Eva said that he was considered to be the handsomest man in all of Canada. As a member of the Garrick Dramatic Club in Hamilton, Bev was involved in amateur theatrical productions. He also claimed membership with the United Empire Loyalists.

As a young man Bev was employed in Hamilton with the Mutual Life Insurance Company. The firm sent him to Montreal to be First Cashier. He was working in Montreal in 1884 when he learned of his father's impending death.

Later in his career Bev became an inspector for the New York Life Insurance Company. While he was working for the company in Columbia, Pennsylvania, he died of heart failure on September 13, 1894. He was 40 years old and unmarried. Bev Johnson's body was brought home to Brantford and a private funeral service was held in the Johnson's home before Bev's remains were laid to rest at the Mohawk Chapel.

Johnson Boys Excel at Lacrosse
by Evelyn Johnson

While Beverly was a member of the Hamilton lacrosse team, Allen played on the Brantford team. The Hamilton players challenged the Brantford team to a game, which was to take place at the Southern Fair Grounds, in Brantford. The boys coaxed Pauline and me to drive from Chiefswood to the game. We did witness the match, and some of the girls asked us which side we were on. We replied that we didn't care who won as we had a brother on each team.[13]

A Singularly Magical Moment

by Jean Waldie

Judge Hardy related that his wife, Mary Elizabeth Curtis, had as a girl frequently visited Chiefswood, the Johnson home. One incident stood out vividly in her mind. It occurred on a summer's evening when she and Pauline and others of the Johnson family were seated outside one of the long windows of the living room, while Pauline's brother, Beverly, an accomplished pianist, entertained them with piano selections at random. Just at the very moment when the moon shone forth in all its silvery splendour, Beverly, by an odd coincidence, broke into the strains of the *Moonlight Sonata*. It seemed to the party assembled a singularly magical moment.[14]

Helen Charlotte Eliza Johnson, 1856-1937

Born on September 22, 1856, and given the names Helen Charlotte Eliza, the first daughter of Chief George and Emily Johnson was known as either "Eva" or "Evelyn" although her father wished her to be called "Josephine," after Napoleon Bonaparte's wife. The baby girl was given the name "Eliza" in honour of her late Aunt Eliza, but the baby's Grandfather Howells suggested she be called "Evangeline" after Longfellow's poem of the same name. This was shortened to "Eva." When Eva was confirmed she took the name "Evelyn" for herself. She was sent to London, Ontario, to study at Hellmuth Ladies' College.

During the years when she and Pauline lived with their widowed mother in Brantford, Eva held a position in the office of the Waterous Engine Works. She recalled in later years that this was the only office job she had during her working life. After her mother's death in 1898 Eva lived in the United States. In Troy, N.Y., she was matron of the Resident Home of the YWCA. In White Plains, N.Y., she was assistant at the Presbyterian Convalescent Home, and later she took charge of a lady's house. In New Jersey she worked as a lady's companion to the Senator's mother, and in Philadelphia she was the assistant to the head of the Sheltering Arms Home.

It was from Philadelphia that she was summoned to Vancouver, B.C., in 1912 to be with her dying sister. After Pauline's funeral in 1913, Eva remained in Vancouver for seven months before returning east, having taken care of her late sister's estate.

Eva Johnson again found employment in New York as a lady's companion. After experiencing ill health and eye trouble, she returned to live in Brantford. She lived alone at the Commercial Chambers on Dalhousie Street. People often saw Miss Johnson, dressed in black, sitting on a bench in Victoria Park. She never married. Eva died at the age of 80 on June 12 of 1937. She outlived her famous sister by 24 years and was the last of the four children of Chief George and Emily Johnson to pass away. Eva Johnson was buried at the Mohawk Chapel.

Allen Wawanosh Johnson, 1858-1923

Allen Johnson was born at Chiefswood, Six Nations, on July 21, 1858. The name "Allen" was given to him as his Godfather, Allen Gleghorne, was one of Chief George Johnson's greatest friends, and the name "Wawanosh" (an Ojibway word) because Chief Wawanosh, a guest at Chiefswood at the time of the boy's birth, requested that his name be given to the newborn. Allen was nicknamed "Kleber" by his father in honour of one of the generals in Napoleon Bonaparte's army.

Allen was sent to the Mohawk Institute but was unhappy there and ran away to the home of his grandfather Chief John Smoke Johnson. Allen was then sent to Miss Osborne's school on the reserve. After that he attended the Collegiate Institute in Brantford. While there he boarded with his uncle, Dr. T.B. Howells.

After completing his education, one of Allen's jobs was as a cashier in Hamilton at the office of the warehouse of Senator James Turner, a friend of the Johnson family. Allen was socially active as a member of the rowing club, the Garrick Dramatic Club and Hamilton's lacrosse club.

Allen became unemployed, and his sister Eva gives this account of a mysterious and prolonged period in her brother's life: "There has been a great deal of misunderstanding about Allen, who came home to Brantford and lived for ten years without working. This attitude was evidently caused by a girl. She had never seen Brantford, although Pauline and I had met her. Some men when disappointed in love will kill, some commit suicide, and some will take to drink. Allen did none of these things, but simply refused to take part in any active support of himself. This inactivity perhaps was due to mother's financing in part his affairs, for which she used most of her money."[15]

Later in his life Allen became engaged to Floretta Katherine Maracle. They married in June of 1908 and both of Allen's sisters attended the ceremony. Floretta was the youngest of six sisters who were raised by two aunts after the girls' parents drowned during a mishap in the Bay of Quinte. Floretta taught school in Ohsweken on the Six Nations Reserve before securing a job with the Indian Department in Ottawa, where she worked for 20 years prior to her wedding. During their marriage Allen and Flo Johnson lived in Toronto, where he served for many years as the vice president of the United Empire Loyalists. In the summer of 1923, Allen became ill and was taken to hospital. He died on June 19 of that year, at the age of 64. He was buried at the Mohawk Chapel.

How the Johnson Children Were Reared
by E. Pauline Johnson

These children were reared on the strictest lines of both Indian and English principles. They were taught the legends, the traditions, the culture and the etiquette of both races to which they belonged; but above all, their mother instilled into them from the very cradle that they were of their father's people, not of hers. Her marriage had made her an Indian by the laws which govern Canada, as well as by the sympathies and yearnings and affections of her own heart. When she married George [Johnson] she had repeated to him the cen-

The first three Johnson children (left to right): Allen, Bev and Eva. This photo was probably taken before Pauline's birth in March of 1861.
(Brant Historical Society #1676)

turies-old vow of allegiance, "Thy people shall be my people, and thy God, my God." She determined that should she ever be mother to his children, those children should be reared as Indians in spirit and patriotism, and in loyalty to their father's face as well as by heritage of blood. The laws of Canada held these children as Indians. They were wards of the Government; they were born on Indian lands, on Indian Reservations. They could own and hold Indian lands, and their mother, English though she was, made it her life service to inspire, foster and elaborate within these children the pride of race, the value of that copper-tinted skin which they all displayed.[16]

mates were totally ignorant, yet her lack of knowledge in which younger children were skilled who had regularly attended public school. She herself maintains that she owes the beginning of her literary career to the knowledge she gained by her assiduous teacher, her pet dog Chip.[17]

Emily Pauline Johnson, photographed in 1872 when she was 11 years old. *(Royal Ontario Museum, Toronto, #930.31.34)*

Pauline's Puppy Trilingual
by E. Pauline Johnson or Evelyn Johnson

Her father one day bought for her a tiny, black, curly-haired dog named "Chip" who was for years her constant companion and pupil. She made for her pet a little coat and cap, and drew him about the house and grounds in a little cart made for that purpose. Chip was unable to understand English when he first became a member of the household, but it was soon discovered that he was well versed in the Mohawk and Tuscarora languages in which it was found necessary to guide and direct him. Little Pauline, however, undertook his early education in English, and during the long winter days she read and recited to him scores of poems and books of prose, and in so doing she memorized verse and prose to such an extent that she became an enigma to her teachers at school who remarked upon her wide knowledge of many subjects in which her older school-

A'bram
by E. Pauline Johnson

He was a curious old customer, industrious but slow, intelligent but superstitious, in short, a typical old Indian to whom honesty was a religion and fidelity a creed. I cannot recall the time when he was not in some capacity or other in the employment of our household-gardener, hostler, harvester, in all he proved himself a priceless retainer and trustworthy friend. Every June of my childhood was particularly identified with A'bram's presence on the old estate, for my father never entrusted the cutting of the June grass and the haying thereof to anyone else, and many of my happiest young hours have been spent in sprawling out in the sunshine on the terraces while I watched him mow the lawns with the big crooked scythe that swathed with such monotonous regularity back and forth, leaving behind it a long heaped-up line of silverish green, and the indescribable freshness and fragrance of newly-cut hay. One morning a week after my final release from the school-room, the familiar swish of the scythe floated in through the old French windows, and in five minutes I had forgotten my young-ladyisms and was lolling out on the grass as of yore, chattering away to the old man, while I watched the hot June sunshine glint along the surface of the river that coiled its sparkling length far round the lowlands, where some lads were tossing the already dried hay into cocks.[18]

This photograph was taken at the Mohawk Chapel on October 1, 1869, on the occasion of the visit of Prince Arthur, son of Queen Victoria, and future Governor-General of Canada. During this reception, attended by several hundred men of the Six Nations, the prince was inducted as an honorary Chief of the Six Nations Indians. Chief John Smoke Johnson, Pauline's grandfather, was appointed as one of two chiefs of the Great Council to conduct the ceremony. Chief George Johnson, Pauline's father, acted as interpreter. Chief George Johnson can be seen to the left of the prince, with his face partly obscured by shadow, but with his distinctive mustache and goatee visible. The chiefs and warriors are posed to form an honour guard for the young royal visitor, while the bough above the chapel door suggests the Six Nations Confederacy's symbolic Tree of Peace. In Pauline's book, *Legends of Vancouver*, she included her account of this famous day, entitled "A Royal Mohawk Chief."
(Ontario Archives, Toronto, #S895)

Horatio Hale Comes to Chiefswood
by Evelyn Johnson

Horatio Hale, the historian, had a very keen interest in Indians, and he wished to obtain every bit of information he could about them. For this reason he often came to our house, and father at these times had different Indians to see him. To assist Mr. Hale in gleaning the required data, John Buck frequently came. He always brought with him his wampum belts, twenty-one in number. These were always carried in a small bag. Mr. Hale, of course, could not speak the Indian languages. Father, therefore, interpreted, and every word uttered by John Buck, or his sister Christine, who sometimes accompanied him, was translated by father to Mr. Hale.[19]

G.H.M. Johnson
by Evelyn Johnson

One time, we had as a guest a young man who told us that until he discovered differently he thought that "G.H.M." (father's initials) meant "Great, High and Mighty." This is one of the few times I can remember father laughing and seeming to heartily enjoy a joke.[20]

George Johnson Encounters a Remorseful Man
by E. Pauline Johnson

George Johnson was a guest of the bishop of his diocese, as he was a lay delegate accompanying Rev. Adam Elliot to the Anglican Synod. The chief's work had reached other ears than those of the Government of Ottawa, and the bishop was making much of the patriot, when an old clergyman approached him with outstretched hand and the words, "I would like you to call bygones just bygones."

"I don't believe I have the honor of knowing you, sir," replied the Indian, with a puzzled but gracious look. "I am your wife's brother-in-law," said the old clergyman, "the man who would not allow her to be married from my house, that is, married to you."

The Indian bit his lip and instinctively stepped backward. Added to his ancestral creed of never forgiving such injury, came a rush of memory-the backward-surging picture of his homeless little sweetheart and all that she had endured. Then came the memory of his dead mother's teaching-teaching she had learned from her own mother, and she in turn from her mother: "Always forget yourself for old people, always honor the old." Instantly George Johnson arose-arose above the prejudices of his blood, above the traditions of his race, arose to the highest plane a man can reach-the memory of his mother's teaching. "I would hardly be here as a lay delegate of my church were I not willing to let bygones be bygones," he said, simply, and laid his hand in that of the old clergyman, about whose eyes there was moisture, perhaps because this opportunity for peacemaking had come so tardily.[21]

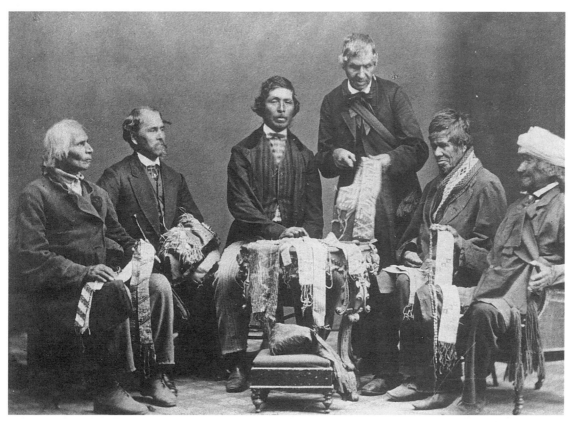

Six Chiefs of the Six Nations Reserve posed for Horatio Hale at Chiefswood on September 14, 1871. The men are deliberately posed to draw attention to the wampum belts. Left to right: Joseph Snow, Onondaga; George Johnson, Mohawk; John Buck, Onondaga (wampum keeper); John Smoke Johnson (standing), Mohawk (council speaker); Isaac Hill, Onondaga (firekeeper); and Seneca Johnson, Seneca. The photographer, Horatio Hale (1817-1896) was from Clinton, Ontario. He was a writer, a lawyer and an ethnologist who studied the Iroquois' political organization for many years. After the death of his friend, Chief George Johnson, Hale wrote a biography of Chief Johnson: *Chief George H.M. Johnson, Onwanonsyshon: His Life and Work Among the Six Nations*, 1885.

Pauline Was Much Annoyed
by Evelyn Johnson

Some Americans called one day, and Pauline apologized for not being dressed for the afternoon. "Why," one lady said, "do you dress for the afternoon?"

"Certainly," said Pauline. "We don't know when anyone may come. Look at yourselves coming unexpectedly." The lady then asked Pauline how she curled her hair, and when Pauline told her it was naturally curly, the lady would not believe her. "Come now, tell me how you curl your hair," she said. Pauline was much annoyed, but answered that she put nothing on it, that she never curled it, and that it was natural as she wore it. The visitor thought that because Pauline was part Indian she would have the proverbial straight hair, but Pauline took after mother with her curly hair.[22]

A portrait of Pauline Johnson, taken in the 1870s. "Eva is like the sun-she dazzles the men; I am like the moon-I drive them crazy."
(Brant Historical Society #563e)

The Celebrated Bell Family at Chiefswood
by E. Pauline Johnson

Upon one occasion he [Alexander Graham Bell] and his parents were spending a day at the writer's home and were to dine with us that evening. I was too tiny a child to make one of the dinner party, but as they were all seated I passed the dining-room door and heard my father say, "Professor Bell, will you please ask a blessing; we would like it in your new sign language." My mother, catching sight of my wistful face at the door, beckoned me to come to her side, and slipping her arm about me held me close as the Professor arose, and standing, "spoke" that strange silent blessing, which consisted of passes made by the fingers and hands from the lips. I watched him intently. Small as I was, I felt the reverence of it; his gestures were so telling, so clear, so plain, even my childish intellect could not mistake his "words." It was a long "blessing," and at its close, the ladies' eyes were wet with emotion.

A studio portrait of outdoor fun-tobogganing. Pauline is in the middle and her brother Bev sits behind her. The girl in the front is unidentified, but could quite likely be Pauline and Bev's cousin Kate who lived in Paris, Ontario, and who was one of Pauline's closest girlhood companions.
(Brant Historical Society #563h)

When our visitors were bidding us good-bye, the Professor shook hands with me and said: "I saw this little girl in the dining-room when I was saying grace," but, turning to me, "you didn't understand what I was doing, did you, dear?"

"Yes, Professor," I answered, gravely, "you were saying 'Our Father.'" It was true. He had said the Lord's Prayer in his wonderful deaf mute language, that was so grandly simple that even a young child understood it.[23]

Chief George Johnson Participates in Making Telecommunications History
by E. Pauline Johnson

When a child I often heard my father relate this story of the initial performance (of the long-distance telephone call) over this unperfected wire that was to grow with years into a necessity more important than at that time they even dared to hope. The young scientist, anxious but confident, had bidden a number of guests to dine at the quaint Bell homestead, and to participate in the pleasure of the experiment. Young Graham and my father personally tacked much of the wire, with non-conducting staples to the fences and trees between Tutela Heights and the city, spending much of the afternoon at the work. Succeeding the dinner came the experiment, which was very satisfactory, the operator in the city being able to distinguish the voices of each guest, until my father was requested to speak in Mohawk. "Can't hear," said the city operator. The greeting was repeated. "Something's

wrong," said the city man. Another Mohawk sentence from my father. "What's that?," from the city. More Mohawk. City man: "Oh! I say professor, you might have invited me, how many cases did you open?" A wild roar of

Alexander Graham Bell (right), in Brantford in July of 1876. This photograph, which also features his cousin, Miss Frances Symonds, was taken shortly after the young inventor had been made an honorary chief of the Mohawks. Bell appears to have borrowed Chief George Johnson's unique buckskin outfit for this appointment with the photographer. Miss Symonds sits wrapped in a blanket (quite likely the red wool blanket that Pauline used years later in her stage presentations) and she is holding the Johnson family's treasured tomahawk-peace pipe.
(Library of Congress, Washington; 409546 LCG9-23-156500-AB)

laughter from the Bell homestead at Tutela Heights and young Graham's voice over my father's shoulder "You've insulted the chief." Apologies from the city man, and general amusement at both ends of the line.[24]

Pauline Instinctively Extinguishes the Lamps
by Jean Waldie

Mrs. Reville (nee Jean Morton) related that, one evening at Chiefswood, where she was a frequent visitor, all the family had retired, save herself and Pauline, who were talking downstairs by lamplight. A sudden disturbance and sound of voices outside caused Pauline with lightning swiftness, in true Indian fashion, instinctively to extinguish the light, and the two girls sat in the darkness for the moment until they heard with relief through the long open window the familiar voices of a couple of boys from town, who had come to call on the girls, as was their wont.[25]

February 14, 1878
Chiefswood, Tuscarora

Cousin Kate Howells:

Think of me when the sun of life has set
And when purple shades of death draw nigh
Look on my grave with just one sweet regret
And for your little gypsy breathe a sigh.

Your loving Pauline[26]

Pauline Succumbs to a Vice
by Evelyn Johnson

One night about eleven or twelve o'clock we were going to bed. Our cousin Kate Howells was visiting my sister. She was Pauline's favourite chum and often spent a vacation at our home. My room was along the hall from Pauline's, and I had to pass the garret stairs to which there was at that time no door. Father was a very light sleeper, and any noise disturbed him; so, this particular night I crept noiselessly past my parents' room which was next to mine and tip-toed along the hall to Pauline's room. Poking my head in the door, I told them in a whisper that I smelled smoke in

A photograph of an adolescent Pauline, undated.
(Brant Historical Society #3790)

the garret. Pauline was lolling in bed, and Katie, at the dressing table, was doing her hair in pig-tails for the night. Pauline, rolling her handkerchief into a ball, threw it at Katie. The handkerchief hit Katie in the back of the neck and rolled down to the floor. Katie was in her petticoat, and when the handkerchief hit her,

she tipped forward on her toes, and as her bare arms and outspread fingers shot downward, she gave a decided squawk. For fear of waking father I popped into the room and closed the door softly. Pauline dived under the bed clothes, and Katie fell into a chair and promptly went into hysterics. When we could recover ourselves, Pauline came up smiling out of the covers, and Katie with a red face said to her, "Can't you go along the hall and see if there is a man smoking in the garret? Can't you see Eva is frightened?" Pauline smiled, but said nothing. I lingered a few moments longer and then retired to my room, but still smelled a faint smoke. Next day it developed that Pauline having a bad cold was smoking a Cuban cigar in bed.[27]

Pauline Cross-Dresses
by Evelyn Johnson

One warm afternoon when we had nothing in particular to do, Pauline thought she would play a joke on (our guest) Nannie; so while I entertained our visitor, Pauline dressed in Allen's clothes. When I thought Pauline was ready I excused myself, and going to the kitchen I stood looking out of a window. Outside stood Pauline, with Allen's hat on the back of her head, her legs apart, and her hands in her pockets. Nannie at my pretended errand in the kitchen went out to look for Pauline, and when she turned the corner of the house she saw someone talking to me. Supposing the person to be a man, she backed away. I said to Pauline, "Here she comes." As Nannie disappeared, Pauline said, "I'm going to chase her," and proceeded to do so. Nannie, thinking that

Pauline is pictured in her canoeing outfit, complete with a tam and fashionable, slip-on shoes.
(Brant Historical Society #624)

Pauline was a man, also ran. They tore around the house; Nannie flew up the steps, and then the stairs with Pauline after her, and finally threw herself on the bed in her own room. Pauline, following her, was discovered and they both enjoyed a hearty laugh.[28]

From Eva's Point of View
by Evelyn Johnson

We were brought up quietly, played among ourselves in our own grounds and garden, and knew little of the outside world. For each

of us the first peep at it was a great novelty, and consequently the first love of each of us was unworthy.[30]

From Pauline's Point of View
by E. Pauline Johnson

An inherited sensitiveness was a perfect bane in our childhood. We were all shy, which mother conquered in us by having us assume a dignity far beyond our years. We learned from her to disguise our wretched bashfulness with a peculiar, cold reserve, that made our schoolfel-

The four Johnson children, January, 1878. Left to right: Pauline (at 16 years of age), Bev, Allen and Eva a.k.a. Evelyn. According to Eva it was "the mixture of bloods, the English and Mohawk, that resulted in our good-looking family."[29]
(Brant Historical Society)

lows call us "stuck-up," and our neighbours' children mock us as "proudy," but it saw us through the exigencies of life, and serves me to this very day. A long public career has never lessened this inherited shyness, but the mask of reserve and dignity learned from my mother has stood me in excellent stead.[31]

Pauline dressed for a cold, Brantford winter, 1880.
(Brant Historical Society #633)

The Christmas Cake That Never Was
by Evelyn Johnson

It was decided one year that Pauline should make our Christmas cake. She was just a young girl, in her early 'teens. It fell to my lot to prepare many of the ingredients. All the raisins had to be stoned; the peel had to be cut, and the currants washed and dried. The night before the cake was to be baked, I made those preparations. Next day about ten o'clock, Pauline began making her Christmas cake. It took several hours to bake in two large pans. About 7:30 that evening, mother and Pauline went to the kitchen to examine the cakes, which they thought had baked long enough. They turned them out of the pans to cool. A currant which stuck to the pan mother put into her mouth. "It is very hot," she said. Pauline said, "Of course it is; it's just out of the oven," and took herself upstairs to her room. When she had gone, mother broke off a small piece of the cake and tasted it and then called my sister. They found that Pauline had used two teaspoonsful of cayenne pepper instead of two of ground mace. Needless to say, we had no Christmas cake that year.[32]

MY LITTLE JEAN

Mine is the fate to watch the evening star,
In yonder dome,
Descending slowly thro' the cobweb bar
That girts the twilight mysteries afar-
Above your home.

Mine is the fate to turn toward the west
When falls the dew,
When dips the sun beyond the woodland
crest
At vesper hour, I think, my loved and
best,
Alone of you.

And mine the happy fate to live for aye
Within the dream
Of knowing that the sun lights not a day
But that some thought of yours to me will
stray,
My little Jean.

The diamond blaze of glory lures me
through
A gilded whirl,
Fame stretches toward me crowns of sap-
phire blue;
But I must fain resist-and choose but you,
My bonny girl.

Your friendship has sufficed, and held its
own
Unsullied still,
What manly voice upon my heart has
grown,
What stronger hand can soothe like yours
alone
My headstrong will?

Life offers me no love but love for you,
My woman's thought
Was never given to test a faith untrue-
Nor drink of passion's spirits drugged with
rue,
Too dearly bought.

They say sometimes my wayward heart
must rise,
To love so strong,
That friendship will grow cold when other
ties
Enslave my heart, that in my soul there
lies
An unknown song.

But yet it is unsung, nor do I care
Its notes to glean;
Give in their place your bonny eyes and
hair,
Your tender voice, your heart, a jewel rare-
My little Jean.[33]

1883, addressed to her friend Jean Morton

THE FIRS

(This poem is a longer, reworked version of
Pauline's poem, The Fourth Act)

Pine trees sobbing a weird unrest
    In saddened strains;
Crows flying slowly into the west
    As daylight wanes;
Breezes that die in a stifled breath,
Leaving a calm that is still as death.

Fir trees reaching toward the sky
    In giant might;
All day long at your feet I lie
    Awaiting night,
While sweet pine needles are falling down
In silent showers of golden brown.

How waves the blue Canadian air
    Amid your arms?
'Tis not so calm down here as there,
    Because your charms
Enhance the world to a sapphire blue,
And change its tone with its change of
hue.

Changed in a thousand trivial ways-
    That shade a life,
Leaving the dregs of yesterdays
    With shadows rife:
Shadows that lie in the fir tops tall,
And fall with the fir cones over all.

For some one's turned their tender eyes
    Away from me,
And dark the sorrow that in them lies
    With misery;
Oh, gentlest pleader my life has known,
I stay as you found me, here-alone.

Alone with the first and the dying day,
    That lived too long;
Alone with the pines that sing alway
    Their strange, wild song.
Ah, darling! unclasp your fair, warm hand,
'Tis better I should misunderstand.[34]

ROVER

Nurse! will you close the window tight?
    The air is bleak;
I cannot bear its breath to-night,
    I am too weak.

You think that I am worse, dear one?
    Just now you cried;
Your tears mean that before the dawn
    I will be dead.

How long you've lived! your hair of snow
    Tells that you've seen
Some three-score years, but I must go
    At seventeen.

So well you've loved and tended me
    Through life's short way,
From my first early infancy,
    To this sad day!

Ah, how the dark pines sigh! I think
    They almost know,
That I am near the river's brink,
    And soon must go.

I do not like their mournful song,
    Nor do I care,
That they are crowns for all the throng
    *

And when he sees you at the gate,
    At home once more,
He'll bark for me and sweetly wait
    Beside the door.

I will not speak or pat his head;
    And he alone
Can't understand that I am dead
    When I go home.

So when in splendor I am laid
    In stately gloom,
Where the stars and flower crosses fade
    In snow-white bloom;

When all the lighted candles blend
    With shadows cast,
Bring Rover in, my best-loved friend-
    To look his last.

Then take him in your arms of snow,
    His future place,
And lift him up, perhaps he'll know
    My poor dead face.

No voice, no step, no greetings kind,
    No laughing eyes,
No clue that his dumb, wondering mind
    Can recognize.

But a year hence, when sorrow's flame
    Has ceased to burn,
My dog will watch and wait in vain
    For my return.[35]

*The fourth line of the sixth stanza is
obscured and cannot be reproduced here.*

At the Expense of a Noble Life

by Horatio Hale

The causes which enfeebled the stalwart frame of John Smoke Johnson's son, and made his last illness fatal, were undoubtedly the injuries which he received in his endeavours to protect the morals and the property of his people from the white outlaws and desperadoes who formerly infested the Reserve. It is somewhat remarkable that an Iroquois chief should, in our peaceful time and among the quiet and law-respecting people of Canada, die from the effect of wounds received from his enemies of European race, as doubtless many of his predecessors had died in the fiercer days of old. But the conditions were strangely reversed. The conflict was still one of civilization with barbarism; but in this case Indian civilization stood at bay before White savagery, and conquered in the end, though at the expense of a noble life.[36]

Pauline's father, Chief George Henry Martin Johnson, as he looked in midlife, proudly wearing his buckskin outfit, complete with fringed leggings, a jacket with a fur collar, and his distinctive hat. Surely his hand is placed in his jacket deliberately, in honour of his hero Napoleon Bonaparte. In remembering his friend, Horatio Hale had this to say: "Few have done more than he accomplished in his humble sphere, in breaking down the absurd and wicked prejudices of race, and proving the essential unity and brotherhood of the human family."[37]
(Brant Historical Society #534)

Pauline Recounts the Circumstances of Her Beloved Father's Death

by E. Pauline Johnson

Cold had settled in all the broken places of his poor body, and he slipped away from her, a sacrifice to his fight against evil on the alter of his nation's good. In his feverish wanderings he returned to the tongue of his childhood, the beautiful, dulcet Mohawk. Then recollecting and commanding himself, he would weakly apologize to his wife: "I forgot; I thought it was my mother," and almost his last words were, "It must be by my mother's side," meaning his resting-place. So his valiant spirit went fearlessly forth.[38]

The ferry across the Grand River at Onondaga, Six Nations Reserve.
(Brant Historical Society #3937)

65

AT THE FERRY

We are waiting in the nightfall by the
river's placid rim,
Summer silence all about us, save where
swallows' pinions skim
The still grey waters sharply, and the
widening circles reach,
With faintest, stillest music, the white
gravel on the beach.
The sun has set long, long ago. Against
the pearly sky
Elm branches lift their etching up in arch-
es slight and high.
Behind us stands the forest, with its black
and lonely pine;
Before us, like a silver thread, the old
Grand River winds.
Far down its banks the village lights are
creeping one by one;
Far up above, with holy torch, the evening
star looks down.

Amid the listening stillness, you and I
have silent grown,
Waiting for the river ferry,-waiting in the
dusk alone.
At last we hear a velvet step, sweet
silence reigns no more;

'Tis a barefoot, sun-burnt little boy upon
the other shore.
Far thro' the waning twilight we can see
him quickly kneel
To lift the heavy chain, then turn the
rusty old cog-wheel;
And the water-logged old ferry-boat moves
slowly from the brink,
Breaking all the star's reflections with the
waves that rise and sink;
While the water dripping gently from the
rising, falling chains,
Is the only interruption to the quiet that
remains
To lull us into golden dreams, to charm
our cares away
With its Lethean waters flowing 'neath the
bridge of yesterday.
Oh! the day was calm and tender, but the
night is calmer still,
As we go aboard the ferry, where we stand
and dream, until
We cross the sleeping river, with its restful
whisperings,
And peace falls, like a feather from some
passing angel's wings.[39]

THE RE-INTERMENT OF RED JACKET

By E. Pauline Johnson,
(A Mohawk Indian girl, daughter of a distinguished sachem lately deceased, and one of the invited guests of the Buffalo Historical Society.)

So still the tranquil air,
One scarcely notes the falling of a leaf,-
But deeper quiet wraps the dusky Chief
Whose ashes slumber there.

Sweet Indian Summer sleeps-
Trusting a foreign and a paler race
To give her gifted son an honored place
Where Death his vigil keeps.

Before that slumber fell,
Those ashes in their eloquence had stirred
The stubborn hearts, whose heirs to-day conferred
A Christian burial.

Through war's o'er-clouded skies
His higher flush of oratory 'woke,
And factious schemes succumbed whene'er he spoke
To bid his people rise.

The keenest flint or stone
That barbed the warrior's arrow in its flight,
Could not outreach the limit of his might
That he attained alone.

Early he learned to speak,
With thought so vast, and liberal, and strong,
He blessed the little good and passed the wrong
Embodied in the weak.

So great his mental sight,
That had his form been growing with his mind,
The fir had been within his hand a wand
With superhuman might.

The world has often seen
His master mind pulse with the waning day,
That sends his waning nation to decay
Where none can intervene.

And few to-day remain:
But copper-tinted face, and smoldering fire
Of wilder life, were left me by my sire
To be my proudest claim.

And so ere Indian Summer sweetly sleeps
She beckons me where old Niagara leaps;
Superbly she extends her greeting hand,
And, smiling, speaks to her adopted land,
Saying, "O, rising nation of the West,
That occupy my lands so richly blest;
O, free, unfettered people that have come
And made America your rightful home-
Forgive the wrongs my children did to you,
And we, the red-skins, will forgive you too.
To-day has seen your noblest action done-
The honored re-intombment of my son."

Chiefswood, Ontario, October 9, 1884[40]

Red Jacket, 1758-1830, a Seneca chief, born in Seneca County, New York. He favoured neutrality during the American Revolution. After the war he spoke out against accepting a peace that he felt would mean inevitable white domination of Iroquois land in New York. He championed Iroquois autonomy, using his considerable skills as an orator.

C H A P T E R   3

Brantford Days
1884-1892

When the Johnson women moved to Brantford in 1884 they adjusted to living in straitened circumstances. There was little spare money for Pauline to finance her visits to friends outside the city. She was not isolated from friends completely; she had a well-developed social life within Brantford and Brant County. During the 1880s, Pauline wrote, canoed, appeared in amateur theatrics, and enjoyed the outdoors in the summer and winter months.

Her set included a number of gentleman callers. According to her sister, "Pauline had many offers of marriage. Few of these were Indians. I know of eight that she received, but of those she had later when she began to travel, I do not know."[1]

Occasionally Pauline went to Hamilton to visit Allen. He escorted her to the theatre and to recitals. She enjoyed attending plays that starred M'lle Rhea, a performer who appealed to her female fans for her extravagant and elegant costumes. In November of 1885, Pauline met the famous actress and the two women became friends.

During this period of her life Pauline was an active member of the Brant Amateurs, a theatre company. In 1886 she appeared as "Mary Moss" in *Old Soldiers*, in which she gave an "excellent representation" of her character according to *The Brantford Courier* of December 15, and as Mrs. Foxton in *Thirty Minutes for Refreshments*. In 1887 she played "Bella" in the four-act comedy *School*.

The city of Brantford commissioned a statue of Captain Joseph Brant at a cost of $16,000. On August 11, 1886 at the cornerstone ceremony in Victoria Park, Chief John Smoke Johnson spoke about meeting with Joseph Brant during the early years of the century.

Smoke Johnson was the only person at the ceremony who had personal memories of the great Six Nations leader. During an interview in 1877, he had this to say about his association with Joseph Brant: "I remember Captain Brant perfectly. I was a kind of pet of his. When I was a boy I accompanied Captain Brant and a delegation of Indians to hold a council with Sir John Johnson at Montreal. We dined with Sir John who treated us very kindly. I remember that Brant and Sir John had a very animated and almost angry discussion upon Indian affairs while we were there. But that was no unusual thing. I remember when a boy attending councils held between our people and English agents or officers. Our Indian orators would stride around the circle and flourish their tomahawks in dangerous proximity to the faces of the British officers, and declaim with great vehemence and energy-and this was done when their intentions were of the most pacificate character. Both Sir John and Brant were men of dignified and haughty manners."[2]

Just 15 days after his public appearance Pauline's grandfather died. He was buried at the Mohawk Chapel. His family placed the Bible and his tomahawk in his coffin. Chief John Smoke Johnson had outlived his wife Helen by 20 years, and his son George by two years.

October 13, 1886 was the day of the unveiling of Brant's monument by Ontario's Lieutenant-Governor Robinson. A memorial ode, composed by Pauline, was read to the throng by Willian Foster Cockshutt, the president of the Cockshutt Plow Company and a budding politician. Before her poem was read, Pauline was conducted to a seat on the platform reserved for dignitaries. At the close of the poem she presented the first copy to Mrs. Robinson. In return, Pauline received applause and a bouquet of flowers.

In the next day's edition of the Toronto newspaper, *The Globe*, a long interview with Miss Johnson appeared on the Women's World page, written by one Garth Grafton. This was the coy pen-name of Sara Jeannette Duncan, a friend of Pauline's from their Brantford school-days. In the 1880s, Sara was making her way in the male-

In this sea of people, gathered for the unveiling of the Brant Memorial in Brantford, 1886, Pauline Johnson can be seen standing on the platform for dignitaries. She is facing left and is speaking to an older woman in black. On close observation the bouquet in Pauline's hands can be seen.
(Brant Historical Society #611)

dominated field of journalism. She is best remembered as the prolific author of 22 books, including the 1904 novel, *The Imperialist*.

Pauline's poem, "Ode To Brant," gained her some publicity in Toronto as well as in her own city. Many invitations for social engagements followed the October 1886 municipal event.

(continued on page 75)

Obituary for Pauline's Grandfather, Chief Smoke Johnson

The Brantford Expositor, August 26, 1886

Many of our citizens will remember the infirm and grey-haired Indian Chief Smoke Johnson, who was present at the laying of the foundation stone of the Brant Memorial. At that time he seemed unusually active for a man of his great age, having passed 94 winters. Today we have to chronicle his death, which occurred at his home on the Reserve, undoubtedly from pure old age. On Monday he seemed in the enjoyment of his usual health, and worked in his garden during the greater portion of the day, but on Tuesday he was taken ill and gradually sank until the end came. Deceased was the oldest Indian on the Reserve and the only one who remembered Chief Joseph Brant, Thayendanegea. He was the father of the generally respected late Chief George H.M. Johnson, and of the following children who survive viz., Mrs. Peter Davis, Mrs. Margaret Elliott, Chief Joseph Johnson, and Mr. Aaron Johnson. His death at this time is all the more to be regretted since it was hoped he would be spared to be present at the unveiling of the Brant Memorial. But it was not to be.[3]

A Memorial Ode

The Brantford Expositor, 1886

Miss E. Pauline Johnson the gifted Indian poetess, daughter of the late distinguished Chief Geo. H.M. Johnson, has written a memorial ode entitled "Brant" which will be offered for sale tomorrow. The poem was written for the Brant Memorial Association, and has been copyrighted. It is cleverly written, and evidences true poetic genius, and will no doubt meet with a ready sale, as a most appropriate souvenir of the occasion.[4]

Pauline, as she might have appeared during her interview with her friend, the journalist, and future novelist, Sara Jeannette Duncan, on the eve of the Brant Memorial unveiling, 1886.
(Brant Historical Society #250)

BRANT
A Memorial Ode

Young Canada with mighty force sweeps on
To gain in power and strength, before the dawn
That brings another era; when the sun
Shall rise again, but only shine upon
Her Indian graves, and Indian memories,
For as the carmine in the twilight skies
Will fade as night comes on, so fades the race
That unto Might and therefore Right gives place,
And as white clouds float hurriedly and high
Across the crimson of a sunset sky,
Altho' their depths are foamy as the snow,
Their beauty lies in their vermilion glow,
So Canada, thy plumes were hardly won
Without allegiance from thy Indian son,
Thy glories, like the cloud enhance their charm
With red reflections from the Mohawk's arm,
Then meet we as one common Brotherhood,
In peace and love, with purpose understood-
To lift a lasting tribute to the name
Of Brant-who linked his own, with Britain's fame

Who bade his people leave their valley home,
Where nature in her fairest aspect shone,
Where rolls the Mohawk river, and the land
Is blessed with every good from Heaven's hand,
To sweep the tide of home affections back
And love the land where waves the Union Jack.
What tho' that home no longer ours! Today
The Six Red Nations have their Canada,
And rest we here, no cause for us to rise
To seek protection under other skies,
Encircling us an arm both true and brave
Extends from far across the great salt wave,
Tho' but a woman's hand 'tis firm and strong
Enough to guard us from all fear of wrong,
A hand on which all British subjects lean-
The loving hand of England's Noble Queen.

"Chiefswood," E. Pauline Johnson,
October 8th, 1886 Te-ka-hion-wa-ke.[5]

Pauline Is Interviewed by Journalist Garth Grafton, a.k.a. Sara Jeannette Duncan
Woman's World, *Toronto Globe*, October, 1886

Among the braves that gathered together their peaceful and warlike belongings and followed the loyal Brant to Canada so long ago was one Jacob Johnson. His son, "Smoke" Johnson, who died a short time ago, well remembered Brant, and his journeys to Montreal and Quebec, whither the young Johnson used to accompany him.

...One of the sons of Smoke and Helen Johnson was the well-known chief of the Six Nations, G.H.M. Johnson, who married an

English lady and brought her to "Chief's Wood," a romantic and secluded home in the Indian Reserve upon the Grand River. And the young poetess whose verses upon the occasion of the unveiling of the Brant Memorial yesterday provoked such a storm of applause, Miss E. Pauline Johnson, is the late Chief Johnson's daughter. I think that in connection with this "auspicious occasion" you ought to know about Miss Johnson, and I intend that you shall.

I have had the pleasure of her acquaintance for some time, and while it is a privilege that cannot, unfortunately, be extended to the general public, it seems to me that all Canadiennes deserve at least to enjoy it by proxy. I found her at her residence in Brantford's North Ward. You want to know what she is like first, of course.

Well, she is tall and slender and dark, with grey eyes, beautifully clean cut features, black hair, a very sweet smile, and a clear, musical, pleasant voice. I have always thought her beautiful and many agree with me. She has certainly that highest attribute of beauty, the rare, fine gift of expression. She is charmingly bright in conversation, and has a vivacity of tone and gesture that is almost French.

"And aren't you connected with Brant in some way?" I asked this graceful olive branch of the Iroquois.

"No," she answered. "There is an impression to that effect. We are not related. But my grandfather, who died a little while ago, remembered Brant perfectly. Poor old grandpapa! It is such a pity he couldn't have lived to see the unveiling to-morrow."

And then Miss Johnson proceeded to tell me all about her romantic family tree.

"Our real name, you know, isn't Johnson," she said, "but Teka-hoon-wa-ke," which sounded very much like Tekkahoonwakky. "That

means *two wampums*, so if it were not for the baptism of my great grandfather, Jacob Johnson, after Sir William, I shouldn't be Miss Johnson, but Miss Te-ka-hoon-wa-ke."

"Oh," I said, "aren't you glad he was baptized? A *wampum* is a sort of a shell, isn't it?"

"It is a kind of bead," said Miss Johnson. "These cuffs that my brother will wear tomorrow in the dance are covered with them."

The cuff consisted of the beads curiously woven with slender leather thongs. They were very old, and some of the purple and white ornaments were chipped and broken. Miss Johnson said the white ones signified peace and that the arrangements of the designs of white beads upon the body of the purple ones was emblematic of the different tribes. Also that the art of making wampum beads is a lost one, and that the shells are supposed to have come from the Gulf of Mexico.

"And this," she said, showing me a superlatively awful looking instrument, "was given to my father by the Cayugas for political services. It's a tomahawk you see, and a pipe of peace combined," and Miss Johnson drew a whiff of nothing more noxious than the common air through the hollow handle. "This is a scalping-knife my father made himself out of a deer's foot. You see the handle is just the polished bone of the deer's leg."

"But don't they-didn't he-I mean isn't it usual for people who indulge in that kind of amusement to do it with their tomahawks?" I inquired rather delicately, for I wasn't at all sure that their fair descendant would relish this allusion to the peculiarities of her warrior ancestors. My compunctions were unnecessary.

"Oh, no!" she laughed. "It would be very awkward to scalp with a tomahawk. You see, this is the way they do it," and she raised some of her own dusky locks and made a mimic circle around it.

"Really!" I said, "Please don't. I always thought that to scalp a person was to deprive him of his hirsute adornment out and out!"

"I know most people think that," she responded, "but it is only a single lock and the portion of scalp it grows on. I saw once a scarf of several hundred and fifty Indian scalps, all braided together with beads and things. It came from one of the Rocky Mountain tribes. These are strings of deer-rattles that the Indians wear about their moccasins when they dance, to make music. You see they are just the ends of the cloven hooves strung together. And this rusty knife," she said, "has quite a history." It was a very rusty knife indeed, all brown and yellow with corrosion, and ragged along the edges. I at once professed my desire to hear the history.

"When my father was a very young man, and had just bought Chief's Wood, an old, old Indian came to him one day, and said, 'Johnson, I hear you've bought Chief's Wood.' My father said he had. 'When I was a youth,' said the old Indian, 'I was very jealous of another young man of the tribe, and he of me. One night he slew my brother. The next day I went to him, and found him sitting on a bench. I threw him back and said, "Did you lend my brother a knife last night?" He said, "Yes." "Then," I said, "I have come to return it," and I stabbed the young man through the heart. Then I drew out the knife, and carried it, dripping with his blood, to the dark side of the tree before your door, and slipped it under the moss at the roots. It has been there seventy-three years. And all those years I can go nowhere up or down the Grand River without seeing the top of that tree though it was cut down long ago, for I know that the knife lies under it still.'

"So then my father and he went to the stump and dug far down, and there surely enough was the knife. It was the last case of blood atonement, according to the old Indian law, that was known among us."

"Why did he take the dark side of the tree?"

"That was the north side. The Indians have a superstition that a dark deed should have a dark burial."

Then Miss Johnson showed me a veritable idol which had been grinning at me for some time beneath the parlor table, and a queer old carved powder horn, and bullet pouch, that bore the date 1807, and had been taken from a Kentuckian by her grandfather in 1812, and several other relics of fascinating interest.

...Miss Johnson's literary work is familiar to all readers of *The Week* in Canada, and to no small public on "the other side." Her poems have a dreamy quality that is very charming, and while she has given us no sustained work as yet, we may doubtless expect it ere long. She writes best of her own people, whom she dearly loves, when her full sympathy with her subject shows itself in every line.[6]

(continued from page 71)

During these Brantford years she often submitted her poems to periodicals. *Gems of Poetry* and *The Week* picked up some of her work for publication. Her poem, *The Sea Queen*, published in 1885, appealed to the poet Charles G.D. Roberts of New Brunswick. He wrote to Pauline to offer her encouragement, thus initiating a friendship and correspondence that lasted for the rest of Pauline's life.

In 1889 two of her poems were chosen by the poet William Douw Lighthall for an anthology of Canadian poetry, published with the title *Songs of the Great Dominion: Voices from the Forests and Waters, the Settlements and Cities of Canada.* After he included her poems "In the Shadows" and "At the Ferry" in this volume, Pauline dubbed Lighthall her "literary father." He called her "a Princess in all respects."

Besides her poems, Pauline was busy writing prose. She submitted articles to quality literary magazines published in New York and Boston. She also submitted several articles to her local newspapers.

Late in 1890, seeking feedback about her writing, Pauline Johnson wrote to the 84-year-old American Quaker, John Greenleaf Whittier. An excerpt of his April, 1891 response to her reads:

My Dear Miss Johnson:

I have received with great pleasure thy poems so kindly sent me. They have strength as well as beauty, and study and patient brooding over thy work will enable thee to write still better. It is fitting that one of their own race should sing the songs of the Mohawk and Iroquois, in the English tongue. There is a splendid opportunity before thee. And I am very glad to see the fine and thoughtful face of the young poet ...With renewed thanks and all good wishes I am thy aged friend,

John G. Whittier[7]

The venerable poet died the next year, the very year that Pauline Johnson's "splendid opportunity" came.

In March of 1891 Pauline turned 30, a milestone in everyone's life. She faced her thirties, unmarried, unengaged, living at home with her widowed mother and spinster sister. Pauline's name was printed in the local newspaper on at least two occasions that year.

In January *The Brantford Expositor* stated: "Last night was the occasion of the most brilliant social event in the city's history-The Bachelor's Ball...Fourteen hundred invitations were sent out, some as far away as Montreal. The hall itself had assumed a gorgeous attire for the evening. The massive walls were hidden in a wealth of beautiful bunting the various forms of the British ensign and Union Jack predominate...Of the Kerby House management too much cannot be said...The whole building was placed at the disposal of the guests. ...Pauline Johnson was beautifully attired in pink silk with a net overdress. The event can only be described as an unqualified success in every particular."[8]

In November the *Expositor* reported: "It is the intention to issue a special Christmas edition this year. It will consist of at least twenty pages of the size employed in *The Dominion Illustrated*. It will give a large number of portraits of Brantfordites, including members of the city council and board of trade, prominent business men, members of the school boards, clergymen, etc. Miss Pauline Johnson is writing a story for the number, as is also Mr. Frank Yeigh."[9]

Frank Yeigh, another of Pauline's friends from her Central schooldays, was responsible for turning her life upside down only a few months later. He had moved to Toronto where, after first working as a journalist, he was the private secretary to the Honourable A.S. Hardy, the Premier of Ontario. Frank continued to write, submitting freelance articles to newspapers. He was part of Toronto's smart professional writers' set, and president of the Young Men's Liberal Club of Ontario.

The club devised a flamboyant nationalist program to publicize its Canadianism policy. As the opening event, Frank proposed a literary evening. To create a list of Canadian poets whom he could invite, Frank turned to *Songs of the Great Dominion*. Probably one of the first people he put on his list was his home town friend, Pauline.

As 1891 turned into 1892, Frank Yeigh's invitation to Pauline arrived at the Johnson home. Eva recollects: "Pauline told me about the invitation as I chatted with her one morning while she made her bed. 'And are you going?' I asked. 'You bet,' was her elegant reply. 'Oh, Ev,' she continued, 'it will be such a help to get me before the profession.' 'What are you going to wear?' I asked, womanlike. 'My grey silk dress,' she replied."[10]

Pauline's Handiwork Undone
by Mrs. W. Garland Foster

Soon after the arrival at Brantford Jean [Morton] came for a visit. Pauline had just finished embroidering a night dress which she had spent weeks completing. It had quantities of very tiny pin tucks and was evidently the joy of Pauline's heart, and she had saved it to wear for Jean's visit. When they were ready to go to their room the pet chipmunk, the favorite of the moment, was missing. He was allowed to roam about the house during the day but was always shut up in a cage for the night. Pauline whistled for him and called but he did not appear. Finally, when they had about given him up, he appeared and was shut up in his cage for the night.

As the girls went upstairs to their room Pauline was talking about the night dress: "It is the best I have ever done. I have spent weeks embroidering it. I am in love with it!"

In those days night gowns were kept under a pillow or in a case below the pillow during the day, and as Pauline proceeded to shake hers out from under the pillow, where she had put it in anticipation of Jean's visit, a cloud of linen bits fell upon the bed where the pet chipmunk had spent many patient hours finishing the embroidery for his beloved mistress.

It was all too much for Jean who burst into peals of laughter. But it was no laughing matter for Paul, as Jean called her, who for once could not see the funny side of a situation. However, so infectious was Jean's laughter, and so absurd the situation that Pauline finally did see the funny side and laughed quite merrily, although she still had regrets for the loss of her gown.[11]

Charming Portrait
by Madge Robertson

This charming portrait (page 79) we are able to give this issue, of Miss Pauline Johnson, the Indian poetess will be very generally admired. The striking attitude, the artistic gown, the face full of thought and feeling, the beautiful tender eyes and the sensitive mouth, combine into a picture worthy of a painter's brush. The palette is needed to bring out the clear dark skin, the masses of black hair and the deep grey of the eyes. The personality of the young poetess shines through her face,

THE RIFT

"The Rift" first appeared in the American publication *Gems of Poetry*, to which Pauline contributed under her nom de plume "Margaret Rox".

Nature has wept today, her pent up grief
In tears still trembles on the lily bell,
Remorseless raindrops fleck its bending leaf,
And crystallize its yellow coronal.

And from the pansy 'neath the almond tree
The purple velvet bloom is dashed away,
The trees are lowering down so heavily
Nature is sadder than a sigh today.

Something has hurt your heart and made you grieve,
The day has been too dark without the sun
Something has proved too hard-but O believe
Others have suffered just as you have done.

Someone has wept today disconsolate
In unison with earth have nursed their pain
And felt the world as harsh and desolate
As the dark mournful trees and dripping rain.

Someone is sad tonight, uncomforted
The heart with all its little woes depressed-
A word perhaps. They fain had left unsaid
Is burning still within that aching breast.

Someone has asked today and been denied-
And in response sent up that saddened cry

That marks some human wish ungratified-
Until their listless hopes all sickened lie.

Someone has craved today a higher sphere
And known the tortures of a pinioned will-
Have felt their efforts baffled, and the clear
Hard tones of fate ring out against them still.

Someone has lost today the gilded prize
That years endeared unto ambition's soul,
Tonight-they near the hardest agonies
Of failures in the race to win the goal.

Someone has harder tasks to bear and do,
Has wilder trails than yours when he contends,
Someone is further off from Heaven than you,
Knows less of kindness and has fewer friends.

Someone is tired tonight-too tired to speak
Of all the hardships of the dark hours past.
With heart and hand so childish and so weak
In struggling for the well won rest at last.

And you are tired tonight-too tired to know
The clouds have clustered in a crimson drift
Too tired to see aloft-God's signet low,
And o'er its prism arch, an azure rift.[12]

Pauline, 1881, aged 20.
(Brant Historical Society #634)

Misguided Becomes Temptation
by Jean Waldie

The poetess gave to Mrs. Reville the manuscript of one of her poems entitled "Misguided." After revision this was published in the *Toronto Saturday Night* under the title "Temptation." In the published version the entire tenor of the poem has been changed by the substitution of the third for the first personal pronoun: "How frail is the craft I am steering" became "How frail is the craft he is steering." Many other changes in this poem indicate the thoroughness of her revision.[15]

A Dress of Rose Cashmere
by Evelyn Johnson

Pauline received an invitation to go to New York. She was very much delighted and began to prepare for her trip. She could sew very nicely and at the time was making a dress of rose cashmere and wine velvet, which she had on a dress-form in the living room and was hastening to complete before she went away. A friend chanced to call, and as it was not very warm in the drawing room we invited him into the living room where we had been sitting. He noticed the half-completed dress on the form and said, "How nice you are able to sew; you can make your own dresses when you are married." Pauline exclaimed, "Indeed! When I am married I do not intend to make my own dresses."[18]

shows itself in every movement, is betrayed in every word she speaks. Of delightful manners-and this means so much!-with the sweetest of soft, low voices, with pretty gestures and the most winning of smiles, who would not have pleasant recollections of an hour passed with Miss Johnson. I have been myself lured into staying, work and the world forgotten, and listening to her conversation, which is more than entertaining, and watching her vividly-expressive face change with each change of feeling.[13]

A REQUEST

To the noble society known as "The Woman's Auxiliary of Missions of the Church of England in Canada,"-who are doing their utmost in the good work of sending Missionaries to the Crees and Blackfeet-the following lines are respectfully and gratefully inscribed. 1886

Beyond the boundaries of all our mighty inland lakes,
Beyond the old Red River shore, where Manitoba breaks
Into the far and fair North-West its limitless extent,
Last year with cannon, shot, and shell the British soldier went.
Full many a city flocked to bid her gallant boys good-bye,
Cheer after cheer went ringing out, and flags were flaunted high;
And well indeed those warriors fought, and surely well they bled,
And surely well some sleep to-day within their silent bed.
Perhaps a soldier's medals are of greater honour when
He wins them at the cost of his own fellow-countrymen-
'Tis not my place to question if their laurel wreath still thrives,
If its fragrance is of Indian blood, its glory Indian lives.
I only know some heart still waits with pulse that beats and burns
For footsteps of the boy who left but nevermore returns,
Another heart still dwells beyond thy banks, Saskatchewan-
O Indian mother, list'ning for the coming of your son
Who left his home a year ago to right the Volunteers,
To meet his death from British guns, his death-song British cheers.
For you I speak to-day, and ask some noble, faithful hands,
To send another band of men to meet you in your lands.
Not as last year these gallant hearts as dogs of war will go,
No swords within their hands, no cause to bring the after-glow
Of blush to Canada's fair cheek, for none can say as then:
"She treats her Indian wards as foes." No! These are different men,
Their strength is not in rank and file, no martial host they lead,
Their mission is the cross of Christ, their arms the Christian creed.
Instead of helmet round their head, a halo shines afar,
'Twill light your prairie pathway up more than the flash of war.
Seek not to find upon this band a coat of crimson glow-
God grant their hands will spotless be as their own robes of snow,
O men who go on missions to the North-West Indian lands,
The thorns may pierce your foreheads and the cross may bruise your hands,
For tho' the goal seems far away, reward seems vague and dim-
If ye Christianise the least of them, "Ye do it unto Him,"
And, perhaps, beyond the river brink the waves of death have laved,
The jewels in your crown will be the Indian souls you've saved.

E. Pauline Johnson.[14]

TEMPTATION
(For Saturday Night, originally entitled "Misguided")

How frail is the craft he is steering, how
rapid the river speeds on,
How many the rocks he is nearing, how lur-
ing the water god's song.

How gay rings his happy young laughter,
tossed in the play of the stream,
Courageous and brave he sails after the fair
golden fleece of his dream.

Once only, the tears rise to blind him, 'tis
when he looks backward and sees,
The Mother and home far behind him-then
trims he again to the breeze.

Ah, me! the reef under the foam crest was
first to grate hard on the keel,
He passed it when leaving the home-nest,
but sharp was the shock he could feel.

Down farther some bold rocks are catching
what driftwood the waters supply,
With careful and diligent watching he
pilots his boat safely by.

And here is a snag where the river runs
dizzily onward and fast,
His shallop flies by with a shiver, thank
Heaven that danger is past.

O! horror, he sees in the distance sand
bars, is he running aground?
But no, with a giant resistance, to clear
them he swings the boat 'round.

Here's a whirlpool, calm seem its terrors,
insensibly he is drawn in,
His eyes can distinguish no errors, his con-
science belittles the sin.

Its grasp is the grasp of a demon, and
whispering faintly a prayer,
With efforts almost superhuman, he pulls
from that deadliest snare.

The struggle has made him so weary he
rests for a space on his oar,
And looks from the river now dreary to the
sweetness of sky and shore.

Red and saffron the clouds glow above
him, the sun in a splendor descends,
The world looks as tho' it could love him,
and he laughs as we laugh on friends.

How brilliant the scene, so much stronger
than shadows which 'round him remain,
He'll watch it but one moment longer, then
look to his helm again.

And so he lies idle, and drifting, forgetting
his life-boat to steer.
Nor seeing some dark rocks uplifting, sure
there can be nothing to fear!

O, fool! had he only but striven to turn
from that sky color-flecked-
Too late, his frail ship is riven, O, god! on
the rock-is wrecked.[16]

Pauline, in her twenties, attired for winter.
(Brant Historical Society #630)

UNGUESSED

The day is warm and fair;
The early summer air
Is resting in the overhanging trees,
And at our feet there leaves
The undulating waves
That wash the shores and fret the sands of
many azure seas.

Beneath the tangled bower
We've idled many an hour
And tossed away too many tender days-
I quite content in love
To watch your face above
The netted couch, in which you lie, that
softly floats and sways.

Did young Apollo wear
A face than yours more fair,
More purely blonde, in beauty more com-
plete?
Beloved, will not you
Unclose those eyes of blue
That hold my world and bless and curse the
life they render sweet?

I wonder how you rest
So calmly, when my breast
Is tortured by the efforts that I make
To strangle love and keep
His ensign from my cheek,
To still the passion in my heart just for our
friendship's sake.

But perfect calm still lies
Within your sleeping eyes,
O'erveiled by lids that soft betoken rest.
Your lips serenely close
In undisturbed repose,
Nor tremble with the gentle, peaceful
heaving of your breast.

Ah! well it is for me
That you, sweet, cannot see
Within my heart so tyrannized by love.
Ah! well it is for you
My friendship you deem true,
Nor know how false the friend that bends
your sleeping form above.

Some stranger far and lone,
By you unseen, unknown,
Could give you calmer fondness in my
stead,
For I have drunk the wine
Distilled from Love's wild vine,
And reeling with its subtle fumes I strike
our friendship dead.

Brantford, June, 1881. E. Pauline Johnson.[17]

Pauline, all dressed up, complete with a hair piece, gloves, and a dress with a train and velvet accents at the bustline and collar.
(Brant Historical Society #632)

WHAT THE SOLDIER SAID

The crisis of the battle neared, the cream
of England's sons
Were in the open, fighting, right beneath
the Russian guns
That were dealing devastation, with shot
that riddled thro'
The "Thin red line" of valiant men that
less and lesser grew,
But one there was who wavered, as the
scarlet columns wheeled,
Who's eyes had caught some colors lying
in the open field,
He waited not for orders, but he left the
ranks to go
To save his comrade, and his flag, to face
the Russian foe,
The deadly bayonets glistened, and the
cannons thundered near,
But his comrade, and his colors he carried
to the rear.

Long afterwards, when June was filtering
her sunshine thro'
The little watery clouds afloat in skies of
English blue,
It seemed to glow the brighter on a lithe
young soldier's face,
As he stood before his sovereign, who
leaned with tender grace,
To pin upon his breast a little bit of
bronze that bore
These words "For Valour," Ah how well he
won it in the war,
"See that you wear it nobly," said his
Captain, "Life won't give
Another such reward as that, so guard it
while you live."
The soldier touched his faded cap, "Your
pardon sir," said he,
"I'm proud of this wee bit of bronze as
any man can be,
It means my honor, Sir, and nought on
earth I honor more,
But Captain, did you never know I wore a
cross before?
It won the glory for me, and I'm none the
prouder now,
Of the cross upon my bosom, than the
cross upon my brow."

For the *Brant Churchman*. 1889[19]

A Forgotten Appointment
by Evelyn Johnson

One evening Cameron Wilson came to our home. He asked for Pauline, who was not at home. I told Cameron that we had expected her back to tea, but that she had probably gone to her great friends, the Goodsons, who lived in Brant Avenue, or the Mackenzies, who lived in Darling Street. Cameron thanked me, but would not come in. When Pauline came home I told her that Cameron had called for her. "Oh," she said, "I forgot that I promised to go up there this evening to coach the young people in a play." Next morning about eleven, Cameron came again. Pauline took him into the drawing room, and after they were seated she said to him, "Cameron, I stayed awake all night trying to think of a good lie to tell you, but I came to the conclusion I had better tell you the truth...I forgot."[20]

FORTUNE'S FAVORS

Some siren drew
Our charmed canoe
To shores of green 'neath skies of blue
In velvet atmosphere-
The heat extreme,
The sun's fierce gleam,
Forbids us paddling up the stream
So rest we idly here.

Hot waning June
Melts to a swoon
The stillness of this still lagoon
Wherein becalmed we lie,
Our tiny sail
Lifts up her pale
Arms longing that some idle gale
Perchance may wander by.

We lie where dim
Still shadows skim
The rushes on the river's rim
That harbor iris rare,
We whistle low,
Subdue and slow
To call the truant winds to blow
And break the silent air.

Some goddess brings
Upon her wings
The breeze desired as near she swings
Her pinions floating past,
With creaking sound
The boom sways round,
Fresh wind our canvas now has found-
It fills-we move at last.

E. Pauline Johnson, 1889[21]

A Thirsty River
by Evelyn Johnson

Pauline had a friend in Michael Mackenzie, whose father was the Rector of Grace Church in Brantford. One day these two canoed down the Grand River to the home of Mr. and Mrs. Sam Styres. Pauline and Michael took their lunch along and tied two bottles of ale to the stern of the canoe, so that the water would keep them cool. They decided to have this on their return journey. The trip to Onondaga from Brantford by road is ten miles, by railway eight, and by river eighteen, so winding is the course. They remained over night and started for Brantford the next day. When the time came for their lunch they left the canoe and spread their table cloth on the river bank. They decided to get the ale the last thing, so that it would be as cold as possible. They pulled it out of the water and were surprised to see that only the two necks of the bottles remained on the string, the weight of the water having broken off the rest.[22]

THE LUMBERMAN'S CHRISTMAS

(at one time entitled "A Backwoods Christmas")

"Well, Carlo, so this here is Chris'mus,
By jingo I almost forgot,
'Taint what you an' me has been used to,
'Afore we come out here to squat.
Seems jist like the rest of the winter,
The same freezin' air, the same snow,
I guess that we can't be mistaken!
This almanac book says it's so.
Well, Carlo, you lazy old beggar,
Right here in the shanty we'll stay
An' celebrate Chris'mus together,
The loggin' will keep for a day.
We'll hang up this bit o' green cedar
Atop our old kerosene light,
It'll make things look somethin' like
Chris'mus,
An' brighten us up a great sight
You're waggin' yer tail, are you, Carlo?
An' puttin' yer head on my knee,
That's one way to say Merry Chris'mus,
An' make believe you're fond o' me;
You scamp, I most think you're not foolin',
I see it right thar in yer eyes,
Don't fail me, old dog, it would kill me,
You're all the possession I prize.
Last Chris'mus-you bet I remember-
We weren't in a shanty that day,
In lumberin' tracts with the railroad
Some sixty an' odd mile away.
No, sir, we were home in the village,
With mother, an' Billy, an' Jack,
An' somehow, I feel like this minnit
I kinder jist want to go back.
An' she was thar too, an' I loved her;
Yes, Carlo, I'll say so to you,
Because you believe that I'm honest
An' them that thinks likewise is few.
You see she had promised to marry
Old Jack, an' my heart kinder broke,

For tryin' to stand by him squar-like
Meant, love-words must never be spoke.
Somehow it got out, an' the neighbors
Said Jack was suspicious o' me;
I carried my heart out too open,
The world as it run by could see.
I stood it until that thar' mornin'
On the Bay, when the storm caught us
squar',
I hoped that we both would be drowned,
An' told her my love then and thar'.
Her voice answered strange like an' bro-
ken,
Her lips they was white and compressed,
"Oh, Jamie, I'm glad you have spoken,
For, dear one, I loved you the best."
An' then, with the storm devils ragin'
Far out of my arms she was thrown.
O, God, when I come to my senses,
I was safe on the shore-but *alone*.
Alone, with her words still a soundin',
Those wild, lovin' words she jist said,
Alone with the terrible sorrow
Of knowin' my darlin' was dead.
Alone, with my brave brother Billy,
Who saved my dishonorable life,
For all says I drowned her a purpose
To keep her from bein' Jack's wife.
I think I'd have borne it quite manly,
But when I looked Jack in the face,
He asked me to give the straight ticket,
I told him my love and disgrace;
But never a word did I mention
About them last words that she spoke,
I'd lost him enough, Heaven knows it,
His heart with my own had been broke.
It's hard on me havin' this achin',
This homelessness here in my breast,
But the hardest to bear is the knowin'
That Jack-well-*he thinks like the rest*.
No, Carlo, we won't be returnin'
To them parts for some time to come,

Tho' knowin' the white-haired old mother
Is waitin' to see us come home;
I guess she looks older this Chris'mus,
An' sadder, mayhap, than I be;
For she an' brave Billy, an' you, sir,
Are all that believes now in me.
Well, Carlo! we'll look up some supper;
By Jingo, the days have growed short-
We've set here for hours jist a-talkin'-

We're two o' the indolent sort.
Well, well, this is Chris'mus, who'd thought it?
The evenin' is goin' to be long,
So we'll have a good smoke an' a fire
An' liven things up with a song.

E. Pauline Johnson, 1889[23]

A Woman One Should Know

by Evelyn Johnson

One day Pauline was at the Mackenzie's for tea, and in the course of the conversation the Reverend Mr. Mackenzie mentioned Mrs. C.H. Waterous. Pauline said she did not know her.

"You do not know Mrs. Waterous?" queried Mr. Mackenzie.

"No," said Pauline.

"Then," said Mr. Mackenzie, "you do not know one of the nicest women in town."

"Well," said Pauline, "she is in the same box."

Mr. Mackenzie looked at Pauline for an instant, and then with his usual bow said, "True, true."[24]

RONDEAU

Some bittersweet that lately grew
When flowers failed and leaves were few,
Tossed thro' the dull November day
Their saucy coral colors gay
Where wind and rain in dashes blew.

A kindly hand upstretching thro'
The vines their clusters downward drew
And broke their stems and took away
Some bitterness.

And brought their berries bright unto
My weary life that lived anew,
Because they made the days less grey.
O! hand that gave, return and stay,
O friend of mine-is all my due
Some bittersweet?

E. Pauline Johnson, 1890[25]

Food For Thought

by Evelyn Johnson

A hard boiled egg was never safe in the house when Pauline was at home, as she was very fond of them. She would go to bed often at the usual hour and then lie awake thinking of some poetry she might have written; whereupon, she would get up and write until perhaps two o'clock. She has even been known to get up hungry in the middle of the night and, going downstairs, forage for what she felt like eating.[26]

IN APRIL

I.
Outlined in red and saffron
Against a ground of gray,
Where last year's sedge o'erhangs the edge
That marks the river's way,
On shores so gray, and dull, and bare,
On shores so seeming dead-
The lips of life are breathing where
The willows turn to red,
Enriching all the somber air
With glints of gold and red.

II.
Without a dash of color,
Untouched by red or gold,
The empty days are garbed in grays,
All passionless and cold,
O! heart of mine so dull and bare,
O! heart so seeming dead,
Thou hast no gems to number where
Love flashes gold and red,
He never limns the somber air
For thee with gold and red.

E. Pauline Johnson, 1890[27]

She Belonged to a Splendid Race

by Theodore Watts-Dunton

Many years ago a beloved friend sent me a book called Songs of the Great Dominion, selected and edited by the poet, William Douw Lighthall. [My friend] knew of the deep interest I have always taken in matters relating to Greater Britain, and especially in everything relating to Canada...He told me that a leading article for the journal upon some weighty subject was wanted, and asked whether the book was important enough to be worth a leader. I turned over its pages and soon satisfied myself as to that point. I found the book rich in poetry-true poetry-by poets, some of whom have since then become great and of world-wide distinction; all of it breathing, more or less, the atmosphere of Canada: that is to say Anglo-Saxon Canada. But in the writings of one poet alone I came upon a new note-the note of the Red Man's Canada. This was the poet that most interested me-Pauline Johnson. I quoted her lovely song "In the Shadows." I at once sat down and wrote a long article...Naturally I turned to his introductory remarks to see who Pauline Johnson was. I was not at all surprised to find that she had Indian blood in her veins but I was surprised and delighted to find that she belonged to a famous Indian family-the Mohawks of Brantford. The Mohawks of Brantford! That splendid race to whose unswerving loyalty, during two centuries, not only Canada, but the entire British Empire owes a debt that can never be repaid. After the appearance of my article I got a beautiful letter from Pauline Johnson, and I found that I had been fortunate enough to enrich my life with a new friendship.[28]

IN THE SHADOWS

I am sailing to the leeward,
Where the current runs to seaward
    Soft and slow,
Where the sleeping river grasses
Brush my paddle as it passes
    To and fro.

On the shore the heat is shaking
All the golden sands awaking
    In the cove;
And the quaint sand-piper, winging
O'er the shallows, ceases singing
    When I move.

On the water's idle pillow
Sleeps the overhanging willow,
    Green and cool;
Where the rushes lift their burnished
Oval heads from out the tarnished
    Emerald pool.

Where the very silence slumbers,
Water lilies grow in numbers,
    Pure and pale;
All the morning they have rested,
Amber crowned, and pearly crested,
    Fair and frail.

Here, impossible romances,
Indefinable sweet fancies,
    Cluster round;

But they do not mar the sweetness
Of this still September fleetness
    With a sound.

I can scarce discern the meeting
Of the shore and stream retreating,
    So remote;
For the laggard river, dozing,
Only wakes from its reposing
    Where I float.

Where the river mists are rising,
All the foliage baptizing
    With their spray;
There the sun gleams far and faintly,
With a shadow soft and saintly,
    In its ray.

And the perfume of some burning
Far-off brushwood, ever turning
    To exhale
All its smoky fragrance dying,
In the arms of evening lying,
    Where I sail.
My canoe is growing lazy,
In the atmosphere so hazy,
    While I dream;
Half in slumber I am guiding,
Eastward indistinctly gliding
    Down the stream.[29]

Flint and Feather

The following poem is an example of Pauline lampooning her own work. "In the Shadows – My Version" was clipped from an unidentified publication and pasted on the inside front cover of one of Pauline's personal scrapbooks. Signed "By the Pasha" is in keeping with Pauline's submitting work to publications using a variety of pen names. This is not the only time that Pauline lampooned her own work. She wrote "The Song My Paddle Sings" in 1892, and mocked it in 1894 when she wrote "His Majesty, the West Wind."

IN THE SHADOWS
My Version.

I am sailing down the river
Calm my craft moves, not a quiver
     Do I feel.
Save when rocky point and jagged
Tho' the boiling rapids, ragged
     Scrapes my keel.

Night-hawks high above me, screaming
Love's eyes turn upon me, beaming
     Trustfully.
All about us night is falling
On the shore a child is squalling
     Bustfully.

Willowy copse and densest umbrage

Cast long shadows, and the foliage
     Tinged with red.
Forms a background for a bumpkin
Sitting on a yellow pumpkin
     Scratching head.

Joyful are the leaping waters
And my boat, light, "teeter-totters"
     On the foam.
And the blue-bloused granger fellow
Smock shock-ful of apples mellow
     Shambles home.

From the Locks as paddling westward
Soon I feel a weakness vestward
     So we lunch.
Leaving naught of all the luncheon
Only sighing for a puncheon
     Of good punch.

Into light from out the shadow
Home is ready and I'm so glad, oh!
     But 'twas bliss.
As we leave the boat house, homing
Naughty thought, I, in the gloaming,
     Snatch a kiss.

By the Pasha.[30]

Pauline in Repose
by Peggy Webling

Pauline is there, stretched at full length, her brown hands clasped under her head, looking at me with that sidelong, Indian glance I know so well, thin lips puckered into a slow smile, grey eyes narrowed by half-shut lids. She even lies upon the ground with more grace and ease than any other woman, no touch of self-consciousness in the stretch and curve of her lithe body, the arms and throat sun-kissed to the colour of bronze, the lines of her young face deep cut already, keen as a hawk, still as an old Redskin.[31]

Brantford

This photograph (date unknown) shows a relaxed Pauline (reclining left) with two unidentified friends. She is wearing her canoeing outfit. The jumble of picnic items would indicate that they are enjoying a summer outing, perhaps along the banks of Pauline's beloved Grand River.
(The William Ready Division of Archives and Research Collections, McMaster University Library, Hamilton, Canada)

THE LAYING OF THE CORNERSTONE

The following song, which is to be sung by the pupils at the laying of the corner stone, was composed by E. Pauline Johnson, a former pupil of the Central School, at the request of Principal Wilkinson-*Air: Onward Christian Soldiers*, 1890

I.
Comrades, we are serving,
'Round instruction's throne,
In our youth we're laying
Wisdom's corner stone.
Flood or fire can never,
Sweep away the towers,
We are building daily,
In our student hours.

Refrain-
Comrades, we are serving,
'Round instruction's throne,
In our youth we're laying,
Wisdom's corner stone.

II.
On the very ashes
Sloth has left behind,
Study lays the ground-work,
Of a scholar's mind.
Every lesson mastered,
Like a little stone,
Helps to raise the structure
Knowledge builds alone.
    Refrain.

III.
On the firm foundation
That our learning lays,
We construct the stronghold
Of our future days.
Sometimes we will carry
Wisdom's flag unfurled,
Underneath that standard
We can face the world.
    Refrain.[32]

Pauline (third from left) relaxes with friends while on holiday on a bright summer day. *(Brant Historical Society #479)*

September 5, 1891

My dear Mr. Hardy:

Your letter has been one of the sincerest pleasures, one of the most acceptable compliments I have ever received. I think I value the moments you have given me as much as I do your words of commendation, for I know what demands an exacting public make upon your time.

Your kind notice of my little poem I will always regard as an imperishable laurel leaf in my tiny wreath, as well as a stimulant, a tonic and an encouragement to better things.

I can scarcely tell you how often an author requires approbation or how dear is the handclasp of encouragement when it does come. Your praise and approval of my work will lighten many a hard road that I must needs tramp over before I reach the heights of Literature I mean to attain. Your letter may have seemed a little thing for you to do, to me it means more than I can thank you for. I will only try to merit your kindness to me.

> Faithfully I am
> Yours
> E. Pauline Johnson[33]

Arthur Hardy was a lawyer, politician and premier of Ontario (1896-99). Pauline probably met him when he practised law in Brantford, and knew him while he was Member of Parliament for South Brant.

SONG

The night-long shadows faded into gray,
    Then slivered into glad and gold sunlight,
Because you came to me, like a new day
    Born of the beauty of an autumn night.

The silence that enfolded me so long
    Stirred to the sweetest music life has known,
Because you came, and coming woke the song
    That slumbered through the years I was alone.

So have you brought the silver from the shade,
    The music and the laughter and the day,
So have you come to me, and coming made
    This life of mine a blossom-bordered way.[34]

Pauline on Holiday
Kitchener-Waterloo Record

One of the many waterways to become immortalized in her writing was the quiet Shadow River that empties into Lake Rosseau at this small Muskoka town (Rosseau, Ontario). Clarence Shaw accompanied Pauline Johnson on her travels. He acted as her guide on a historic canoe trip up the Shadow River before the turn of the century. The experience became a poem. She returned often to give public poetry recitals in Rosseau's biggest building, the Monteith Inn Dance Hall, which held 500 people. For many years she vacationed with the Fred Wilkes family. Her memorable trips up the Shadow River were made in original Ditchburn Brothers canoes, once built in the town of Rosseau by ancestors of the Ditchburn family.[35]

EVERGREENS

  A jovial lot are they
  Who fill the lumber sleigh,
And by their merriment the woodman gleans
  That through the storm and cold,
  With boyish hearts and bold,
The little choristers have come to haul the Christmas greens.

  And quickly, too, they heap
  The boughs where, soft asleep,
A subtle perfume loves to long abide;
  So wild and sweet and free,
  It always seems to be
Twin sister of the music that we hear at Christmas-tide.

  Adown the long white road
  The axeman drives his load
Of fragrant greens through puffs and drifts of snow
  Until his happy eyes
  See in the twilight skies
The village spire, and well he knows who waits for him below.

  Anon he halts before
  The church's open door,
And pretty faces greet him with a smile.
  Is it the light and heat
  That makes his pulses beat,
Or but a pair of laughing eyes he meets across the aisle?

Brantford, E. Pauline Johnson, 1891

TWO WOMEN

She stands where a thousand candles
Broadcast their yellow rays,
Where laugh and song ring all night
long,
And music sweeps and sways,
A woman pure and peerless as
The diamonds in her hair,
Her regal footsteps never pass
But heroes worship there,
For queen of all 'mid song and light,
She's conquered every heart to-night.

Alone with the night, a woman,
Watches a setting star,
Her heaving breast, her lips compressed
Bespeak a soul at war,
In pure and peerless womanhood,
She threw her world away,
And suffered for another's good
Self sacrifice to-day,
The victor in a noble fight,
She's queen of but herself to-night.[37]

A glamorous photograph of Pauline. According to her sister, Pauline favoured soft shades of blues and pinks for her garments. She strongly objected to, and avoided wearing, black.
(Brant Historical Society #625)

Star!

1892-1897

*A*fter Pauline accepted Frank Yeigh's invitation to recite during a literary evening to benefit the Young Men's Liberal Club of Toronto, she travelled alone to Toronto and took a room at the Rossin House.

On January 16, 1892, an audience of 400 gathered in Association Hall to hear modern Canadian poets present their work. Pauline was in good company, for the programme that evening included, among others, William Wilfrid Campbell, Duncan Campbell Scott, Helen Merrill, William Douw Lighthall, and Hereward K. Cocklin. Among those who sent their regrets was Archibald Lampman.

The 1890s was a decade of poetic endeavour in Canada. Readers and critics became aware of "the Northern school of poets," also referred to as "the later poets" or "the Confederation poets." This group of seven writers had a lasting impact on the literature of Canada.

The group included Pauline Johnson (born 1861), William Wilfrid Campbell (born 1861), Bliss Carman (born 1861), Archibald Lampman (born 1861), Sir Charles G.D. Roberts (born 1860), Frederick George Scott (born 1861) and Duncan Campbell Scott (born 1862). The early years of the 1860s had borne poetic fruit.

Frank Yeigh invited Toronto journalists to the poetry event. They left a record of Pauline's triumph. From memory she recited "A Cry from an Indian Wife." The poem was based on the battle at Cut Knife Creek during the Riel Rebellion. Her recitation so startled and moved the audience that, in the finest tradition of theatrical lore, a star was born. Pauline entered the collective Canadian conscience that evening, and she never left it. Pauline's stated desire was "to set people on fire." That she did, between 1892 and her retirement from the stage in 1909.

After her Toronto triumph, Pauline returned to Brantford while Frank made arrangements for her to headline a second Toronto concert. The February 19 event was a great success, despite the fact that she dried up in the middle of one poem. Pauline must have thought that her fledgling stage career was ending almost before it had begun.

Early in 1892 she had written "The Song My Paddle Sings," and at the second Toronto concert she recited it from memory. It was during this poem that she forgot her words, and had to rely on diverting the audience's attention. She slowly and deliberately disassembled a fresh rose. She then told the audience that she would move to another selection, and return to "The Song My Paddle Sings" later in the programme. Thus, through sheer personality and theatrical instinct, her stage career was saved.

Her sister, Eva, relates that one of Pauline's friends was in the audience that evening. "When Pauline forgot her piece Harry felt the blood rush all over his face to his head. 'But,' he said, 'I knew that girl would recover herself, for I myself trained her in the Garrick Dramatic Club in Hamilton, with others for an entertainment there.'"[1] Recover she did, and the stage was set for her successful stage career.

Walter McRaye, Pauline's stage partner and manager from 1901 to 1909, wrote, "The Song My Paddle Sings" was submitted and accepted by *Toronto Saturday Night*, which sent the sum of three dollars. She had submitted it also to *The Youth's Companion* of Boston, which sent her a cheque for fifty dollars which she had to return."[2]

Acting as her manager, Frank Yeigh booked other performance dates for Pauline. At first she appeared on stage in her best gowns. It wasn't until late in 1892 or early in 1893 that she

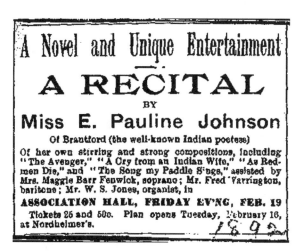

This newspaper advertisement announces Pauline's second Toronto concert of 1892.
(The William Ready Division of Archives and Research Collections, McMaster University Library, Hamilton, Canada.)

donned the buckskin garment that was to be her trademark-the Mohawk Princess was fast becoming an established sight on Ontario stages.

Biographer Mrs. Foster commented: "in her own province, she was variously accepted. Some of the older people, strange as it may seem today [1931], were not a little shocked at her unconventional costume, which somewhat modified their appreciation of her art. Many pioneers still remembered the atrocities of the Iroquois. They were still too near those days to hold such things as the fortune of war as merely reprisals for past conditions thrust upon them by rival nations chiefly concerned with the fur trade. Not so long ago the name Mohawk had struck terror to the hearts of white men and alien Indian tribes alike."[3]

In 1892, federal government policies affected Pauline's people, the First Nations of Canada. *The Statistical Year-Book of Canada* reveals the overriding attitude in one passage: "It is the policy of the government to endeavor as much as possible to persuade Indians to give up their wandering habits and stay on their reserves. Only those brought into personal contact with the Indians can understand the ignorance, superstition and laziness that have to be overcome before the Indians can be persuaded to take genuine interest and perseverance in the simplest farming operations."[4]

If anyone had an uphill battle to prove this

kind of thinking wrong, it was Pauline. Her stage appearances offered Euro-Canadians an opportunity to be "brought into personal contact with the Indians." As Canada moved toward the twentieth century, Pauline, the sweet singer of the Mohawks, was generally accepted, first as a curiosity, then as a familiar friend who delivered a good evening of entertainment. Her buckskin skirt and blouse, reserved for stage appearances only, offended the sensibilities of some, for it was low-cut in the front, one of her arms was visible, and the hem did not reach the floor.

A necklace helped with the first problem, the left sleeve made of rabbit pelts reached the elbow, and Pauline followed the conventions of the day by making sure her legs were covered, with buckskin leg wraps. While wearing the somewhat daring stage outfit, Pauline went a step further and literally let her hair down. It fell around her shoulders-something mature women of that era enjoyed only in the privacy of their own bedrooms.

It remains unclear just when Pauline adopted for her own use her great grandfather's name, Tekahionwake. It is clear that she was exceedingly fond of the name and used it throughout her performing and writing careers. Pronounced Dega-hewn'-wagay, "Tekahionwake" served Pauline well as her personal trademark. She once remarked that she preferred to be remembered by people "not as Pauline Johnson, but as Tekahionwake."

She cut an attractive, exotic and alluring figure, and audiences loved her. Her personality was appealing, her poetry was dramatic, and she quickly became a popular performer with both men and women audience members.

The Dominion Day holiday of July, 1892, found Pauline relaxing with friends on a canoeing trip. A look back at events in the recent months must have given her great satisfaction, while a glimpse forward into her future must have held boundless excitement.

In November of that year Frank suggested that Pauline team up with a vaudeville performer, Owen Smiley. She did so and they toured together for five years, until late in 1897. Pauline and Owen accepted engagements in small communities that were seeking performers for benefit performances. For example, in November of 1893 she was in Stratford, Ontario, as a guest of the Young Woman's Guild and the Women's Chapter of St. James Anglican Church. While her fee was $25 plus expenses, the receipts for the evening were $137. The host organizations collected $112 for their good works.

Causes, such as raising funds for a new church steeple, a bicycle club house, or a town clock, gave Pauline an opportunity to give something to the community and the country. At the same time the opportunity to perform lined her own pockets, and brought her one step closer to accumulating enough money to travel abroad to find a publisher for the book of poetry of which she dreamed.

In February of 1893, *The Dominion Illustrated* published her short story, "A Red Girl's Reasoning." In 1892 this piece had been awarded the first prize for fiction by the magazine. Through the story's lead character, Christe Robinson, Pauline speaks eloquently from her Mohawk heart about respect for the sanctity of tribal marriage ceremonies. She writes of her protagonist Christie: "Personally she looked much the same as her sisters, all Canada through, who are the offspring of red and white parentage-olive-complexioned, grey-eyed, black-haired, with figure slight and delicate, and the wistful, unfathomable expression in her whole face that turns one so heart-sick as they glance at the young Indians of to-day-it is the forerunner too frequently of 'the white man's disease,' consumption."[5]

Mother and daughter. Emily Johnson sits for a formal photograph with her successful and famous poet/performer daughter. The photograph was taken at a Brantford studio in 1894.
(Royal Ontario Museum, Toronto Ontario #930.31.55)

In the summer of 1893, Pauline and Owen travelled to Canada's east coast and the eastern United States. They toured New Jersey, New York, Connecticut and Massachusetts on behalf of the Indian Historical Societies. In August she attended the American Canoe Association meet on the St. Lawrence River in Kingston, Ontario. A newspaper reported the event: "The members of the Cataraqui Canoe Club of Kingston held a most successful and enjoyable entertainment at their beautifully-situated encampment last evening... Certainly the attraction of the evening was a series of recitations by Miss E. Pauline Johnson, the well-known Indian poetess, in Indian costume. She was encored time and again, and got a special three cheers from her hosts, who feel the success of their entertainment was due in a very large measure to her able efforts."[6] Her mother accompanied Pauline on this occasion, and took great pride in her daughter's success.

At this event Pauline met Arthur Henry (Harry) O'Brien, a young lawyer then practising in Toronto. Pauline and Mr. O'Brien struck up a close friendship that lasted until her death in 1913. Pauline had a knack for creating and sustaining life-long friendships, with men and women alike, despite her nomadic lifestyle.

As 1893 passed into 1894, Pauline took a moment to reflect on all the "firsts" in her life. Since the beginning of 1892 she had given her first recital in Toronto and acquired both her first manager, Frank, and her first partner, Owen. She had worn her buckskin stage outfit and had toured both the Canadian Maritimes and the American Eastern seaboard, both for the first time.

In April of 1894 she marked yet another important first-a trip to England, the land of her mother's birth. Pauline packed her buckskin outfit, and was prepared to perform should the occasion arise, but her motivation for making the trans-Atlantic voyage was to find a publisher, secure a contract, and see her book of collected verse available for sale.

The people of Brantford gave her a rousing send-off at a reception in her honour at Kerby House on April 26, 1894. By early May she had settled into a small studio apartment at 25 Portland Road, Holland Park W., London-a proper address for a proper young lady, abroad for the first time *and* unchaperoned.

With a collection of letters of introduction solicited from prominent members of Ontario society, she was introduced to Lord and Lady Ripon. After a successful first meeting Lady Ripon asked Pauline to give a drawing-room recital at her home. Pauline gladly obliged. This was the first of many parlour presentations given during her months in London. At one of these, Prince Arthur, the Duke of Connaught and son of Queen Victoria, was a spectator. He sent an aide to ask Pauline what had become of the red blanket which had been part of the ceremony in 1866 in which the Prince had become a Six Nations chief. Pauline replied that after acting as a dust cover for the family's piano at Chiefswood, the blanket now served as a dramatic accessory for her buckskin stage outfit.

Pauline's visit to England was brief but exhilarating. She spent Dominion Day at a celebration at Westminster Palace Hotel, visited Sir Charles Tupper, then Canadian High Commissioner to London, and met artists, playwrights, actors, theatre managers and writers. She saw both Eleanor Duse and Sarah Bernhardt perform during two separate visits to Daly's Theatre, Ellen Terry and Henry Irving at the Lyceum Theatre, and Lily Langtry at the Opera Comique. As she sat in these darkened theatres she took mental notes from the great actresses of her era, in order to apply their stage business to her own performances.

Foremost in Pauline's mind, however, was finding a publisher for her poems. At the home of

Sir Gilbert and Lady Parker, Pauline had the opportunity to meet Clement Scott, a famous critic. Mr. Scott recommended her to John Lane, part owner and senior editor of The Bodley Head, the premier publisher of all new English poetry and the greatest warehouse of poetry in the Commonwealth. Mr. Lane sent Pauline's manuscript to two well-known literary critics, John Davidson and Percy White, who declared Pauline's poetry worthy of publication.

According to Hector Charlesworth, "John Lane of The Bodley Head was just then making a fight for the recognition of the younger poets, which did much to influence British literature in the nineties, and on meeting Pauline Johnson at once arranged to publish a volume of her lyrics. The man to whom he assigned the task of selection, from the material she had brought with her, was the ill-fated John Davidson, one of the most brilliant poets of the nineteenth century...Pauline afterwards told me how fond she became of Davidson, a very brusque man with a broad Scottish accent and characteristic frankness in expressing his opinions. Some of her lines he would damn emphatically, but would raise his voice in acclaim of the originality of others."[7]

Pauline chose the title *The White Wampum* for her soon-to-be published collection: "As wampum to the Redman, so to the Poet are his songs; chiselled alike from that which is the purest of his possessions, woven alike with meaning into belt and book, fraught alike with the corresponding message of peace, the breathing of tradition, the value of more than coin, and the seal of fellowship with all men. So do I offer this belt of verse-wampum to those two who have taught me most of its spirit-my Mother, whose encouragement has been my mainstay in its weaving; my Father, whose feet have long since wandered to the Happy Hunting Grounds."[8] So wrote Pauline in her first book.

Five more books would follow; three during her lifetime and two posthumously, adding up to three volumes of poetry and three of prose.

By July, Pauline was back with her mother and sister in the little house in Brantford. She told them to expect to see *The White Wampum* in October of that year. The book, however, did not make its appearance until July of 1895. It was a slim volume of only 88 pages, containing 36 poems.

Only one month after her return from England, Pauline and Owen embarked on yet another first-a trip across Western Canada to the Pacific coast.

The low point of the year was the death of her elder brother, Beverly. While in Medicine Hat, Pauline received a telegram informing her of her brother's sudden death, as a result of heart failure. He had been far from his childhood home of Brant County, for he died while on business in Philadelphia, Pennsylvania. Pauline had made commitments to perform in Pincher Creek, Lethbridge, Fort Macleod, Calgary, Banff, Golden, Vancouver, New Westminster, Nanaimo and Victoria, before she could head home in October to be with her grieving family. It was to be a subdued Christmas of '94 at the Johnson's home.

1895 and 1896 were years in which Pauline, accompanied by Owen, toured Canada extensively. Her appearance on the concert stage couldn't help but promote her book of verse, and soon *The White Wampum* was sold out. There were no plans for a reprint.

As she toured, Pauline's path crossed with other touring performers and theatre companies. In the 1890s Canadian audiences were treated to singers, violinists, cartoonists, comedians, lecturers, elocutionists, bell ringers, vaudevillians, circuses, boxing matches, animal exhibits and lantern slide shows, besides a variety of melodramatic and comedic plays. Pauline and Owen carved a niche for themselves despite these competing diversions.

1897 was another year of touring. By August she was again in Winnipeg, preparing for another tour of the west. Comfortably settled into a suite at the Manitoba Hotel, Pauline felt at home in the prairie city. One of the primary reasons for her sense of settledness must have been her relationship with a man named Charles Drayton. How they met is unrecorded, but because he was stationed in Winnipeg for his banking career and because of her many visits in the prairie city, Pauline and Charles probably first encountered each another in that city.

Although no announcement was made until 1898, late in 1897 Pauline's relationship with handsome, young Mr. Drayton was turning serious. It soon became official when his proposal of marriage was accepted. In November, Pauline left the city and headed for Ontario. In Toronto she and Owen Smiley parted ways and their fruitful and eventful partnership came to an end.

Pauline toured Ontario by herself during December, and returned to her mother's and sister's home for a family Christmas-unbeknownst to them, the last family Christmas in Brantford.

By December 29, Pauline was back in Winnipeg to give a concert at the Grand Opera House. After the curtain fell she received visitors backstage. One of these was a young man who brashly introduced himself as the entertainer Walter McRaye.

As 1897 drew to a close Pauline was looking forward to a future with Charles Drayton. On top of the world-an accomplished, famous and much sought-after performer, courted by a devoted young businessman-how could Pauline have guessed that the stranger whom she had just met, Walter McRaye, would play a more prominent and enduring role in her life than the man with whom she was in love?

Off to a Good Start
by Frank Yeigh

By this time [1892] some of Pauline Johnson's writings had appeared in the press, and so she was asked to come to Toronto...A crowded hall greeted the reciters, including some of the then famous ones. Truth to say their respective personalities interested the audience more than their renditions, for most of them read or recited their productions very badly and inaudibly. It was becoming a dull and sad affair, once the novelty of the personalities wore off, when the young Brantford girl came on. Rarely has a newcomer made such a hit with her poem "A Cry From An Indian Wife." Perhaps it was partly on account of the striking contrast of her manner and matter that woke up a somewhat somnolent audience, but they went wild with applause. The bashful and frightened Indian Princess-Maiden had captured the town with this and other numbers. She captured the press critics as well, and the next day they sounded her praises to the skies while letting the others "off easily." She was off to a good start.[9]

(The decision by Pauline to recite this poem at a novel evening of Canadian poets reciting Canadian poems was a bold one. Unlike other poems of the era, it did not celebrate the glamour of war; it was written in the first person-and in a woman's voice at that; and it unequivocally stated a Native point of view.   – Author)

A CRY FROM AN INDIAN WIFE

My Forest Brave, my Red-skin love, farewell;
We may not meet to-morrow; who can tell
What mighty ills befall our little band,
Or what you'll suffer from the white man's hand?
Here is your knife! I thought 'twas sheathed for aye.
No roaming bison calls for it to-day;
No hide of prairie cattle will it maim;
The plains are bare, it seeks a nobler game:
'Twill drink the life-blood of a soldier host.
Go; rise and strike, no matter what the cost.
Yet stay. Revolt not at the Union Jack,
Nor raise Thy hand against this stripling pack
Of white-faced warriors, marching West to quell
Our fallen tribe that rises to rebel.
They all are young and beautiful and good;
Curse to the war that drinks their harmless blood.
Curse to the fate that brought them from the East
To be our chiefs-to make our nation least
That breathes the air of this vast continent.
Still their new rule and council is well meant.
They but forget we Indians owned the land
From ocean until ocean; that they stand
Upon a soil that centuries agone
Was our sole kingdom and our right alone.
They never think how they would feel to-day,
If some great nation came from far away,
Wresting their country from their hapless braves,
Giving what they gave us-but wars and graves.
Then go and strike for liberty and life,
And bring back honour to your Indian wife.
Your wife? Ah, what of that, who cares for me?
Who pities my poor love and agony?

What white-robed priest prays for your safety here,
As prayer is said for every volunteer
That swells the ranks that Canada sends out?
Who prays for vict'ry for the Indian scout?
Who prays for our poor nation lying low?
None-therefore take your tomahawk and go.
My heart may break and burn into its core,
But I am strong to bid you go to war.
Yet stay, my heart is not the only one
That grieves the loss of husband and of son;
Think of the mothers o'er the inland seas;
Think of the pale-faced maiden on her knees;
One pleads her God to guard some sweet-faced child
That marches on toward the North-West wild.
The other prays to shield her love from harm,
To strengthen his young, proud uplifted arm.
Ah, how her white face quivers thus to think,
Your tomahawk his life's best blood will drink.
She never thinks of my wild aching breast,
Nor prays for your dark face and eagle crest
Endangered by a thousand rifle balls,
My heart the target if my warrior falls.
O! coward self I hesitate no more;
Go forth and win the glories of the war.
Go forth, nor bend to greed of white men's hands,
By right, by birth we Indians own these lands,
Though starved, crushed, plundered, lies our nation low...
Perhaps the white man's God has willed it so.[10]

Flint and Feather

Stage Fright
by Frank Yeigh

Answering many demands, a recital was arranged for a few nights later-a somewhat risky venture. Would she be able to fill the whole programme? She would, and did, showing a diversity of gifts that surprised another large and fashionable audience-not only as a dramatic and sometimes a melodramatic reciter of hair-raising and "scalp" Indian poems, but of nature and descriptive poems that lent themselves to platform delivery. But she nearly "came a cropper" on this occasion.

After giving the first verse of her first number "The Song My Paddle Sings," she suddenly stopped and for some seconds quietly pulled a rose to pieces. "What has happened?" everyone anxiously wondered. With apparent self-control she said, "I'm sorry I've forgotten the rest of the piece, and if you don't mind I'll give another in its place."

Stage fright had attacked her at the start, but this solution of the difficulty made another hit with the audience. Later in the evening she recalled the forgotten lines and did not go through a similar experience. If she had studied it as a bit of stage business it could not have worked better, but it was too real for that. She told me afterward that her one thought was, "What will Yeigh-Man say! I'm disgracing him!"[11]

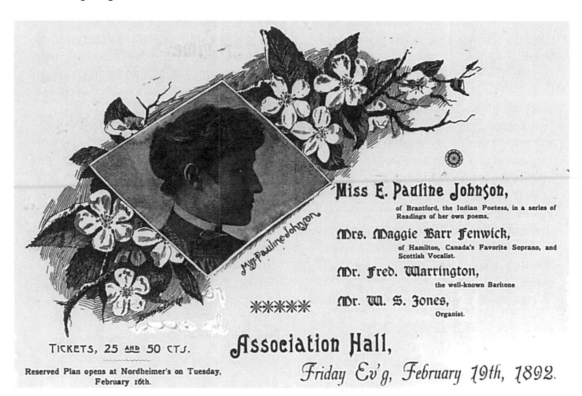

A flyer advertising the second Toronto appearance of Pauline, during which she dried up during "The Song My Paddle Sings." She managed to recover her composure.
(The William Ready Division of Archives and Research Collections, McMaster University Library, Hamilton, Canada)

The Gift of Song

by E. Pauline Johnson

Much of my poetry has been dreamed of in my boat, and I would have my canoe asso-ciated always with the songs I give the world, for it was father to most of them; and above all I am proud of my Iroquois blood and of my noble Mohawk ancestors, from whose wild, beautiful life, and through whose lovely poetry of belief I have inherited whatever gift of song I may possess.[12]

THE SONG MY PADDLE SINGS

West wind blow from your prairie nest?
Blow from the mountains, blow from the
west.
The sail is idle, the sailor too;
O! wind of the west, we wait for you.
Blow, blow!
I have wooed you so,
But never a favour you bestow.
You rock your cradle the hills between,
But scorn to notice my white lateen.

I stow the sail, unship the mast:
I wooed you long but my wooing's past;
My paddle will lull you into rest.
O! drowsy wind of the drowsy west,
Sleep, sleep,
By your mountain steep,
Or down where the prairie grasses sweep!
Now fold in slumber your laggard wings,
For soft is the song my paddle sings.

August is laughing across the sky,
Laughing while paddle, canoe and I,
Drift, drift,
Where the hills uplift
On either side of the current swift.

The river rolls in its rocky bed;
My paddle is plying its way ahead;
Dip, dip,
While the waters flip

In foam as over their breast we slip.

And oh, the river runs swifter now;
The eddies circle about my bow.
Swirl, swirl!
How the ripples curl
In many a dangerous pool awhirl!

And forward far the rapids roar,
Fretting their margin for evermore.
Dash, dash,
With a mighty crash,
They seethe, and boil, and bound, and
splash.

Be strong, O paddle! be brave, canoe!
The reckless waves you must plunge into.
Reel, reel,
On your trembling keel,
But never a fear my craft will feel.

We've raced the rapid, we're far ahead!
The river slips through its silent bed.
Sway, sway,
As the bubbles spray
And fall in tinkling tunes away.

And up on the hills against the sky,
A fir tree rocking its lullaby,
Swings, swings,
Its emerald wings,
Swelling the song that my paddle sings.[13]

Flint and Feather

An Aptitude for Public Appearance

Toronto newspaper clipping, February 21, 1892

The fact that Miss Johnson recited her own magnificent poetry lent much to the good effect of her appearance, but there was some interesting dramatic study in her recitations, too. In the first place, she has something which is heard all too seldom nowadays, a clear, distinct and correct enunciation and a voice that carries well, and this does a great deal for anybody...I must add that she has a face surprisingly mobile, a good presence, and is thus well equipped for the expression of emotions...Even in her selection "The Avenger," when she was obviously most nervous, the feeling which she expressed had the upper hand of the very natural sensations of one making a first appearance of the kind, and scorn, contempt and sarcasm were admirably expressed in her rendition.[14]

(While this poem in its entirety remains one of Pauline's "lost poems," Walter McRaye, in his book *Pauline Johnson and Her Friends*, quotes a short passage from "The Avenger."   – Author)

> His eyes aglow
> With hate and triumph as he hisses thro'
> Locked teeth: Last night thou lendest a knife unto
> My brother; Come I now, O Cherokee,
> To give thy bloody weapon back to thee,
> An evil curse-a flash of steel-a-leap -
> A thrust above the heart, well aimed and deep,

> Plunged to the very hilt in blood the blade,
> While a vengeance gloating yells, "The debt is paid."

Forty-Five Miles on the Grand

by E. Pauline Johnson

Canoeing has sprung into marvellous popularity in Canada within the last five years, and, apart from the great sporting centres, there exist no clubs of more active organization than those of Galt and Brantford, on the Grand. A stretch of thirty-five miles of water lies between these points, and a lovelier run cannot be found in the Province...One warm June morning two of us made the run in a little, cruising Peterboro' that we had shipped by rail across country the previous day. Our taut little craft slipped between the rocky shores upon which the slumbering old town of Galt crowds its grey stone houses, and in the fourth of an hour we had left streets and buildings and people behind the rolling hills and pasture lands, and were dancing along on the sunny breast of the Grand that very soon changed its shores from green country sides and meadow lands, to wild, cedar-crested banks, where shy birds hushed their song at the sound of our voices, and where pathless woods and underbrush stretched along the very water's edge....We slipped very slowly into Brantford, for many waste waters, dams and mill races take the life out of the stream above the town. But if it lacks character above, it certainly

Pauline in her canoe, which she named "Wild Cat", on the shore of the Grand River in Brant County, Ontario. This photograph dates from the early 1890s.
(Brant Historical Society #563)

regains its natural temper and tone, as it whirls away from the little city, like a steed broken loose from charing harness, and whatever bondage it suffers to serve the good townsfolk, is but a tonic and stimulant to further vivacity, and rejuvenates all its up-stream vitality.[15]

A Strong Race Opinion on the Indian Girl in Modern Fiction

by E. Pauline Johnson

She must not be one of womankind at large, neither must she have an originality, a singuality that is not definitely "Indian." I quote "Indian" as there seems to be an impression amongst authors that such a thing as tribal distinction does not exist amongst the North American aborigines.

The term "Indian" signifies about as much as the term "European" but I cannot recall ever having read a story where the heroine was described as "a European." The Indian girl we meet in cold type, however, is rarely distressed by having to belong to any tribe, or to reflect any tribal characteristics. She is merely a wholesale sort of admixture of any band existing between the MicMacs of Gaspé and the Kwaw-Kwliths of British Columbia, yet strange to say, that notwithstanding the numerous tribes with their aggregate numbers reaching more than 122,000 souls in Canada alone, our Canadian authors can cull from this huge revenue of character, but one Indian girl and stranger still that this lonely little heroine never had a prototype in breathing flesh and blood existence!

It is a deplorable fact but there is only one of her. The story writer who can create a new kind of Indian girl or better still portray a "real live" Indian girl will do something in Canadian literature that has never been done but once. The general author gives the reader the impression that he has concocted the plot, created his characters, arranged his action, and at the last moment has been seized with the idea that the regulation Indian maiden will make a very harmonious background whereon to paint his picture, that he, never having met this interesting individual, stretches forth his hand to the library shelves, grasps the first Canadian novelist he sees, reads up his subject and duplicates it in his own work.

After a half dozen writers have done this, the reader might as well leave the tale unread as far as the interest touches upon the Indian character, for an unvarying experience tells him that his convenient personage will repeat herself with monotonous accuracy. He knows what she did and how she died in other romances by other romancers and she will do and die likewise in this (she always does die, and one feels relieved that this is so, for she is too unhealthy and too unnatural to live.)

...Half of our authors who write up Indian stuff have never been on an Indian reserve, have never met a "real live Redman,"...what wonder that their conception of a people they are ignorant of, save by hearsay, is dwarfed, erroneous and delusive.

And here follows the thought-do authors who write Indian romances love the nation they endeavor successfully or unsuccessfully to describe? Do they, like Tecumseh, say, "And I, who love your nation, which is just, when deeds deserve it," or is the Indian introduced into literature but to lend a dash of vivid coloring to an otherwise tame and somber picture of colonial life: it looks suspiciously like the latter reason, or why should the Indian always get beaten in the battles of romance, or the Indian girl get inevitably the cold shoulder in the war of love?

Surely the Redman has lost enough, has suffered enough without additional losses and sorrows being heaped upon him in romance. There are many combats he has won in history...there are many girls who have placed dainty red feet figuratively upon the white man's neck...Let us not only hear, but read something of the North American Indian "besting" some one at least once in a decade, and above all things let the Indian girl in fiction develop from the "dog-like," "fawn-like," "deer-footed," "fire-eyed," "crouching," "submissive" book heroine into something of the quiet, sweet womanly woman she is if wild, or the everyday, natural, laughing girl she is if cultivated and educated; let her be natural even if the author is not competent to give her tribal characteristics.[16]

THE DEATH CRY

Moonless the skies, unlit the forest way,
Black hangs the night o'er Northern Canada.
Parting the silence comes the hoot of owls,
A stray fox barks-afar some strange dog howls:
In such forebodings crouches death-

Uplifted in the crisis of hot strife
Has drunk vermilion draughts, its hostile blow
Has stilled the hostile blood of some dark foe.
Noiselessly the victor thro' the midnight creeps
Towards the forest stream, which silent sleeps-
Leans he low down over the snake-like flood
To tell his world that law is blood for blood,
Bold from his parted lips the death-cry leaps
Adown the waters, icily it sweeps,
Weird, strange, and chilling, awfullest of cries
That on the distant darkness floats-then dies.

The Mohawk listens! All is still as death,
Aye, death itself seems dead-once more that breath
Curdles the air with savage eloquence,
Vibrating thro' the forest black and dense.
One moment more of gloom, ghost-like and drear,
Then the red warrior's cat-like, listening ear
Catches a seeming echo-a reply
From miles adown the stream-his wild death-cry
Has floated with the waters, and 'tis passed
From mouth to mouth, the deed is known at last.
Unmoved he hears the far-off eerie wail,
Then turns to take again the midnight trail,
He parts the boughs-bends low his eagle plume
And merges in the depths of forest gloom.[18]

Pauline Planning Ahead

by a contemporary

In the autumn of 1892, after she had achieved her first dramatic success as a reader, I heard her in Strathroy in a recital which I have never forgotten. The musical voice which seemed to hold the echoes of both the forest and river, and the slender swaying form, made a startling appeal to Canadian audiences, accustomed to the conventional elocution of the young graduate from the school of oratory. On the day following the recital we were in the train together and she told me of the warm reception she had met in Toronto and of her plans for an English tour. She was full of hope and enthusiasm and warmly grateful to those who were interested in her career. Then she turned to talk of her childhood and of the days along the river. I had been in Muskoka for the first time the summer before and had learned the magic of the Muskoka which the tourist never sees. So she told me of the many little lakes and streams she had found in her wanderings in the north country, and the dreamy days of paddling on the rivers which flowed through the land of pines. She said gaily as we parted, "I'm going to have a great time in England."[19]

HELD BY THE ENEMY

Oh! dainty little cousin May,
I hear your girlish laughter gay
Each time I near the wide stairway,
Each time I leave the dance.
You little witch, how well I know
The deadly dagger you can throw,
You meet your unprotected foe
With laughter as your lance.

The music murmurs thro' the rooms
And throbs atween the rich perfumes
That drift from lips of summer blooms,
But sweeter than the flute,
And clearer than the clarionet,
I hear your merry voice, my pet.
Oh! roguish May, where did you get
The laughter of the lute?

I know quite well you're sitting where
The light is shaded from the stair,
For seven dances you've been there
With some poor college boy,
I know so well your feathered fan
Is resting near your mouth, a plan
You always have to tease a man,
The thing you most enjoy.

I know your eyes of melting grey
Are not too often turned his way,
Nor have you very much to say,
But oh, you scamp, you're playing
The very deuce with that poor chap
For whom you never cared a rap,
Unless it was to test the trap
Of coquetry you're laying.

Ah! coy demoniac and divine,
The boy must go-this dance is mine,
I see your eyes with radiance shine
The while I resume him
From out the toils he's sure to rue,
For now that I'm alone with you
I know you're loyal, staunch and true
In heart to Cousin Jim.[20]

Pauline Creates Her Stage Attire
by Evelyn Johnson

I was going upstairs one day when Pauline called me into her room. She was working on an Indian costume in which she afterwards frequently appeared on the platform. "I don't like this, Ev," she said. "Neither do I," I replied. She held out both her arms to show me the buckskin strips about two inches in width, which were to serve as a covering for her arms. These were embroidered from shoulder to wrist. On either side of the strip was buckskin fringe about five inches long. This part of the garment she had sent to the North-West for. The rest of her Indian costume and silver brooches were copied from a picture which we had of Minnehaha.* The short skirt was cut at the bottom into a fringe about four inches long. After contemplating the dress for a few minutes I said to Pauline, "Why not leave one sleeve the way it is and make the other of the wild beast skins you have?" Pauline thought a moment then said, "That is exactly what I shall do."[21]

*In Longfellow's poem, "Hiawatha," Minnehaha was the daughter of the old arrow-maker of the Daco-tahs, and wife of Hiawatha.

A Sunday Service Disrupted
by E. Pauline Johnson

Once, soon after I began my recital tours I was marooned over Sunday in a small settlement in the backwoods of Ontario, and a very nice young Anglican clergyman happened to be staying at the same house I was. He invited me to go with him to the service he was to hold in the afternoon, and I went. There was no church building so the people met in the schoolhouse. It was a little one-room school, and in those days the beginners studied their lessons from large cardboard placards hung on the walls. I noticed these big cards hanging round, all of them bearing one-syllable words, but I wasn't prepared for what happened. The nice young clergyman stood directly underneath one of the placards, and when I looked at him from my seat, there, hanging over his head, was the question: "Is it an ox or an ass?" I gasped, but read on: "Lo, it is an ass. Can the ass bray? Yes, the ass can bray. Go on, old ass, and bray." I was convulsed, but finally shamed myself into control, and glanced up at the clergyman again. "Is it an ox or an ass?" the card asked me, and away I went once more, but pulled myself together and sat at attention. "Go on, old ass, and bray," leapt at me the instant I raised my eyes to the young man's face. It was hopeless. I laughed all through the service, and the more ashamed I was the more helpless I became. The poor young man was red with embarrassment, but went through with his work. He must have had great will power. After the service I apologized and showed him what had been hanging over his head, but he saw nothing funny in the card and never forgave me.[22]

Vice-Regal Party Pays Pauline the Courtesy of Staying Put for her Entire Programme
Toronto Globe

During her late tour of Ontario, Miss E. Pauline Johnson recited in Ottawa before a crowded house, which numbered among the audience, in addition to some of the leading literary and political lights of the capital, Lord and Lady Stanley and the entire governmental suite. It is very rarely that the vice-regal party sit out an entire programme, and that they did on this occasion was a tribute to the artiste, which she deserved. Miss Johnson has prepared an entirely new programme for her dual recital with Mr. Owen H. Smiley, in Association Hall, on the 19th. Among the selections, her arrangement of "The Red Girl's Reasoning" [sic], which gained the prize in *The Dominion Illustrated*, as a dialogue in which Mr. Smiley takes part, will be a special feature of the programme.[23]

Onwanonsyshon's Daughter: Pauline Johnson, the Mohawk Poet and Reader
The Boston Herald, 1893

...as she threw aside her Indian mink-trimmed garment in which she had been bundled, and

---

KEEPSAKES

"Keepsakes?" she asked, then grew her sweet eyes grave,
    "Why yes, old-fashioned as it is, my dear,
I hoard some treasures Cousin Malcolm gave
    To me before he went away last year.

"Three gems he left me, then came a good-bye;
    Then crossed he to that 'far-off-land-alone,
But those three treasures are a prisoner's tie
    That bind us thro' the distance where he's gone.

"One is a plain and heavy hoop of gold;
    To others 'tis an ordinary ring,
But unto me it means a wealth untold-
    His faith and mine are in that wedding ring.

"I count so royal his untarnished name
    And strive to wear it worthily alway-
To keep it clothed in honor, just the same
    As Malcolm gave it ere he went away.

"Blue blessed eyes and hair of golden light
    My crowning jewel has-so like to his,
God help me lead our little child aright
    Till I may follow where my darling is."[24]

stretched out a welcoming hand to the reporter yesterday one would never suspect her as being the granddaughter of "Disappearing of the Indian Summer Mist."

"Ah, I understand your look," she said, smilingly, displaying two rows of fine white teeth. "You will say I am not like other Indians, that I am not a representative. That is not strange. Cultivate an Indian, let him show his aptness, and you Americans say he is an exception. Let a bad quality crop out and you will stamp him as an Indian immediately."

Miss Johnson is a stalwart enthusiast over her Indian ancestry. From end to end of Canada her name is known as a literary woman of unusual ability. In conversation she is brilliant, in appearance handsome and attractive. When she read before the Massachusetts Indian Association she captivated all who heard her. Her short visit to Boston will be replete with social attentions, and already she has been lionized by the Hub's bright literary set.[25]

Ernest Thompson Seton (1860-1946), author, naturalist, artist. He and Pauline became friends upon their first meeting in 1893 when she attended a viewing of his paintings of wolves. Pauline felt that she and the artist were kin for she was Mohawk of the Wolf Clan. After their first meeting she sent him a small, silver wolf. He gave her a collection of bear claws, which she strung and wore around her neck during the buckskin part of her stage performance. Pauline and Ernest remained friends until her death.
(National Archives of Canada C52221)

RONDEAU
The Skater

On wings of steel the bold athlete
Brooks rival none, for none so fleet
As speeding under wintry skies,
Before the nor'land gale he flies,
And flying, frets the ice to sleet.

Like Mercury's, his wing'd feet
Skim o'er the river's crystal street,
And dread and danger he defies
On wings of steel.

What tho' the blast about him beat?
His dauntless heart athrob with heat
Of warm, young blood-his eager eyes
Essay no effort to disguise
That life to him is rare and sweet
On wings of steel.[26]

THE PORTAGE

Now for a careful beach, atween the towering
Grey rocks a'yawn like tombs.
Aft lies the lake, blurred by our pad-
dle's scouring.
Forward the Portage looms,
Beyond its fastnesses, a river creeping,
Then rapids leaping.

Now for a bracing up of stalwart shoul-
ders,
And now a load to lift,
An uphill tramp through tangled briars
and boulders,
The irksome weight to shift,
And through it all, the far incessant
calling
Of waters falling.

What of the heat? the toil? the sun's
red glaring,
The blistered fingers, too?
What of the muscles, teased and
strained, in bearing
The fearless, fleet canoe?
Brief is the labor, then the wild sweet
laughter
Of rapids after.[27]

A portrait of Pauline, showing to advantage her direct gaze and her long, curly brown hair. The beaded choker at her neck had not yet been replaced by the bear claws given her by Ernest Thompson Seton.

That Dusky-Skinned Lady

by Arthur Stringer

The following evening [after one of Pauline's Toronto recitals] James A. Tucker took me down to a rather shabby side-street hotel and introduced me to "Tekahionwake," to give the lady her proper Mohawk name. That dusky-skinned lady, at the moment, was busy ironing one of her stage dresses. The strange thing, the arresting thing, was that Pauline in no way stood ashamed of her flat-iron. She went on with her work as calm-eyed as a Chinaman in a wooden-fronted Coast laundry. It was typical of a certain grand simplicity about her, a simplicity which worldly success left quite unsullied. Mixed up with that simplicity was an almost aboriginal love of the unconventional. Yet imposed on what looked like a woodland sang-froid was an uncommonly cool and acute intelligence. As she flattened out her gown-wrinkles, that night with Tucker and me, she talked of poetry reading and audience reaction, discussed her contemporaries and their merits and defects, maintained we should all be more Canadian in our note, and confessed she wanted to make enough money out of her trouper-recitals to go to London and find an English publisher for her poetry.[28]

Brantford,
February 4, 1894

My dear Mr. O'Brien

Why do I write to you-perhaps to thank you for your personal interest and kindness in attending to those railway tickets for me, and yet I think it is more for another reason, to exonerate myself from a self-asserted failing, and yet I know you would partially understand me, tho' not quite, not thoroughly. I felt that you looked at me with unforgivable eyes when I tricked myself into the confession that I played to the public. That I must make myself a favorite, whether it reflected credit upon my literary work or not...the public will not listen to lyrics, will not appreciate real poetry, will in fact not have me as an entertainer if I give them nothing but rhythm, cadence, beauty, thought....I have had dreams of "educating" the vulgar taste to Poetry, not action...

What am I writing? You see I am in a "mood"; I often have them. I have no excuse for writing to you like this-save perhaps the ever recurring haunting memory of your silent disapproval...I wish that you would feel confidence enough in me and

my good judgement, and liberal ideas to know that of all things I desire-improvement is the greatest...

Goodnight, what a strange woman you will think me-And yet as I said before I believe you will understand and excuse me. Faithfully I am yours,

E. Pauline Johnson -

My cold is dreadful, I am really quite ill it with.

postscript: I enclose my two studies of this week-Always you must pay some bitter price for the friendship of a poet-They *will* ask you to read their stuff-[29]

Arthur Henry (Harry) O'Brien met Pauline in 1893 during a canoeing event. He practised law in Toronto. He and Pauline corresponded for many years.

A Golden Send-Off
by Evelyn Johnson

The committee, who had charge of the entertainment to be given for Pauline in Brantford a few days before her departure [for England], asked her whether she would rather have money or a piece of jewelry as a gift. Pauline said that she would rather have the money to help her on her undertaking. The day before she left on her trip the citizens of Brantford presented her with a purse of gold.

An early publicity photograph of a dramatic, theatrical Pauline in her two piece stage outfit, made from pearl-coloured buckskin and accented with red broadcloth at the yoke, under the arms and at the hem. While the outfit's bodice stayed the same throughout Pauline's 16-year stage career, at some point she changed the skirt. The first skirt was distinguished by its straight-cut fringed buckskin at the hem, while the second skirt boasted a tear-drop-shaped fringe. Today, Pauline's outfit is at the city of Vancouver Museum, where she wished it to reside, as outlined in her will. From 1894 onward this was the image the public had of Pauline Johnson, Mohawk poet/performer.
(Rare photograph courtesy of Marion W. Macdonald, Simcoe, Ontario)

As we dressed on the evening of the entertainment, Mrs. Geoffrey Hale, a friend who lived a block away, sent a note with her young daughter, Jessie, asking what Pauline intended wearing. Pauline sent back word that she would probably wear a hat, inferring that she would not be in evening dress, and that her dress would be of white cashmere trimmed with heliotrope velvet. This gown had a short train. Jessie went home, and Mrs. Hale sent her back again, this time with flowers for Pauline.

We all drove down to the Kerby House where the entertainment was to take place. Just as we stepped out of the cab, the Reverend Mr. Mackenzie came forward to assist Pauline and the rest of us. He said, "This is the very thing that should have happened: your clergyman to meet you and escort you up the stairs."

The ladies kept on their hats, and the gentlemen wore evening dress. Two of the leading ladies received with Pauline. After the address was read, Pauline made a little speech and recited one of her poems. The remainder of the evening consisted of conversing socially, and at an early hour the gathering broke up. This presentation and entertainment were a great benefit to Pauline financially and an encouragement towards making her trip a success.[30]

A Brilliant Reception
The Brantford Courier

At the G.T.R. depot this morning a few intimate friends assembled to see Miss Johnson on the train and she was accompanied as far as Harrisburg by her brother and sister.

She sails from New York to-morrow by one of the Cunard steamers. It is satisfactory to know that Miss Johnson goes to London well armed with a number of letters of introduction to distinguished people.[31]

An English Journalist Chats with Pauline Johnson
The Gazette, London, England, summer, 1894

"You ask me why I have come to England," said Miss E. Pauline Johnson, the young Iroquois poetess and reciter, Tekahionwake, to the writer last week. "I have come here because my Indian people are very much misunderstood among you English. You do not believe them to be poetic, artistic, and as beautifully moral in their religion as they are. You have a poor idea of the grandeur of the Red Man's nature, and you do him an injustice."

"An injustice? I thought the Indians were so well treated in Canada!" I exclaimed.

"Yes, the Canadian government treats us with the greatest consideration, while the United States government does not study the Indians at all. We of the Six Nations tribe-that is the Iroquois tribe – have our own government. We are, of course, under white law, but the Canadian government never does a thing without asking the chiefs of the Iroquois in council, and when the chiefs pass a bill in our council it is submitted to the Canadian parliament. But there is never any dissension. They do not impose on us, and we do not impose on them. But then, we are one reserve out of hundreds."

"You spoke of an injustice?"

"You do the Indian an injustice by the way you think, and speak and write of him. I am an Iroquois, and, of course, I think the Iroquois are the best Indians in civilization and birth, just as you English think you are better than the Turks. Do you know that the Iroquois have done more in the last hundred years than it took the native Britons all their time to do? Indian families who fifty years ago were worshipping the Great Spirit, in the old Indian way, have turned into professional men and finely-educated women who hold responsible positions. One of the best government land surveyors Canada has is a full-blooded young Indian, and one of the best assistants in the Indian Department at Ottawa is a little Mohawk lady. You cannot, perhaps, count such cases by scores, but they show of what the Red Man is capable. He is no savage if only given a chance."

"How is he handicapped now?"

"For one thing, by the awful class of white people near our reserves. When an Indian mixes in cultured white society, he becomes, in five years, a cultured man. When I was a child I was never allowed to have any white friends except those of the missionary's family. They drag the Indian down. Yet I would not say that the Indians have now any real grievance, so far as the government is concerned, though they had at the time of the North-West Rebellion. The only thing is this. Suppose we came over to England as a powerful people. Suppose you gave us welcome to English soil, worshipped us as gods, as we worshipped you white people when you first came to Canada; and suppose we encroached upon your homeland and drove you back and back, and then said, 'Oh, well, we will present you with a few acres – a few acres of your own dear land. What would you think of it all? So we think. We are without a coun-try. I cannot say America is my country. The whole continent belongs to us by right of lineage. We welcomed you as friends, we worshipped you, and you drove us up into a little corner.

"But you white men may well think better of the Indian than you do. Why, do you know that the Iroquois have one of the most marvellous constitutions that the world has seen? Hiawatha-not the god that dear dead Longfellow painted him, but the greatest statesman Indian civilization ever produced-he found the Indians in eternal feud with one another, killing each other out, and he conceived the idea of making one vast nation called the Iroquois to sweep the continent of America as Napoleon swept Europe. He got fifty-two representatives of each tribe, who were all fighting with one another, to meet, as Disraeli gathered the Berlin Conference together. He got them to agree and instead of fighting among themselves, they fought for the British. To get quarrelling Indian tribes together to do that, and give them a constitution which has lasted for four hundred years, was no small achievement.

"I will read you what Horatio Hale, the historian, says: 'The laws and policy framed by Hiawatha, and his associates more than four centuries ago are still in force among their descendants on the Grand River Reserve, near Brantford, Ontario. The territory has shrunk by many sales made at the well-meant instance of the protecting government to an extent of little more than 20,000 acres, with a population of some 3,000 souls. But in this small domain the chiefs are still elected, the councils are still conducted, and the civil policy is decided as nearly as possible by the rules of their ancient league. Not many persons are aware that there exists in the heart of Canada this relic of the oldest constitutional government of America-a free commonwealth, older even than any in Europe, except those of England and Switzerland, and perhaps two semi-independent republics which lurk in the Pyrenees and the Appennines.'

"That was what Horatio Hale wrote, and he and Parkman and, of course, Thoreau, are the most accurate recorders of Indian affairs, though Parkman did abuse the Iroquois somewhat unjustly.

"And it makes one feel sad to think that, despite all these historic associations, the national character, the Indian is going to die out like the Pole and the Jew. Yes, I know the Iroquois are increasing in numbers a little now; but while we are today, say, 5,000, there must have been 30,000 of us a hundred years ago. The same sad tale must be told of the Crees, the Blackfeet, and the

A broadly smiling Pauline, wearing a fetching hat.
This photograph was probably taken in 1894.
(Brant Historical Society #3789)

Sioux-all of splendid lineage. The Onondagas are blue-blooded-not a drop of any other blood in them, and they generally remain conservative in their habits. They will not embrace Christianity. I know an Onondaga family which can count back nine hundred years in direct line, and a great many Crees and Sioux Indians are the same. The Tuscaroras have a little Osaga blood in them, I think-some Florida Indian blood."

"But come, Miss Johnson," I said rallying her; "you yourself would hardly be leading your present life of culture had it not been for the white man's invasion."

"Perhaps not the same kind of life; but there are two of me. Sometimes I feel I must get away to the Highlands among a people who seem somehow akin to mine."

Then Miss Johnson went on to show me the precious wampum belts which form a part of her Indian costume in recitals. "The white wampum," she explained, "always signifies peace, and is far more valuable and rare than the purple. Wampum is the history, literature, seal and coinage of the Iroquois. The art of carving the head from the shell is lost, and the art of reading the belts is also lost, save in one or two instances where a pupil has learned by rote the meaning of certain belts. The diagonal lines on a belt always proclaim it as Iroquois. This purple wampum, the 'Belt of Hospitality', signifies the freedom of the camp or settlement or lodge to a visitor. The circles are emblematic of the polished basswood bowl wherein is served the national dish, beaver-tail soup. No, I have never tasted our national dish. You have killed off nearly all our beavers. This white wampum here, the 'Ladies' Belt', is one that has seen service in its own peculiar capacity. In a case of murder, the old Indian law of 'blood for blood' is invariable, save in some instances where an unmarried female relation of the murderer presents this belt to the avenger and petitions that he allow the offender to go unavenged; the avenger is

121

bound to accept the offering of peace."

Among other treasures at Miss Johnson's studio is the copy of the Toronto *Globe*, of October 2, 1869, bearing a superscription addressed to Chief G.H.M. Johnson, thus: "With kind regards, from your brother chief, Arthur." It gives a full account of the ceremony when the Duke of Connaught was made chief of the Iroquois by Miss Johnson's father and grandfather in full Indian conclave. I wonder whether H.R.H. ever wears the woollen and red-beaded scarf with his ribbon of the Garter to indicate his Indian chieftainship.[32]

How To Secure a Publisher
by E. Pauline Johnson

When you are getting a book published never be actuated by motives of charity. When *The White Wampum* was ready for its English publication, I took the manuscript over to London and said to myself: 'Now I will hunt up some poor worthy girl who has a mother and a little brother to support, or who is trying to educate herself, and get her to do the typing for me.' I did not go near an agency bureau but spent five days hunting up my worthy girl. I gave her the manuscript and finally the work was done. She said her charge was a guinea-I had expected to pay two-Oh, it was awful! I do not know how long it took me to correct it. There were words spelled wrong, whole lines left out, dreadful punctuation and other things you can imagine. I determined I would not have it done over, however, so I took it to Clement Scott, the great English critic. I had a note of introduction and recommendation from Professor Clark of Trinity University, and it was

the best thing I could have secured, for a word of recommendation from him is considered in England to be the greatest honour any of the colonies could give. I was told that I would be very fortunate if I could secure an interview with Scott, but decided to leave no stone unturned. On inquiring for him I was told he was busy.

"I must see him," I said, and finally was show into his den.

He was a regular lion and glanced up through an awful scowl, growling out: "Well?" There is only one way to deal with a man-that is through his vanity-so I turned to the door again saying "I'm afraid to come in."

"Come back here!" he growled louder. "What are you afraid of?"

I went back, "I'm always afraid of a man who can make one or ruin one with a stroke of his pen," I answered.

He looked over my work then scribbled a line of recommendation to John Lane, the best London publisher. I went to Lane and submitted my copy to him. As soon as he saw it he roared:

"What do you mean by getting this copy typewritten?"

"Why," I said, "I thought it was necessary."

"No," he snapped, "it is not. I never take a book for publication without the expectation that my author will be great, and how would this look in the British Museum labelled, *Original Manuscript of Miss Johnson's First Book*?"

I had expected to go to about twenty publishers before I could secure one, and had arranged to spend three months in England for the purpose; but Lane accepted it, with the result that I was made.

"I would not dare," he told me, "to refuse anything that Clement Scott recommended."[33]

Do You Sell Canoes?

by Walter McRaye

A good story Pauline told was an incident that happened while she and Miss Beverley Robinson were being shown through the great

"This was taken in 1894 just after I returned from my first London season. The frock is my first English dinner dress. It was made at Barkers, High Street, Kensington, S.W." – Pauline, written on the back of the photo.
(Brant Historical Society #635)

department store of Whiteley's. Sir Charles Tupper (then Canada's representative in London) had told them they could "get anything under the sun" in the store. "Why," he said, "they will secure you guests for your dinner, if others fail. They will marry you here, sell you cradles for your babies, and finally make arrangements for your funeral."

Pauline, with a twinkle in her eye, informed Sir Charles that there was one thing she was quite sure could not be purchased in the store.

"And what is that?" he asked.

"A William English-Peterboro' canoe," she replied.

"We will see," said Canada's representative, "and to make it interesting I will wager you a pair of gloves that you are wrong."

Calling a floor walker, the question was asked, "Have you any William English-Peterboro canoes?"

The answer came quick as a flash, "Yes, Madame, fourth floor up. Take the lift."

There were dozens of them in stock![34]

Will That Be Moccasins? or Toboggans?

M.A.P. magazine, England

Of course Tekahionwake wears moccasins when she appears in her Indian dress. More than once they have proved a source of great interest and curiosity on this side of the Atlantic, where we rarely see them. When a friend's lady's maid was helping her to dress, Miss Johnson thought it better to explain at once that her soft leather boot coverings were not to be worn on the hands, like gloves, or hanging from the belt, like tobacco

Pauline in a publicity photograph, showing her buckskin stage dress and all its accessories to advantage. She is wearing the famous bear claw necklace. Suspended from her waist is a beaded belt (left) and a wampum belt (right).
(Cochran of Ontario Collection, Vancouver Public Library, Vancouver B.C., #9429)

pouches. "Oh, no, ma'am, I quite understand!" said the lady's maid. "I've often heard that Canadian ladies wear toboggans on their feet."[35]

Rat Portage, Ontario,
August, 1894

My dear Mr. O'Brien
Was it not from Merrie England that I last wrote to you?...Well, I have left England behind me, left it and its warm hearts, its applause, its possible laurel wreaths, and out here I am forgetting it. The little island has dropped many thousand miles behind me, many, many days away from me. What I see now kills memory of it, and the real heartache I had at leaving it just when I had made dear friendships there. This "great lone land" of course is so absorbing, so lovely, so magnificent, that my eyes forget the beauties of the older land. Ah! There are no such airs as these in England, no such skies, no such forest scents and wild sweet perfumes...We are getting into Indian country now. Every town is full of splendid complexioned Ojibawas, whose copper colouring makes me ashamed of my washed out Mohawk skin, thinned with European blood, I look yellow and "Chinesey" beside these Indians...I send our route on the other page. Perhaps you will find time to drop me a wee letter, I know you will have the disposition.

Sincerely I am your friend,
E. Pauline Johnson[36]

My Aim, My Joy, My Pride...
by E. Pauline Johnson

Never let anyone call me a white woman. There are those who think they pay me a compliment in saying that I am just like a white woman. My aim, my joy, my pride is to sing the glories of my own people. Ours was the race that gave the world its measure of heroism, its standard of physical prowess. Ours was the race that taught the world that avarice veiled by any name is crime. Ours were the people of the blue air and the green woods, and ours the faith that taught men to live without greed and to die without fear. Ours were the fighting men that, man to man-yes, one to three-could meet and win against the world. But for our few numbers, our simple faith that others were as true as we to keep their honor bright and hold as bond inviolable their plighted word, we should have owned American to-day.[37]

A Brantford Man
newspaper clipping

Columbia, Pennsylvania, September 14, 1894 - Harry B. [sic] Johnson, superintendent of the agencies of the Anglo-American Savings and Loan Association, of New York, who has been here since April, was found dead on the street last night. Death resulted from heart failure, superinduced, it is said, by excessive smoking of cigarettes. Mr. Johnson was 35 [sic] years of age and a native of Brantford, Ont., where his mother and sister reside.[38]

Beverly Johnson in his business attire. He sent this photograph to his mother and inscribed it: "Your loving son Bev. 21 Jan 1890." Bev died in 1894, at the age of 40. *(Brant Historical Society #491)*

Banff Springs Hotel, Banff, Alberta, September 21, 1894

My dear Mr. O'Brien
It is not usual with me to reply to letters so rapidly, but yours came to me yesterday at Calgary-just when I most wanted a good friendly letter, and now I feel just like answering the friendliness of the letter at once.

Banff, with its wondrous beauties, is lost to us, we are here but a single day, and the entire scenery, with its mountain grandeur and superb forests of fir, is shrouded in a snow storm. We can see nothing, and go absolutely nowhere, for we are both down with awful colds...Now you know before I tell you-you know from the foregoing lines that I am "in grey days"...I have just lost my dear eldest brother. He died last week in Pennsylvania and they brought him home to be buried...I was too far west to get home in time, and so I go on night after night before the public-for when one is under signed contract they may not have a heart. It was worst while he lay dead, and I in gay gowns, and with laughter on my face and tears in my heart, went on and on-the mere doll of the people and slave to money. Well, I must not make you blue my good friend-I am mastering myself-and after all work, and work alone helps one in these things.

I have gone on the same as ever, driving across the prairies, seeing the wild Western Indians, taking late suppers with hospitable townspeople, studying new parts, and today I laughed like my old self, and shall do henceforth. Owen's kindness and dear friendly care of me has helped me along wonderfully. This life is all so new to me, and coming just after the London days it is more distinct by contrast. I like it, even though the travelling is hard. The great brown prairies I love, we have been in them for the last month, and yet it was good to see trees and mountains once more today at daybreak, when we entered the Rockies. After all, now more than beautiful our dear old Canada is, this trip, a revelation to me.

I shall see you in two weeks' time I hope, I shall be myself by that time, and I hope you will have quite your old rollicking laughter-and a good warm hand clasp for your Sincere friend,

E. Pauline Johnson[39]

Many times in Pauline's life story, more than one version of the same event is documented. The two stories (on the next page) about the inspiration for her poem, "A Prodigal," is just one instance of a recurring pattern in the retelling of the life of Pauline Johnson-which story is "real" and which is "myth"?

DEPTHS

Serene dark pool with all your colours dulled,
Your dreamless waves by twilight slumber lulled;

Your warmth that flamed because the hot sun hushed
Your lip vermilion that his kisses crushed;

Wan are the tints he left of gold and tem
For dusk's soft, cloudy grays have smothered them.

Where yonder shore's tree-terraced outlines melt,
The shadows circle like a velvet belt;

And down, far down within the sable deep
A white star-soul awakens from its sleep.

O! little lake with twilight interlink'd
Your darkling shores, your margin indistinct-

More in your depth's uncertainty there lies

Than when you imagine all the sunset dyes.

Like to the poet's soul you seem to be
A depth no hand can touch, no eye can see.

And melancholy's dusky clouds drift thro'
The singer's songs, as twilight drifts o'er you.

O! life that saddens for the colours fled,
Within your depths a diamond 'wakes instead.

Perchance in spheres remote, and fair and far,
There breathes a twin soul to my soul's white star,

Or have we touched already, and passed by
Unconscious that affinity was nigh?

O! soul, perchance so near me, yet unknown,
Some day we'll 'wake within fate's velvet zone.[40]

Pauline Visits the Cathedral at St. Boniface
newspaper clipping, Vancouver

Some say that "A Prodigal" is the best poem Pauline Johnson, has ever written. Sitting in her room at the Hotel Vancouver I learnt for the first time of how this poem came to be written.

"It was at Red River, Winnipeg," commenced Miss Johnson. "I had gone over to visit the cathedral at St. Boniface, which you will remember from Whittier's poem. As I stood outside the railings I saw in the churchyard a beautiful little French nun. I asked her to show me the grave of Louis Riel, and as she did so we talked together.

"'Sister,' I said, 'you are very young to be here.'

"'Yes,' she answered, 'I am young-but very happy.'

"As I went away, she said to me, 'Some day you will come back?' I told her that I could not say, and she answered-'O yes, some day you will be glad to come back.'

"And as I looked back and saw her standing there I wondered to myself what it was that had taken one so young and so beautiful into that convent. Out of the incident I wrote the poem, thinking that perhaps some such reason as it embodies might have driven her to shut herself up so closely with God."[41]

A PRODIGAL

My heart forgot its God for love of you,
    And you forgot me, other loves to learn;
Now through a wilderness of thorn and rue
    Back to my God I turn.

And just because my God forgets the past,
    And in forgetting does not ask to know
Why I once left His arms for yours, at last
    Back to my God I go.[42]

Flint and Feather

Pauline Encounters a Sister of Charity
by Mrs. W. Garland Foster

The story behind "The Prodigal" [sic] is of a poignancy to stir the hidden pools of life. Pauline was one day wandering about the tombs in the churchyard of the old St. Boniface Cathedral at Winnipeg, reading the strange legends set over the last resting places of wanderers, traders, settlers, on their way to the land of the setting sun. Strange half tales here to stir the imagination, stranger still to hush the heart beats could the whole be known. Looking up from her culling of old memories, she saw a little Sister of Charity placing an offering of flowers as she knelt beside an unmarked, but well kept grave. Wondering and vaguely stirred the Indian maiden drew nearer the black robed figure as she rose. With that soft protective air, so kindly, so incurious, Tekahion-wake smiled sadly, as one who knew. The little Sister returned the shadow of a smile, and they both stood looking down at the unmarked grave.

"No stone, no marking," breathed Pauline.

"No name," returned the Sister, sighing softly. "She was just a girl. We never knew her name," she continued, fingering the crucifix at her side. "We respected her pride. We nursed her, and when she died, we laid her here with her just-born daughter by her side. But they seem so lonely, those two in their sadness, that I come always to care for the spot and leave a token of flowers with a prayer to the Virgin, Mother of God."[43]

WINNIPEG AT SUNSET

Sink in your pillows, O Sun King that reigns
    From East unto West,
Bury your yellow head out on the plains,
    Wind-beaten breast.

Sink in your cradle of colour and cloud,
    King of the day,
Leaving us only the shadows and shroud
    Of on-coming grey.

Twilight is lingering over the rim
    Of prairie and sky,
Its purple and amethyst, born in the dim
    Horizon, to die.

The city is blinking her myriad eyes
    Of glimmering lights,

And the summer moon, in the summer skies
    Sails up the heights.

While her thousand vassals of stars step forth
    The nights to greet,
Where the city, Queen of the West and North,
    Stands at their feet.

She who in garment of loveliness dressed,
    Regally reigns,
Queen of the Prairie-Land, Queen of the West,
    Queen of the Plains.[44]

There and Back

by Miss Poetry (E. Pauline Johnson) and Mr. Prose (Owen Smiley), *The Toronto Globe*

...This article will leave the important events out. It is merely intended to be an impressionist sketch of the experience of two Torontonians who journeyed from ocean to ocean, making numerous pauses during their three months of travel for the noble purpose of furnishing divers dramatic and literary critics with items for their columns. It will be something of a panorama in make-up.

...At our first western stopping place-the "Soo"-...Miss Poetry nosed out a dusky Chippewa pilot, and went tearing down the rapids, acquiring such a reckless taste for this sort of water-tobogganing that she narrowly escaped missing the train, arriving at the station out of breath, but spray-soaked from head to foot, just in time to swing gracefully (perhaps) on the last car as it moved out. Miss Poetry caught some music from the rapids, in addition to a fine large cold in the head.

...It is not till you wake up at Winnipeg that you are in touch with the plains, and after a few hundred miles of piled-up rocks you appreciate them, but long before the Rockies are reached you grow desperately tired of them again, and turn from the view outside to your fellow-passengers for something to interest you. There is such a variety of nationalities to be found in the colonist cars that this is easy to discover. 'Arries from England, Murphys from Ireland, Sandies from Scotland, all are there, but Chinamen seemed to be in the majority most of the time.

Pauline, hat and all, is pictured seated in a canoe between two guides, as they ferry her across the Ste. Marie River in Northern Ontario, 1894.
(Brant Historical Society #239)

THE PRAIRIE

I may not catch the largeness or its
meaning,
So infinite and perfected the whole,
But this child-wisdom I am slowly
gleaning,
That thro' its silence I can reach its
soul.

I stand and watch its limitless out-
reaching,
Its velvet browness to the sky unroll,
And tho' I may not understand its
teaching,
Its silence has revealed to me its soul.

In this poem Pauline lampoons her wildly successful poem "The Song My Paddle Sings."

HIS MAJESTY, THE WEST WIND

Once in a fit of mental aberration
I wrote some stanzas to the western
wind,
A very stupid, maudlin invocation,
That into ears of audiences I've
dinned.

A song about a sail, canoe and paddle
Recited I, in sailor flannels dressed,
And when they heard it people would
skiddadle,
Particularly those who had been west.

For they, alas, had knowledge, I was
striving

To write of something I had never
known,
That I had ne'er experienced the
driving
Of western winds across a prairie
blown.

I never thought when grinding out
those stanzas,
I'd live to swallow pecks of prairie
dust,
That I'd deny my old extravaganzas,
And wish his Majesty distinctly-
cussed.

In order to clear up any doubt there may be upon the subject, I wish to state clearly that his well-known and respected highness the west wind lives two miles west of Fort Macleod. The west wind comes in its full force through this town...If you drop a dollar-bill say good-bye to it, unless you are on horse-back. The prairie is so flat that anything as light as paper keeps on the move all the time. We had some most exciting races with two pages of newspaper, which we tore into small pieces and let the wind carry along. Mr. Prose's fragments won most of the contests, however, as he had a copy of *The New York Herald*, while Miss Poetry was handicapped with a scientific journal, which was so slow in comparison with *The Yankee Times* that, to even matters up, she tore out all the more ponderous words, but even then *The Herald* took a jump over the cliff into the Old Man River (the goal) first every time.

KICKING-HORSE RIVER

It does not care for grandeur,
It does not care for state,
It flips its little fingers
In the very face of fate,
And when its course is thwarted,
Its current set at bay,
It just kicks up its saucy heels,
And-takes another way.

It laughs among the monarchs,
It giggles at the kings,
It dances in the gorges,
While a comic song it sings;
It ripples into waterfalls,
It tipples into spray,
And when they raise their eyebrows up,
It-takes another way.

It does not care a button
For the granite of the rocks,
It never gets discouraged,
For it's never in a box.
When mountains contradict it,
And canyons have their way,
It kicks a little higher,
And-takes another way.

...And now we shall bring this diary of impressions to a close...and we will
ring down the CURTAIN

Scene, final;
    Setting, modern;
        House, interior.
Left centre, window open to the west;
Right centre, swing door (showing some exterior
And eastern garden seats, where one may rest).
Dramatis Personae,
    Two wandering spirits,
Who speak their lines, then flit across the stage,
Trusting the audience to applaud their merits,
Hoping their failures earn not failure's wage.
Enter
The "Gentle Reader" with this paper-
Then, warning tinkle of the curtain-bell;
The footlights lower; something like a vapor
Comes to the eyes that westward look farewell;
The rising audience dons its coat and tilling
(The "Gentle Reader" stays until the close);
Then, with the customary bowing, smiling,
Exit Miss Poetry and Mr. Prose.[45]

Pauline, celebrity poet, strikes a romantic, sensuous pose for the camera and for her growing legion of fans. Peggy Webling, a friend, tells us that "when Pauline Johnson was touring Canada, a chairman in Manitoba thought it necessary to plead for a fair reading for a Redskin, so he said, with due emphasis: 'Now friends, before Miss Johnson's exercises begin, I want you all to remember that Injuns, like us, is folks.'"[46]
(*The William Ready Division of Archives and Research Collections, McMaster University Library, Hamilton, Canada*)

The Windsor Hotel,
Montreal,
June 9, 1895

My dear Mr. O'Brien

Your note came to me last evening, for which I thank you. I send herewith the promised poem and hope you will like it. Small and brief as it is I consider it one of my best of recent efforts, and you see I have kept to your colors- *The White and the Green*. Tomorrow I am going to look for silk to make the promised pennant. If I succeed in getting the right quality I shall let you know and at all events you shall have something pretty for your Regatta, made by very willing and interested hands. This place is deadly dull, we have played to poor business, as have also the Caghlans who have been here all the week. There is absolutely nothing going on and Mr. Smiley and I are forced to drive about the mountain daily, at the imminent threat of everlasting poverty in consequence of such extravagance, but if we did not do something, we would grow heartily tired of one another and probably quarrel-Horrors! What a life. The hotel is as usual, big, dull, ponderous. The waiters proud in their majesty and refusing to run even for a "quarter." Tuesday, however, we leave for the small towns, where we shall probably long for the Windsor again and refuse to be comforted because we are not here. We are going to have a few days rest on Lake Champlain, which I think we shall enjoy greatly. I'm glad you would like to hear sometimes how and where I am-You shall, and later in the season the pennant will follow-With my warm regards,

Yours faithfully

E. Pauline Johnson

postscript: I lunched at Sir Wm. Van Horne's today "They put up something very good" as the out-west senator said. His pictures are glorious. Rosseau, Carot, Dore, Reynolds, Danbigny-all the great names-Ah! it was a feast worth having-that hour with his beautiful paintings. EPJ[47]

This poem was written for Pauline's friend, Mr. O'Brien, for his canoe club's *Year Book*.

THE WHITE AND THE GREEN

I.

It is winter in the lakeland, and the sleeping islands lie,

Wrapped in pearl-embroidered ermine, crowned with milk-white ivory.

For many days have come and gone, and many hours are old,

Since the plover passed to southward, at the coming of the cold.

II.

It is summer in the lakeland, and the islands lie serene,

All garmented in emerald, within a world of green.

For many days have come and gone, and many hours are old,

Since the plover passed to northward, and the April suns were gold.[48]

Sir Charles G.D. Roberts (1860-1943), poet and lecturer, was knighted in 1935. Although he and Pauline had corresponded for years it was not until 1895 that they met one another, during her tour of Canada's eastern provinces. After Pauline's recital in Fredericton, N.B., Charles' father invited Pauline to be their guest at their home. During her stay Charles travelled from his home in Nova Scotia to visit with Pauline. Before she left to continue her recital tour, Charles presented her with a copy of his book, *Songs of the Common Day*, published in 1893, as well as the pen with which he had written the book. Later, Pauline sent him a poem entitled "The Douglas Shore." This poem remains one of Pauline's lost poems.
(University of New Brunswick, Harriet Irving Library, Archives and Special Collections)

Pauline's Volume of Poetry is Published!...And Comes under the Scrutiny of the Critics

newspaper review, 1895

Pauline in a typical publicity shot. When dressed in her buckskin dress, she preferred to show photographers and the public her profile, thinking that this angle pronounced her Mohawk features, more than a photograph of her full face would have done. Horatio Hale, a friend of the Johnson family, had this to say of her: "A graceful figure, and pleasing face, prepossess the audience at once. The warmth of feeling, the unstudied utterance, the alternate fire and softness of her intonations, the apt appealing gestures, all tell of the hereditary instinct of eloquence, which has come down to her from a line of chiefs and councillors with whom persuasive oratory was the very life and mainspring of tribal policies."[51]
(The William Ready Division of Archives and Research Collections, McMaster University Library, Hamilton, Canada)

*T*he White Wampum by E. Pauline Johnson, "Tekahionwake" – Miss Johnson is undoubtedly something of a poet, but we do not think that the idea of posing as an Indian bard can be counted among her happiest inspirations. It is true that she has so successfully caught the Mohawk frenzy as to break quite naturally into the cry of "Wah," and to warn her enemies, in rather doubtful rhyme, of the day when –

> *Reeking, red, and raw*
> *Their scalps will deck the belts of Iroquois.*

But on the whole, though we like to hear of the Indians' virtues, and fully believe at least in their wrongs, the fiery strains of "Tekahionwake" leave us unmoved; and we much prefer the poems in which Miss Johnson, who is, it appears, a Canadian, condescends to touch the humbler lyre of the palefaces. Such verses as "Workworn," "Overlooked," "Christmastide," and "Brier," if they contain nothing very original either in style or matter, are alike graceful in form and touching in sentiment. In the Canadian canoe, if not in the Indian wigwam, Miss Johnson is thoroughly at home, and if, as she herself says, the shadows and the dreaming suit her better than storm and stress, it must be allowed that she dreams very prettily.[49]

Pauline scribbled a note on this review from England: "This is the notice *Black & White* gave the roast to. *The Guardian* did not know I was Indian."[49]

...She Is a Pretty Poet...
newspaper review, 1895

I am not prepared to say what *White Wampum* means, but it is the title of a book of verse by Miss Pauline Johnson, lately issued from The Bodley Head. The subjects are mostly Indian, in praise of the Redman and of his country. One gathers that Miss Johnson lives in Canada, and has an intimate knowledge of the fast-dying race. Her poems sing their virtues and heroism in a sympathetic fashion, but, though possibly this poetess knows a great deal more about the red-skins at first-hand than did Longfellow, she describes them in a far more outside fashion than he. In the verses with human subjects, there is none of the strange fascination that creeps on us as we read *Hiawatha*. Not that her point of view is more prosaic, but only that her art is less. In nature poetry she is better skilled. Longfellow and Whittier have done more for the red-man she loves and champions. But she is a pretty poet, all the same, when she sings of the land he lives in, and still more when she tries to utter the dreams that lie about her there.[50]

Pauline as Wife Material
by Mrs. W. Garland Foster

She gave a recital at Medicine Hat. A man who was leaving the hall was overheard saying: "Isn't she savage! I wouldn't like her for a wife."[52]

Trails of the Old Tillicums
by E. Pauline Johnson

It was in 1895 that I first saw this Chief ride up from the south-eastern horizon into Fort Macleod. He was followed by at least 50 of his tribe. The Blood of Southern Alberta. They all wore fringed buckskin leggings, and were stripped to the waist, their bodies stained and painted in soft pastel tints, and over-lined with streaks of scarlet and dark brilliant blue.

At his belt, the Chief wore, by actual count, 17 scalps, all taken in wars across the border, when the Bloods invaded the territory of the Sioux and trouble continued for years, that had first been stirred up by the wars in Sitting Bull's time. This particular Chief was a great "Britisher," and an American Indian's scalp was, to him, a veritable Victoria Cross.

The desire of my life had been to possess an Indian scalp, a Sioux scalp particularly, so I interviewed the inspector of the N.W.M.P. and asked what chance there was of securing the treasure. He shook his head gravely.

"None, I am afraid," he replied. Then I offered a sum of money far in advance of what I was able to spare, but the Inspector said money would not count with the great Blood Chief; that he was worth at least $50,000, which he had made in cattle.

"However," said the policeman, with the gallantry and effort to please, that so strikes the Easterner when they first meet any of the force, "I shall try my best to secure one for you; perhaps we can appeal to him through your ancestors, the Mohawks always fought for the British-did they not?"

"Always," I affirmed; "my great grandfather fought against Washington for King George, my grandfather fought as a boy of 16 under Sir Isaac Brock at Queenston Heights. My father carried dispatches from Niagara Falls to Hamilton during the 'Fenian Raid'."

"Then we've got our good friend the Chief, and I think you have got your Sioux scalp," laughed the inspector.

Afterwards I heard how it happened. The inspector approached the Chief, and diplomatically opened negotiations. The Chief sat and smoked for a full hour in silence, then he asked, thoughtfully:

"You say this lady's father, and his fathers before him were great warriors?"

"Yes, great warriors," replied the inspector.

"Who did they fight for-Yankees or Queen?" demanded the Chief, with suspicion.

"Oh, the Queen, always, and the British crown before the Queen was born," the inspector assured him.

The Chief removed a single scalp from his belt, and rising to his feet, said: "Send this to the lady who comes from the Land of the Morning, and tell her I take no money from the daughter of fighting men."

"But you never would have got it," the inspector told me, "no matter how well your ancestors may have fought, had they not fought for the British."

It is a beautiful braid of long brown-black hair, the flesh "cured" and encased in tightly-stitched buckskin, and coiled about it close rows of turquoise blue "Hudson's Bay" beads.[53]

The Most Popular Figure in Canadian Literature
by Hector Charlesworth, 1895

For the past five years Miss Pauline Johnson has been the most popular figure in Canadian literature, and in many respects the most prominent one. There is something more or less remarkable in all this, since her prominence and popularity were accomplished merely by a few occasional lyrics in fugitive publications. Recently Miss Johnson has been figuring throughout Canada in a bardic capacity as the reciter of her own works, but her fame was made before such a course became possible. Instances of a poet's achieving actual fame years before he or she has issued a single volume are sufficiently unique to be remarkable, and now that a collection of Miss Johnson's songs is actually between covers we are enabled to realize something of the charm and power and music that had enabled her to achieve her previous importance.[54]

The following exchange between Pauline and Hector Charlesworth took place on a scrap of paper. The poem to which she refers is a mystery.

But all the poem was soul of me
Launched out, and wrecked upon a sea
I hoped would float it tenderly,
But portless it is toss't-
E. Pauline Johnson

And perhaps if I could catch it
'mong the notes that tinkle low
There's a bar of grand sphere-music
in the singing 'neath the snow.
Hector Charlesworth[55]

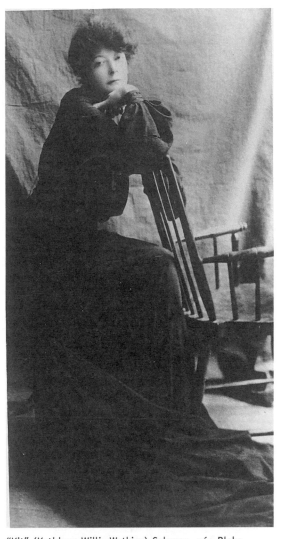

"Kit" (Kathleen Willis Watkins) Coleman, née Blake (1864-1915). Canada's first women's page editor, columnist, history's first accredited woman war correspondent (Spanish-American War, 1898), first president of the Canadian Women's Press Club, Canada's first syndicated columnist, and friend and supporter of Pauline.
(National Archives of Canada, Ottawa, #PA164916)

Prominent Female Columnist Writes of Pauline

by Kit Coleman

The Indian poetess is a very clever woman. Her voice is exquisitely tender, her facial power wonderful, and her gestures graceful and telling. It was with intense pleasure I listened to her rendering of her own beautiful compositions, some of which seemed to be almost beyond reach of our more commonplace minds. Her passionate, dark face expressed every shade of feeling. She was a revelation to me. Her Indian costume, which must have cost an immensity, was accurate in every detail, and most becoming to its wearer. Miss Johnson now and then showed how intensely sarcastic she can be, as well as how passionately devoted she is to her own people, for all of which I love her.[56]

A Rose by Any Other Name
by Walter McRaye

Katherine Blake Coleman, "Kit" of the old *Mail and Empire*, was a great friend of Pauline. Kit was a brilliant journalist, who had for years edited the woman's page of the above mentioned paper. She was beautiful, and charming of manner. When I met her she was living at Copper Cliff [Ontario], where her husband, Dr. Coleman, was physician to the miners. Copper Cliff had huge copper smelters, and the sulphur fumes killed all vegetation in the place. There was nothing green within miles. "Kit" had sent to Toronto for a bouquet of roses to present to Pauline at the performance. She kept them in a refrigerator. They wilted to a dark brown on their journey to the hall, much to the disappointment of our hostess.[57]

Adventures in Nakusp, British Columbia
by Mrs. W. Garland Foster

The town hall at Nakusp, B.C., on Arrow Lake, saw several of Pauline's concerts. Tom Abriel was always on hand to rent the hall and incidentally enjoy a bit of repartee. On one occasion, Pauline requested Mr. Abriel to be sure and see that none of the children were allowed to interrupt her by making a noise during the recital. For like all small towns, where all the family turned out to hear Pauline, there were always small children in the audience, and naturally she hated to be disturbed in the midst of her more tragic selections by a child's cry. So fervent promises were obtained from Mr. Abriel that not a child should whimper that night. All went well, but toward the end of the programme, when she was giving a tragic selection, an infant, with a particularly powerful pair of western lungs, set up a howl and there seemed for a time a question of who had the stage. The following morning Pauline took Mr. Abriel aside and admonished him that, whatever else he attempted in the future, never make any rash promises about controlling crying infants, for as a child's nurse he left much to be desired.

On another occasion at Nakusp, one summer evening, when the last minute of daylight was being utilized by the farmer inhabitants who would presently arrive for the concert, Pauline and her manager were kicking their heels idly about the entrance of the hall. The Abriel cow, whose duty it was to crop the grass about the hall in lieu of a lawn mower, was wandering about when Pauline, seized with a spirit of mischief, gently let down the bars into a nearby field of clover remarking that the cow would have a good feed before she was discovered. It so happened that Pauline's eloquence must have prevented the owner from seeing the cow that night, with the result that she was not released until the next morning, when her owner's fury could not be expended upon her lest she explode.[58]

An Unexpected Concert in B.C.

by Mrs. W. Garland Foster

Several concerts were also given in the Nelson opera house, as this town was a convenient stopping place on the way in and out of the smaller places. While the Silver King Mine was in operation, Nelson was only a little less lively than Rossland. Unexpected concerts were sometimes given, as on one occasion, when going down to Nelson on the S.S. Moyie, which carried the Crow's Nest passengers from Kootenay Landing, Pauline's company was hailed as the boat put into Kuskanook. This landing was in its transition stage and looked much like a lumber pile. The man on the dock who recognized Pauline and her manager proved to be Gus Fraser, whom they had often met when he was featuring melodrama in the Mollie Jeffreys company. After the company had failed the remnant of the cast had settled down in Kuskanook awaiting for something to happen. So it happened that Pauline's company was persuaded to remain for one night. There were half a dozen saloons, but no church or hall, so Gus Fraser suggested that they might do a benefit in aid of a church, which he opined was sadly needed. In order to ensure an audience several small boys were sent about with bells shouting: "Pauline Johnson to-night! Show to-night!"

A billiard room was equipped for a theatre. The billiard table in a corner served as a stage, while a few boxes did duty as steps, and Hudson's Bay blankets screened off the dressing rooms. Such a setting would be no bar to Pauline, who always rose to such occasions. The entertainment lasted two hours and the audi-ence was well pleased with the programme.[59]

The Johnson-Smiley Combination Give a Delightful Entertainment

Terre Haute Express, December, 1896

Quite a surprise greeted the audience which filled the Congregational Church last evening to hear the Johnson-Smiley combination. The programme was a delightful one from beginning to end, and it is safe to say that should the company ever come here again none of the halls in the city will hold the throng which would greet them. The dramatic part of the entertainment as given by Mr. Smiley showed his wonderful power of impersonation...Miss Johnson, the Indian poetess, was attired in a native costume. Her recitations were all of her native life and showed her to have great power and originality...Mr. Smiley's musical sketch *Music in Three Flats*, was especially fine. The plot being laid in a flat in a large city. A fair maiden lived on the lower floor, while her lover lived on the third. Unfortunately a crusty old bachelor lived between them. They were in the habit after having spent most of their time together during the day of singing their love to each other after separating. They would always become more sentimental in song than they were in life. They would raise their windows and sing responsively. The old bachelor buys a piano and joins in the love-making only to cause a falling out. Mr. Smiley produces all the scenes incidental to this little drama.[60]

Johnson-and-Smiley in Cleveland, Ohio
by Evelyn Johnson

Pauline and a fellow reciter, Mr. Owen Smiley, whom we all admired, were once preparing the platform for an evening's entertainment in the church of which the Reverend Mr. Tuttle had charge in Cleveland, Ohio. Coming upon the baptistry, Pauline said "Oh, Mr. Tuttle, suppose one of us should fall in there?" "Well," said Mr. Tuttle with a twinkle in his eye, "I think you would be improved."

"And now, " said Pauline, "my fellow worker and I have been wondering ever since whether Mr. Tuttle meant physically or morally."[61]

Red, White and Blue
by Evelyn Johnson

Pauline won the prize which *The Mail and Empire* offered for the best Conservative poem on the coming elections, when Sir Charles Tupper was Premier. *The Mail and Empire* stipulated that the poem be written so that it could be sung to some patriotic air. During that time Sir Charles Tupper spoke in the Armouries in Brantford and Pauline's poem was sung by a number of men just before his speech. The Premier mentioned Pauline's poem with high praise and said that he had seen her in England and also that he had given her a letter of introduction for use in England.

Pauline had wanted very much to present a flag or flowers to the Premier. She could get red and white flowers, but was unable to obtain blue ones. That afternoon someone suggested that she get wild flowers in blue. I forget where she got the blue flowers, but she had the three colours combined in a flag of flowers for presentation that evening. She handed the flowers to some gentlemen on the platform, but they insisted that she herself ascend the platform and present them to Sir Charles Tupper. She told me afterwards that Mr. Arthur Bunnell, among others "fairly kicked her up onto the platform," and she was obliged to present her flowers. Sir Charles Tupper after his thanks to Pauline again spoke highly of her to the audience.[62]

Pauline dressed in a gown, with a long train, expansive sleeves, and rich velvet trim.
(Brant Historical Society #627)

THE GOOD OLD N.P.

Miss E. Pauline Johnson has been awarded the first prize of the three offered by the Industrial League for the best campaign song. The following verses comprise the song that she submitted: (Air - The Red, White and Blue)

I.
Now rise up men of the nation,
    Rise up at your country's command,
Come forward whatever your station,
    And shoulder-to-shoulder we'll stand,
We may differ in creed and in colour,
    French, and English and Red men are we,
But we're one for our cause and our country,
    We are one for the good old N.P.

Chorus
Then three cheers for the good old N.P.
    Give a hearty three times three,
We are one for our cause and our country,
    We are one for the good old N.P.

II.
It has nourished the son of the city,
    It has nourished the son of the soil,
Surrounded the workman with plenty,
    Awarding with wages his toil,
It has fed both the lordly and lowly,
    And Master and Man will agree,
And its foes are admitting, tho' slowly,
    Success means the good old N.P.
Chorus

III.
So rally ye sons of Protection,
    And shoulder-to-shoulder we'll stand,
We'll gather from every direction,
    From seaboard and lakeside and land;
For the tariff that fostered and fed us,
    From the hour of its birth we began
To know, to prosperity it led us
    And we'll stand by it now to a man.
Chorus[63]

The "N.P.," or National Policy League, advanced tariff protection for Canadian manufactured goods.

Literary Gossip

The Magnet Magazine, January, 1897

"Tekahionwake," Miss Pauline E. Johnson [sic], the Red Indian poetess, who recently gave us a very fresh and delightful book of songs, under the title of *The White Wampum*, is proud of her descent from the Mohawks, who form the great Iroquois nation. Her name is already known all over Canada and the States as a talented reciter and a strong and vigorous writer...In conversation she is brilliant, in appearance handsome and attractive-charms that are enhanced by a musical voice and bright, unconventional manners. She invariably recites in her national dress, which consists of a short, sleeveless dress of red woollen material, over which falls a tunic of buckskin trimmed with ermine tails and coloured beads, and wearing bear's claws and panther's teeth for her "wampums." She is, perhaps, distinguished as the most unique figure in the literary world of today.[64]

Mr James Brown July, 1897
Department of Education
Regina, North-West Territories

Dear Mr. James Brown
Some months ago my friend Mr. Fred Jones wrote me and mentioned having spoken to you regarding the entertainment given by Mr. Owen Smiley and myself. Since that time I have been seriously ill, and am only just now arranging our tour of the West.

I take the liberty to send you by this mail samples of our printing, press notices, etc. and of making you an offer for some date early in September. Our usual rates are $75.00 a performance, but as we did not visit Regina on our last trip west, and are anxious to do so this time we will cut to $60.00 and if you have any reason a house that causes you to fear loss, we will make a rebate of $10.00 so that in event of a poor house our charges will not exceed $50.00.

We supply gratis lithographs, the same as samples sent, also press-notice circulars and programmes, for the evening.

September is a good month for entertainment we always find, the harvest money is in, the schools open etc. This is all business detail, but we must all take small things into consideration in these matters.

I have made these rates the lowest figure that we could make even a small margin on, and I trust you will see your way clear to engage our services on behalf of either Church or State. If so, an early reply will greatly oblige us.

Faithfully I am yours,
E. Pauline Johnson[65]

Pauline-star!
(Brant Historical Society #620)

Music and Drama
Winnipeg Free Press, December, 1897

Winnipeg has been visited at various times by writers of note who have given readings from their own productions and have drawn good houses; in the majority of instances, however, the public interest has centred in the personality of the reader and the reading itself has possessed no special merit.

Miss E. Pauline Johnson is a reader or reciter of talent as well as a writer. It may be that she has inherited from her Indian ancestors a communion with nature which is denied to most people of white blood; at any rate she gave last night in the Grand Opera House an entertainment which the talent of a pale face could hardly be thought of as originating.

In the first part of the programme she appeared in picturesque Indian costume, and in every gesture, in the glances of her eye, in the varying expressions of her face, and in the working of the different emotions and passions she was a pure Indian. She portrayed the heathen Indian so that the audience could see him live and move, and could appreciate his views of Christianity and civilization.

Some of the blunders in the attempts made to Christianize him and educate his children were made to appear. The titles of her readings in this part were "Ojistoh," "The Cattle Thief," and "His Sister's Son." The wrongs done the Indian by the white man and the hatred and revenge of the latter were strongly depicted.

When Miss Johnson, in the second part of the programme, appeared in a rich and beautiful dress made in fashionable, civilized style, the impression upon the audience was entirely changed. People then thought she must surely be at least almost white, in her features and her complexion they could see nothing of the Indian.

But one characteristic she did not lose, namely, the power to interpret nature which comes from, or is dependent upon, keenness of observation. She showed herself to be an observer of human nature as well as of external nature. In her reading, "The Success of the Season," she afforded much amusement by her pictures of the follies and insincerities of fashionable, or would-be fashionable, society...The concluding reading "Canadian Born" was full of patriotic sentiment. Miss Johnson may expect good houses at future appearances in Winnipeg, for her recital last evening gave genuine pleasure and its merits were recognized by those who heard her.[66]

TEKAHIONWAKE

RRSkye

On Her Own

1898-1901

*B*etween 1892 and 1897 Pauline experienced more ups than downs. The death of her brother Bev seems to have been the only low point in a chapter in her life that was marked by joyous occasions and exhilarating firsts. Starting in 1898, however, Pauline was in for a spot of rough weather. "Grey days," as she referred to her times of low spirit, were plentiful in the coming three and a half years.

All was well early in 1898. Pauline left Winnipeg accompanied by the young performer Walter McRaye. They toured American towns south of Manitoba before returning to Winnipeg to give a concert in the city on January 18. If Walter was using the brief tour to audition to be Pauline's new performing partner, he was sorely disappointed. He was sent on his way because Pauline was ready to announce her engagement to Charles Drayton. This item appeared in the January 26, 1898 edition of one of Pauline's hometown newspapers:

"The engagement is announced of Miss E. Pauline Johnson, daughter of the late Chief G.H.M. Johnson of the Six Nations Indians, and Mr. Charles R.L. Drayton, assistant inspector for the Western Loan and Savings Company, Winnipeg, and whose home is in Toronto, where he is widely and favorably known. The young couple are the recipients of the warmest congratulations on all sides in Winnipeg, in which no doubt Miss Johnson's many friends in this city will most heartily join."[1]

The next day *The Brantford Courier* had this to say about the news: "The announcement of the engagement of Miss E. Pauline Johnson to Mr. Charles Drayton of Winnipeg came as a surprise to those not intimately connected with the family. That her rare accomplishments and pleasing personality should win many bids in the matrimonial market was to be expected, but Miss Johnson was enthroned by her genius far above the commonplace of life and getting married is such an ordinary thing to do that it was the last thing expected of her..."[2]

And what of the man whose proposal Pauline accepted? Charles Drayton was

Pauline. This photograph was taken in 1897 during a tour of Ontario. It is, perhaps, Pauline's most striking portrait.
(Brant Historical Society #539)

born in 1872, in Barbados where his father served as an officer of Her Majesty's 16th Rifles. Of British descent, the Draytons settled in Ontario in 1874 where Mr. Drayton, Sr., lectured at Osgoode Hall in Toronto. Charles was educated at a private school in England and Upper Canada College in Toronto.

In 1890 Charles began his apprenticeship with the Western Canada Savings and Loan Company. The next year he transferred to the company's Winnipeg office where he was a cashier. By 1897 he was an assistant inspector and living at the Clarendon Hotel, adjacent to Pauline's Winnipeg base, the Manitoba Hotel.

Pauline let it be known that the wedding date would not be until "next September," presumably September of 1899. In the meantime she had plans to spend the summer of 1898 in New York City, supervising the publication of a book of her short stories. This did not come to pass, for whatever reason. In February, just one month after the announcement of her forthcoming wedding, Pauline received a telegram from Allen telling of their mother's grave ill health. Foul weather made the homeward journey a lengthy and stressful one. Pauline arrived at Emily's death bed with little time to spare, for her mother died within forty-five minutes of her arrival.

Mrs. George Johnson was buried at the Mohawk Chapel. After the funeral Pauline fell sick with a severe throat infection. When she recovered she left Brantford to perform in Toronto, Ottawa and Sudbury. Engagements in the United States kept her busy until mid-June, when she fell victim to a recurrence of her throat infection and returned to Brantford. Her sister nursed her back to health.

In July, Pauline went to Toronto to meet Charles and attend the funeral of his mother. She returned to Brantford alone to help Eva pack and move out of the home the family had known for the past 14 years.

At the Woodland Cultural Centre in Brantford there is a framed photograph, taken on a warm summer day, of Mrs. Johnson with Eva and Pauline posing in front of #7 Napoleon St. On the back of this rare photograph Eva wrote a dedication to her sister on the occasion of her engagement.

Having finished the emotional task of organizing the family's possessions and clearing out the Brantford home, Pauline went to Ottawa for another concert appearance before travelling to Winnipeg. A weary Pauline spent most of August and September fighting further illness. By late September she had signed with a new manager, Thomas E. Cornyn, and was embarking on another tour. The rest of 1898 was spent on the road giving performances in small prairie towns like Portage La Prairie, Minnedosa, Rapid City, Birtle, Binscarth, Russell, and Yorkton.

Despite starting on a high note, with the announcement of her engagement, 1898 had seen Pauline weather the deaths of both her beloved mother and her intended mother-in-law, as well as frequent and intense periods of ill health. She must have hoped that 1899 would bring fairer weather.

Thomas Cornyn kept his client on the road continuously throughout 1899. Before Christmas of that year she had been west as far as Vancouver Island, to the Kootenays, to Calgary, to Minnesota, to the Qu'Appelle Valley in Saskatchewan, and back to Winnipeg.

The engagement of Charles Drayton and Pauline Johnson typified the long-distance relationship, for not only was Pauline "on the road," but Charles' job took him on lengthy business trips throughout Canada's west. Who knows how often the paths of the lovers crossed during this, the second year of their engagement, before their intended wedding date of September 1899?

Although the engagement was greeted with contentment by Charles' family, and although Pauline seemed prepared to make a commitment to marriage, sometime between Christmas of 1899 and January 9, 1900, the engagement between Pauline and Charles Drayton was dissolved.

Soon after, Pauline was on an eastbound train, heading for Toronto's Massey Music Hall where she was to headline two concerts in aid of Canadian soldiers engaged in the Boer War in South Africa. For these appearances Pauline chose to recite "Riders of the Plains" and "Canadian Born."

By February of 1900 she was again embarked on a series of concerts, this time in towns throughout Ontario. By spring she was east of Ontario. Two train ticket stubs (found among the Johnson papers located at The William Ready Division of Archives and Research Collections, McMaster University Library, Hamilton, Canada) place Pauline on a train from Montreal to St. Agathe, Quebec in the company of a Mr. Charles H. Wuerz. Written on the ticket stubs, in the space marked "On account of...," both travellers have written "Advertising." The date of departure was May 28, 1900.

Charles Wuerz is a mystery man in Pauline's life; where and when she met him and under what circumstances are facts that either were not recorded or have not been uncovered. There are only three clues that give some information about Mr. Wuerz besides the train ticket stubs. In the June 2, 1900, edition of *The Halifax Herald* this brief appears: "Mr. Wurz [sic] who is directing the Canadian tour of Miss E. Pauline Johnson, the famous Canadian poet reciter, arrived in the city yesterday from Quebec. Arrangements have already been made for Miss Johnson's appearances at Halifax, Dartmouth,

Amherst, Springhill, Truro, New Glasgow, Windsor, Kentville, Wolfville, Digby, Yarmouth and a dozen other towns will be announced later. After leaving Nova Scotia, Miss Johnson will appear in a few cities in the United States and in the fall will leave for Australia and Great Britain."[3] Just when the management of Pauline's career changed from Thomas Cornyn's hands to Charles Wuerz's hands is unknown.

This photograph of Pauline shows the image she projected in Charles Wuerz's promotional material.
(The William Ready Division of Archives and Research Collections, McMaster University Library, Hamilton, Canada)

Another clue to Mr. Wuerz is the appearance of his name on Pauline's letterhead of this period (1900): *Tour of the World, E. Pauline Johnson – Tekahionwake, The Iroquois Indian Poet Reciter, In Dramatic Recitals Of Her Own Works in Correct Costumes, Direction of Mr. Chas. H. Wuerz.* He was nothing if not ambitious for his client.

After completing concerts at some of the places listed in *The Halifax Herald*, Pauline fell ill in late June and remained confined to a Halifax hotel room for approximately a week. After that she resumed her concert commitments in Nova Scotia. In late July she wrote to Prime Minister Sir Wilfrid Laurier seeking a letter of introduction to Newfoundland. She arrived in St. John's on September 12 and was accorded the patronage of Lady McCallum, wife of the island's Governor-General. In November, 1900, she performed in a show at the Odd Fellows' Hall in Marysville, N.B., on November 24 she was in Fredericton, and on December 6 she performed in Saint John at the Mechanics' Institute in aid of the New Baptist Tabernacle.

At the McMaster University Library (Hamilton, Ontario) there is a poem in Pauline's handwriting on letterhead from the Queen Hotel, Fredericton, N.B., with the date 190- incomplete. This poem, simply entitled "To C.H.W.," is the final clue with regard to the mysterious Mr. Wuerz.

This poem must speak for itself, and readers must draw their own conclusions. Pauline's friend, Isabel Ecclestone MacKay, later wrote, "Some curiosity has been indulged in regarding Pauline Johnson's love affairs. That she had them, should go without saying, in the case of one who radiated energy and vitality as she did. Fascinating in person, charming in conversation, with a tempting trick of repartee it could not be otherwise. There were several engagements, but something always intervened...Pauline was once asked in an interview as to whether many of her poems are reflections of moods and experiences. She smilingly replied: 'Well, not entirely so, of course. One must allow for imagination which brings to the verse writer an inspired second-hand knowledge of experiences which she

---

TO C.H.W.

I

In Heidelberg, where you were born
The sunshine must be fine and rare
To leave such warmth within your heart
Such warmth of yellow in your hair,
To touch your thought and soul with that
Which neither suns nor stars impart,
That strange exquisite gift of God,
That fine and fairy thing called art.
Did Fate decree your art and mine
Should weave into a future skein
When you were born in Heidelberg
And I was born in Vain?

II

In Heidelberg where you were born
The day dawn must wear strange disguise
Now, it has left its wealth of grey
And melting shadows in your eyes
From whose deep sombre beauty all
Your soul God-given speaks the clear
Unblemished strength of all your art
And writes that soul, a soul sincere,
Did Fate decree your promise hour
Meet mine of storm and stress and rain
When you were born in Heidelberg
And I was born in Vain?[4]

herself may never have passed through. Indeed, one of the secrets of good writing of any kind is the power of being someone else.'"[5]

While the client/manager relationship between Pauline and Charles Wuerz appears straightforward, nothing is certain regarding any other type of relationship between the two.

Where she spent Christmas Day, 1900; New Year's Day, 1901; or February and March of the new year is unknown, but on April Fool's Day she was in Havelock in eastern Ontario writing a letter to her friend Frank Yeigh:

"My dear fond friend-Now, when I wrote you-or rather wired you not to bother about that loan I was begging of you I felt like an escaped convict-independent, free-everything that is glorious, albeit I am in a network of tragedy-too sad for human tongue to tell-Now-could you, without great inconvenience lend me the half of that amount I was so frantic about last week. That is-fifteen dollars to be repaid in a month's time-you could never quite imagine just "where I am at," or you would forgive me writing and asking this.

Here I am, in Holy Week in Havelock, an economic town to pray in, also to eat in, and I shall be here all week.

This is all a horrid shame and I would not have Mr. O'Brien or Miss Maracle know for worlds what I am asking of you. Someday, when I see you again, I shall tell you all of it, and grasp your good warm hands and congratulate you from my true Indian heart, that your own has anchored in the harbour of a fond woman's love.

If you will write to me here-do-if you can spare that little fifteen dollars, you will do more than churches, nor yet priests can do for me and yourself in the great Hereafter.

Thine E. Pauline Johnson[6]

Rondeau
Morrow-Land

In Morrow-Land there lies a day
In shadows clad, in garments grey
When sunless hours will come, My Dear
And skies will lose their lustre clear
Because I shall be leagues away.

Has Fate no other-kindlier way?
No gentler hands on me to lay,
Than I to go-Than you to stay here
In Morrow-Land?

And O! These days will be so dear-
Throughout the cold and coming year,
This Passion Week of gold and grey
Will haunt my heart and bless my way
In Morrow-Land.[7]

During that same Holy Week, Pauline took a sheet of her "Tour of the World" letterhead, complete with C. Wuerz named as director of the tour, and wrote the following poem:

In the corner she wrote "E.P.J. to M----- (illegible) to Amuse."

In the middle of 1901 Pauline was again under the management of Thomas Cornyn. He sent her on a tour of Canada's east coast in the company of his wife, Clara, a classical pianist. In August the women were in Newfoundland where Pauline gathered material for magazine articles on the island's features.

By mid-October, Pauline was in Ottawa. There she parted company with the Cornyns and, in November, entered into a business partnership with Walter McRaye, whom she had first met in Winnipeg in the winter of 1897.

On November 7, 1901 a new chapter in Pauline's stage career began with the debut of the Johnson-McRaye performing team in Ottawa under the patronage of their Excellencies, the Earl and Countess of Minto, before a discerning audience that included the Lauriers and the Honourable Clifford Sifton, federal minister of the interior and superintendent general of Indian Affairs. But whatever she had endured emotionally over the past 12 months remains Pauline's secret.

Mrs. Emily Johnson's Obituary
The Brantford Courier

Many friends will be sincerely sorry to hear of the death of Mrs. G.H.M. Johnson, which occurred last evening at her home. Deceased, who was the widow of the late Chief Johnson, head Chief of the Mohawk Band of the Six Nations, had been ill for some time past, suffering from the weakness of old age. Her condition was so serious that some days ago her daughter, Miss E. Pauline Johnson, was telegraphed to come home from Winnipeg. Unfortunately she was snow bound on the road and only arrived last evening just before the end and after her mother had become unconscious. The deceased was sincerely beloved by all who knew her and her true Christian life and

many estimable qualities endeared her to all with whom she came in contact. She was a cousin of the famous American author, W. Dean Howells. A son and two daughters are left to mourn her great loss and they will have the sincere sympathy of all in the hour of their deep affliction.[8]

Emily Johnson, widow of Chief George Johnson. This photograph was taken in 1894, ten years after her husband's death, and four years before her own. She chose to wear mourning each day of her life after the passing of her beloved husband.
(Brant Historical Society #S1306)

Pauline Leaves Brantford

The Brantford Courier, July, 1898

Countless friends and admirers of Brantford's talented authoress, Miss E. Pauline Johnson, will be sorry to learn that she is about to sever the ties which have hitherto bound her to this community. Tomorrow she leaves on an eastern tour then followed by a trip through the North-West. After this her marriage takes place in Winnipeg when she will take up her permanent home in the Prairie city. Brantfordites generally will experience a sincere sorrow over her departure, and wish her every future prosperity and happiness.[9]

Winter Weather Wreaks Havoc with Tour of 1898

by E. Pauline Johnson

It was at Saltcoats in Saskatchewan in the winter of '98 that I "hugged" the large stove with its roaring fire, while outside a blizzard ripped through the unsheltered prairie, and the thermometer registered 40 degrees below zero. The motherly hostess of the little hotel now lives in British Columbia; but, if she reads this, she will remember that day when Trooper Hamilton flung open the door, his bridle across his arm, cheeks that particular white of frozen flesh, his eyelashes frost fringed and gummy with ice. The snow skirled in through the open door, and the wind struck us like a whiplash as all sprang to our feet, and our hostess hurried toward him with anxious concern.[10]

Pauline Storm-Stayed Again

by Mrs. W. Garland Foster

That winter of '98 Pauline was storm-stayed at Duck Lake for several days. The hotel was full so she was the guest of the wife of the officer in charge of the police barracks, Reverend Lewis Hooper and Mrs. Hooper. She was often a guest at these homes, and life, which was a quiet routine for the wife of a Mounted Policeman, was gay, while Pauline entertained with her talk of adventures.[11]

Brantford,
February, 1900

My dear Mr. Sifton,
Will you grant me one more favour, one that is urgent, and will most greatly assist me at this time when I am financially embarrassed and seeking backing for my proposed Australian tour.

I called upon Supt. Cameron here today to learn if I could raise $500.00 at once on the rent of my share of our Indian Reserve property. He informed me there would be no difficulty in getting an advance on rent under official loan if the Department would approve of it as the security of this lease is number one. Will you do me the inestimable favour of having the Department approve without delay if possible. I need this money very urgently. Mr. Cameron said he would write the Department at once about it.

If you will see that the Department

sanctions this for me, I shall be most greatly in your debt, and you will be doing me a kindness inexpressible.

I have the honour to be yours most faithfully,

E. Pauline Johnson[12]

Sir Clifford Sifton was a lawyer, politician, businessman, Member of Parliament for Brandon, Manitoba. In 1896 he became federal minister of the interior and superintendent general of Indian affairs. He met Pauline and corresponded with her on many occasions.

gated colours had just come out, and of this she was making pansies in purple shades, to give away to her friends.

Her conversation, that day, diverting as it proved, gave many glimpses of the difficulties of her career. She had hoped to give a recital at Woodstock at this time, but the local committee had not been able to promote it, and here was the Fredericton affair cancelled with the prospects of having to pay for the hall. The trains, on this occasion, were not released until evening, when all hope of the concert for that night was over.[13]

Pauline Loses Much-Needed Revenue

by Mrs. W. Garland Foster

She had given a programme in St. Stephen, and the following day was on the way to Fredericton for another engagement. Arriving at McAdam Junction she found the trains were likely to be delayed owing to the heavy snowfall, which had started early that morning.

As there was a whole day in which to get through she was not at first anxious, but as time went on and no trains appeared, she became doubtful of being able to keep her appointment. Fortunately, another lady, on the way from Woodstock to Halifax to catch a boat for Europe, was no better off, except that she had brought lunch, for there were no dining facilities at McAdam in those days. Over the lunch the two discussed many things. Pauline was crocheting-she always had some sort of needle work on hand to while away the time when travelling. A new kind of thread in varie-

Bill Stickers Beware!

clipping, *M.A.P. Magazine*, 1906

Miss Johnson tells a good yarn of a certain little town in Newfoundland. Arriving on the day of the performance, she was annoyed to find that the walls were very poorly billed. The local bill-poster was summoned and questioned. He indignantly protested that he had done his best, and took Miss Johnson to the end of the main street. There he posted up a couple of bills, and asked her to retreat to a little distance and watch. After a while a herd of goats appeared upon the scene, and made straight for the posters, stripping them off the walls to lick the paste underneath. "Guess the goats want to digest your show!" said the bill-poster.[14]

Only one panel of an extravagant, four-panel flyer promoting Pauline's 1900/01 tour of the Maritimes.
(The William Ready Division of Archives and Research Collections, McMaster University Library, Hamilton, Canada)

Halifax,
July, 1900

My dear Sir Wilfrid-
Some months ago when I called upon you you graciously promised to give me letters of presentation to the various Governors in Australia. I have not yet arranged the date of my trip there but am intending to visit Newfoundland within the next two weeks. Your graciousness regarding the letters to Australia has led me to think you will be just as willing to give me an introduction to His Excellency the governor of Newfoundland. Such a letter would be a matter of great advantage to me. I wish to make use of it in the matter of begging the patronage of Their Excellencies at one of my public recitals. If you will extend to me this favour I shall be most greatly indebted to you, and shall do my utmost to merit your kindness.
I am my dear Sir Wilfrid

Yours most faithfully,
E. Pauline Johnson[15]

American News Flashed to Newfoundland
by E. Pauline Johnson

At the great transatlantic cable station of Hearts' Content, in Newfoundland, I had idled away the afternoon. It was amazing to watch the news that touched the world's heartstrings being flashed from hemisphere to hemisphere. As I stood beside the dispatching operator, I heard him give a smothered exclamation, an odd thing for one who must necessarily handle the sudden news that daily assails these stations. Then, from long custom his fingers tapped the key steadily. The news was flashing underneath the ocean to England. "What is it?" asked the superintendent, on his rounds. He knew through years of experience the signs of agitation in one of his employees.

"President McKinley of the United States assassinated in Buffalo," responded the operator, his fingers still tapping the keys. "This message is official; going to the American ambassador at the court of St. James."

I turned away weakly. What a horrible shadow to fall across the vast world to the south of us, all that wonderful country that divides Canada and this ancient British colony of Newfoundland from the tropics.[16]

AFTERMATH

The wide, warm acres stretching lazily,
Roll out their russet silence to the sea,
Bared to the winds that whisper
ceaselessly
Of homing time and landward-lying things.

Along the uplands, vagrant locusts whirr
Themselves through sunshine, and within
the blur
Of purple distances, the faint, far stir
Of some lone haymaker that scythes and
sings.

Across the marsh, reclaimed from the seas
that creep
Against the sheltering dykes, the droning
sweep
Of sickles, where the long salt grasses
sleep,
Hushed in the peace that near fulfilment
brings.[17]

This poem refers to the land of Henry Wadsworth Longfellow's heroine, in "Evangeline."

CHAPTER 6

Johnson and McRaye

1901-1909

The performing partnership Pauline formed with Walter McRaye held the promise that her period of rough weather was behind her. But she faced one more trial before she could move on with renewed confidence.

Pauline and Walter toured Ontario small towns throughout November and December of 1901. One town was Orillia where the *Orillia Packet* informed its readers that Pauline was now doing comedy. Orillia audiences, however, were not treated to this comedic concert. Pauline fell ill and spent Christmas delirious in an Orillia hotel room. A doctor came to find his famous patient suffering from a severe attack of erysipelas.

In this highly contagious disease, the skin, and usually the tissues just under the skin, are infected, become swollen, and take on a fiery red, glazed appearance. The affliction often starts with a small scratch on the skin. Cheeks and ears become involved. The infection, nicknamed St. Anthony's Fire, is accompanied by a burning fever, giving the sufferer the sensation of being consumed by flames.

While red patches spread across her face, the doctor could do nothing for Pauline except administer morphine to kill the pain. Before the year was out the illness had passed its peak and Pauline and Walter left Orillia. Although the partners had scheduled concerts in communities across Northern Ontario, they notified sponsoring groups that the show could not go on. Pauline sought sanctuary with her cousin Kate (Howells) Washington in Hamilton. Walter's ambitions for a stellar career as Pauline's partner were on hold.

Not only did her face show the ravage of her recent illness, the erysipelas also caused Pauline's long, curly brown hair to fall out, a blow for anyone, but for Pauline, who made her living by appearing before the public, a traumatic experience.

By February 7, 1902, Pauline had recovered enough to perform in London, Ontario. She and Walter then headed for Northern Ontario for more concerts. At the end of May, Kit Coleman filed this review with Toronto's *The Mail and Empire*, from

While this poster advertises the team of Pauline Johnson and Walter McRaye, only Pauline appears. Instead of her bear claw necklace, Pauline chose to wear this unique necklace made from elk's teeth. In her hair is a solitary feather. *(courtesy of the late Ralph Miller, of Marburg, Ontario)*

Copper Cliff, near Sudbury: "As for Miss Johnson – Tekahionwake's companion, Mr. Walter McRaye, he is fast making a name for himself in Canada. He is richly armed for the fray.

Humour, rare goddess, is his and his also is romance. He is par excellence the best reader of dainty poems I have ever heard, and I pretty well know the elocutionists half the world over. If he works he has a great future before him. He is a true artist."[1]

Pauline and Walter travelled west to Winnipeg in June, 1902. Later that month the partners were at Government House in Regina to give a concert in celebration of the coronation of Edward VII. A register of names of visitors to Government House, dated June 29, 1902, includes the signatures of both E. Pauline Johnson and J. Walter McRaye. Both wrote "Brantford" under the column marked "residence," even though it had been five years since she left that city after the death of her mother.

The coronation concert lasted two hours and, according to Pauline's notes in the margin of the programme, it was "full of laughter and good humour." Besides poetry, the partners performed a playlet entitled "At The Ball." Pauline seems to have put all her trouble and illness behind her and was at last moving forward and enjoying a new phase of her extraordinary, enduring career.

On the way to Calgary, Pauline's train was stranded for two days at the Gleichen, North-West Territories, station. The adventure provided Pauline with good material for an article she wrote about the mid-summer delay on the prairies.

Moving west from Calgary, the partners headed into mining country. Walter reports: "In Phoenix [near Red Deer, Alberta], we gave an entertainment under the auspices of the Orange Lodge in aid of a R.C. Irishman, McCluskey, whose eyes had been blown out in a blast."[2]

Pauline spent Christmas of 1902 with her brother Allen back east. Summing up that first year of their partnership, Walter wrote: "Pauline Johnson and I made our first tour across Canada in 1902. Leaving Toronto, we were gone six months, and covered every Province and penetrated to the farthest outposts of the Dominion. Her popularity and fame were such that all that was necessary was to send out a batch of postal cards announcing her coming, and committees would form and arrange evenings, glad of the opportunity."[3]

Besides more touring with Walter, 1903 brought the publication of Pauline's second book of poetry. Entitled *Canadian Born*, this 67-page volume containing 31 poems was published by George Morang Publishing Company of Toronto. The author's inscription read: "Let him who is Canadian born regard these poems as written to himself-whether he be my Paleface compatriot who has given to me his right hand of good fellowship, in the years I have appealed to him by pen and platform, or whether he be that dear Red brother of whatsoever tribe or Province, it matters not-White Race and Red are one if they are but Canadian born."[4]

Two poems of this period were commissioned pieces, commercial poems for which Pauline received a fee: "Canada for the Canadians" written in 1902 for the Summerland (B.C.) Development Company and "Made-in-Canada," 1903, for the Manufacturers' Association banquet in Brantford. Pauline was also submitting prose pieces to various magazines.

As the partnership of Pauline and Walter solidified, Pauline's cares were lightened by Walter's management skills. Reflecting on the years spent in Pauline's company, Walter wrote: "Those years were packed with experiences and incidents full of tragedy and comedy to us, railroad and boat wrecks, late trains, fires that burned our hotels and opera houses, drives across the prairie in weather that registered forty below, being frozen in the Straits of Northumberland – all accepted by Pauline Johnson as part of the game. She was in truth a "Well Beloved Vagabond" who loved any trail, old or new... There is hardly a town or settlement in Canada that we did not visit several times during those years. Throughout it all Pauline Johnson kept her splendid spirit of optimism. Life, with its many ups and downs, its successes and failures, never grew stale."[5]

By 1904 Pauline had already spent 12 years on the road. By the age of 43 she had gained her stride as a touring performer. In 1904 alone she and Walter travelled west to Saskatoon, Vancouver, Nanaimo, the Fraser River Valley, Edmonton, the Kootenay mining towns, and the Okanagan Valley, and that was before August. That month the time seemed right for her to embark on a long-anticipated adventure, a trip on the Cariboo Trail to Barkerville in the interior of present-day British Columbia.

She and Walter acquired a $250 travelling outfit of driver, horses and vehicles. After giving a concert at Ashcroft, where audience members paid $1.00 to enjoy the entertainment, they started on their trip, 400 miles north, then 400 miles south again. Along the way they found accommodation at log mile-houses. Instead of opera houses, performances were given in cedar shake sheds or barns. As they travelled north the admittance price went up, from $1 to $1.25 to $2.00. By the time they reached their destination, Barkerville, the price had risen to $2.50 per person.

After the 20-day round trip Pauline and Walter were in Vancouver to give a concert at City Hall. They took a CPR train east to Calgary where they met noted journalist and editor Bob

Edwards, founder of a string of newspapers which he called *The Eye Opener*. After this eventful year, the partners spent a quiet Christmas in Regina, the guests of Henrietta Forget, mistress of Government House.

By 1905, Pauline and Walter had worked out a stage routine that suited them and pleased their audiences. With Pauline's poetry and Walter's recitation of Dr. Drummond's "Habitant" poetry, audiences experienced an evening of 100% Canadian content. This year was spent giving concerts in Ontario, New York State, New Brunswick, Manitoba and Alberta, with only two weeks of rest in Ontario.

The profits earned from concerts given during the first months of 1906 were earmarked to finance a trip to England. Walter's participation in this overseas venture was not welcomed by Eva Johnson, who recorded: "On her second trip to England, Pauline took with her a reciter of whom neither Allen nor I approved. Of course, just as we said, Pauline failed. Although people were nice to her on this trip, she never regained her former popularity."[6] Walter was held in such contempt by Eva that she deliberately avoided mentioning his name.

In contrast to Eva's description of the trip as a failure, Walter had this to say: "We sailed on Good Friday, March 13, 1906. During the trip across, the San Francisco earthquake occurred, and when we landed we heard the first news at Liverpool. Many friends greeted Pauline in London. Again she was invited everywhere. The twelve years of her absence had changed many customs. 'Drawing Rooms' were no longer popular; other forms of entertainment had taken their place."[7]

The partners settled into separate apartments at 53 St. James Square, London. Pauline wrote to various publications asking if they would print her stories. She met with success from the publication *Canada*, but was turned down by *Chums* and others. She and Walter visited the offices of the Keith Powse Entertainment Agency and signed up, hoping to be booked for performances in the city. Unfortunately not many engagements were forthcoming.

Thanks to a letter of introduction from Prime Minister Laurier, the partners were accorded the patronage of Lord and Lady Strathcona. Lord Strathcona, 86 years of age, was the Canadian High Commissioner in London. Pauline and Walter were inactive in June, but Pauline did enjoy tea on the terrace of the House of Commons on June 22. There she met Sir Arthur Pearson. He owned 30 newspapers and asked her to write a series of articles which he would publish. At the annual Dominion Day party at the Imperial Institute in South Kensington, where Pauline was the guest of her patrons, she recited *Canadian Born.*

She was one of 1,500 guests at Lord and Lady Strathcona's garden party on July 14, at Kenilworth Hall. Also on the guest list was Sir Charles Tupper, whom Pauline had met on several occasions, and who she would meet again, under very different circumstances, during her retirement years in Vancouver, B.C.

During their London sojourn Pauline and Walter visited with the Webling family. There were six Webling sisters and Pauline knew the family because the girls' uncle had lived in Brantford during the 1880s. One of the sisters, Lucy Betty Webling, became Mrs. Walter McRaye three years later.

Pauline and Walter were booked to perform at Steinway Hall on July 16. The concert went well according to reviewers from eleven papers and periodicals. The eminent critic, Theodore Watts-Dunton, also attended. He had reviewed the anthology *Songs of the Great Dominion* in 1889 and had lavished praise on Pauline's two poems. 1906 was the first opportunity for the poet and the critic to meet. When Watts-Dunton went backstage at Steinway Hall, Pauline expressed her sincere gratitude to him for his enthusiastic review of her work. Eva Johnson records what Watts-Dunton said when the two long-distance friends met at last: "My God! How young you are! How young you are!"[8] The success of the evening must have made Pauline feel, and appear, younger than her 45 years.

Two days after their triumph, Pauline and Walter left London to holiday at a rented country house in Berkshire. It was while they were out of the heat and dust of London that Pauline heard of the arrival in London of three chiefs representing west coast Natives. They had come that vast distance to meet with the King and Queen.

The delegation included Chief Joe Capilano, a Squamish; Chief Charlie Silpaymilt of Cowichan; Chief Basil Bonaparte from Ashcroft; and interpreter Simon Pierre of the Keatzie Reserve, Port Hammond. They had made the journey despite the lack of an appointment with the sovereign. A London businessman who had worked in Vancouver introduced Chief Joe to Lord Strathcona. Strathcona did not know how to fulfil the Chief's request to meet King Edward.

Pauline's name was mentioned as someone who could meet with the west coast Natives. She happily travelled from her rural holiday house to London to offer what assistance she could. As Pauline's first biographer Mrs. Foster relates: "The few Indian words that she had picked up on her various trips to the coast of British Columbia were used to great advantage in cementing a friendship with Chief Capilano."[9] That meeting of Pauline and Chief Joe marked the beginning of a special and close friendship between the two. They shared a burning pride in their Native heritage. On August 13, the King and Queen met

Three west-coast Chiefs during their 1906 visit to England, where they met with King Edward VII and Queen Alexandra. They brought grievances from Canada's west coast Natives. From left to right: Simon Pierre (interpreter), Chief Charlie Silpaymilt, Chief Joe Capilano (born Sahp-luk in 1850, died 1910), and Chief Basil Bonaparte. Chief Joe Capilano was a leader on his reserve near Moodyville, British Columbia. He crusaded all his life for Native rights. He and Pauline were true friends.
(The William Ready Division of Archives and Research Collections, McMaster University Library, Hamilton, Canada)

with the three Chiefs, and two days later the Chiefs left England and sailed for Canada.

Meanwhile, the Keith Powse Agency had drawn up a schedule of engagements for Pauline and Walter, keeping them busy throughout September and October. In early November they performed in a benefit for the Liverpool Seamen's Orphan Institute. Pauline was one of 18 performers in the programme, and performed the sketch "Miss Stuart's Five O'Clock Tea." In mid-November, the partners returned to Canada.

The new year started with performances in northern New Brunswick and English-speaking parts of Quebec. By March Pauline was in Ontario, staying at the Hamilton home of her cousin Kate.

In April 1907 she was England-bound once again, unaccompanied. Just five months after her most recent visit she was back at 53 St. James Square, London. What drew her back? What occupied her time in London? No-one knows. She set sail for Canada again in mid-June, after only two months in London.

In 1908, *The Brockville Times* in Ontario printed a 12-page booklet of Pauline's poems called *When George Was King and Other Poems*, by E. Pauline Johnson (Tekahionwake). The foreword on the cover reads:

Know by the thread of Music woven through
This fragile web of cadences I bring,
That song is soul, and soul is song, if you
Re-echo in your hearts-the songs I sing.

One of these poems, "Autumn's Orchestra," she "inscribed to one beyond seas." The third stanza evokes time spent with the "one beyond seas":

There is a lonely minor chord that sings
Faintly and far along the forest ways
When the first finger faintly on the string
Of that rare violin the night wind plays,
Just as it whispered once to you and me
Beneath the English pines beyond the sea.

The "Orchestra" ends with these haunting lines:

But through the night time I shall hear within
The murmur of these trees,
The calling of your distant violin
Sobbing across the seas
And waking wind, and star reflected light
Shall voice my answering. Goodnight, Goodnight.[10]
Flint and Feather

Could this poem hold the key to understanding Pauline's solitary, brief visit to England?

Pauline could not have relished what lay ahead. The Johnson-McRaye partners had arranged with the American Slayton Lyceum Society to join the Chautauqua tour in the midwestern states. She knew, from having spoken to other performers on the concert circuit, that Chautauqua tours were gruelling. But with *The White Wampum* and *Canadian Born* out of print and having spent funds on two recent overseas trips, quite simply, she needed the money.

Early in July, 1907, Pauline and Walter travelled to Indiana, joining the Chautauqua that would take them to Michigan, Iowa, Nebraska, Colorado, Kansas, Missouri, Illinois and Oklahoma. They performed in huge, humid outdoor tents to audiences that were not always in a mood to listen to Canadian poetry.

Promotional material from this Chautauqua reads: "The name Chautauqua has now become a well known synonym for the most popular and instructive series of entertainments ever presented in the country. You can not only listen to and see the greatest lecturers, orators and entertainers in the country, but at the same time enjoy a ten days' outing at a time of the year when you can and should gladly take a short rest, and recreation from your regular daily business and home affairs. And then the cost is so little. For only $1.50 or .15 cents a day, you can enjoy what in any other way would cost you many dollars. Buy a season ticket, and hear them all-over 60 entertainments."[11]

It took stamina and perseverance for Pauline and Walter to keep up the pace, travelling by train one day, performing that evening, then travelling the next day to another town, another tent, another inattentive audience.

By early September Pauline and Walter were free from their Chautauqua commitment and travelled east to give a special concert in Boston for the Massachusetts Indian Association. They took a well-earned rest in East Aurora, New York, at the Roycroft Hotel, established by author/philosopher Elbert Hubbard, the author of a series of booklets called *Little Journeys*.

In October the partners performed in Manitoba, and in November they were in Edmonton, where Pauline enjoyed a visit with her friend, Ernest Thompson Seton, whom she hadn't seen for four years. The rest of the year was spent performing in prairie towns.

In early 1908, the partners travelled east to the Maritimes where they performed in Nova Scotia. By February they were back in Ontario, where they played The Grand Opera House in London. They headed east again for dates in New Brunswick, Nova Scotia and Prince Edward Island. Walter recalls that "springtime in the Annapolis Valley was always a delight to Pauline Johnson. The train ran so close to the apple trees in that hundred mile orchard that one could almost pick the blossoms from the car windows. Pauline always loved the grey old Provinces by the sea, the leisured culture of the people, their hospitality, the homes full of beautiful old furniture brought by the United Empire Loyalists from the American Colonies at the time of the Revolution."[12]

Family beckoned and Pauline travelled to Toronto to attend the wedding of her brother Allen. On June 25, 1908, Allen, aged 49, took as his wife Floretta Kathryn Maracle, 39. The marriage register lists Allen as a bachelor, a member of the Church of England, and an insurance agent, while Floretta is listed as a spinster and a member of the same church. The happy occasion was a rare opportunity for the three surviving Johnson siblings to come together. Pauline's itinerant life differed so greatly from the lives of Allen and Eva.

The wedding over, Pauline headed west alone. She stayed at the Hotel Vancouver for a full month's rest. During this time she and her friend Chief Joe Capilano paddled their canoes along the shorelines of Burrard Inlet, English Bay and Coal Harbour. Pauline was reliving joyous days of her girlhood on the Grand River.

After her pleasant stay in Vancouver, Pauline travelled east to meet Walter. Together they toured Ontario towns and that autumn headed south to perform in Cleveland and Pittsburg. By Christmas Pauline was with Cousin Kate in Hamilton. During a visit with her brother and sister-in-law, she probably took the opportunity to discuss her thoughts about retirement from the stage. She had been on the move since 1892, and her career in the public eye was now entering its 16th year. Eager to make a change in her life, eager to put an end to the demands of

Five head-and-shoulder shots of Pauline, probably taken during the early years of the century. She wears a smart hat, a locket on a chain around her neck, as well as a maple leaf which says "Canada" at her throat.
(Brant Historical Society #540)

Pauline, as she appeared in her late 40s.
(Brant Historical Society #563a)

playing for the public, Pauline first had to accumulate some funds with which to retire.

January of 1909 found her and Walter on the cold, windy prairies. They spent the next five months performing in communities of every size, from crossroads to whistle-stops, from hamlets to villages, from towns to cities. Early in May Pauline and Walter performed in Vancouver, and from there travelled up the Fraser River Valley to the Okanagan and the Nicola Valley. In mid-August they were in Kamloops, B.C.

At the close of the Kamloops performance, Pauline folded her buckskin outfit and her red blanket into her Saratoga trunk, and discreetly and without fanfare exited from her very public life.

A Johnson-McRaye Recital

undated clipping, Hagersville, Ontario

The Johnson-McRaye recital in the Presbyterian church on Tuesday evening last proved a very enjoyable affair. The attendance was not so large as it should have been owing to a variety of causes which kept many away who would otherwise have been present. Those who did attend, however, were delighted with the excellent work of the artists. Interest was added to Miss Johnson's selections from the fact that she is an exceedingly promising poet as well as a clever elocutionist. By training and mental and physical superiority she was enabled to personify character and poetry vividly, the aspirations of the human heart and the emotions of the soul. In her own productions she is seen possibly at her best.

Mr. McRaye's numbers proved most enjoyable. His humour is pleasing and he was particularly entertaining in Dr. Drummond's "Habitant" poems.[13]

THE CANADIAN MAGPIE

excerpted from William Henry Drummond

Mos' ev'rywan lak de robin
An' it's pleasan' for hear heem sing,
Affer de winter's over
An' it's comin' anoder spring.
De snow's hardly off de mountain
An' it's cole too among de pine
But you know w'en he sing, de sout' win'
Is crowdin' heem close behin'.[14]

⚏ + ⚏ + ⚏ + ⚏ + ⚏ + ⚏

Pauline Johnson Receives Friends;
Well Known Lady Entertainer Shows Traces of Recent Illness

The Telegram, Winnipeg, Manitoba, June, 1902

A portrait of Pauline. Her short hair is either her own, growing back slowly after her 1901 illness, or a wig worn over what remained of her own hair after it all fell out. *(Brant Historical Society #1652)*

Miss E. Pauline Johnson arrived in Winnipeg yesterday, but her many friends here were disappointed to find that she would be in the city for one day only, and that no opportunity was to be had of hearing her or the talented entertainer, Walter McRaye, who accompanied her. Miss Johnson and Mr. McRaye intend touring the Territories and will go through to the coast, after which they leave for California. It is likely they will open the fall season in Winnipeg.

When seen at the Leland Hotel yesterday, Miss Johnson was surrounded by old friends. Though traces of her recent severe illness are noticeable, she is fast regaining strength. Of course, her beautiful hair is gone, a severe attack of brain fever being the cause of this. A friend asked her how she managed to dress for the stage with such shortly cropped tresses.

"Well, I'll tell you," she replied. "I wear a wig, but it bothers me, seeming to irritate my head; when I don evening dress I imitate the chorus girl and appear in a large hat, which, people say, is very becoming; and no one suspects the tragedy underneath." Miss Johnson's bright and pleasing manner is one of her chief charms.[15]

⚏ + ⚏ + ⚏ + ⚏ + ⚏ + ⚏

Pauline's Namesake
by Walter McRaye

There is a girl teaching school in Manitoba today who is called Pauline, and wears a locket sent her by Pauline Johnson. We were coming out of Regina on the early morning train and found the coaches crowded. The only seat to be had was with a woman who had four small children, each crying more loudly than the others. The woman looked not only tired but worn out. Pauline took the baby from her. The woman told us the children were her brother's, and that he had died the day before, leaving them destitute and alone. She was a farmer's wife with several children of her own. "But," she said, "they have no one to go to. We are poor but we will get along somehow." Pauline never lost track of them throughout the years. She wrote and sent clothes to the baby, whom the foster mother named Pauline. Several years ago in a Manitoba town a handsome young woman came up to me, after a Chautauqua programme, and introduced herself as Pauline. She said that her mother had told her to be sure and tell me that she was the baby of the train episode.[16]

Among the Blackfoots: Interesting Results of Blockade on the C.P.R.
by E. Pauline Johnson

We were aboard No. 1, the C.P.R. westbound, and it was the 4th of July. We

---

HIS MAJESTY THE KING

I.
There's a man in the Isle of England, he's Lord of a vast Empire-
The son of a woman dear, and dead, the son of a noble sire.
A man who was born a Briton, born in the British hearts to dwell;
And they call him the King of England- but, he reigns in the West as well.

II.
There's a man in the Isle of England whose rule we are proud to own,
In the purple, and gold, and ermine, and the splendor of England's throne.
He has come to the heart of a nation too vast for the tongue to tell,
And they call him the King of England, but he's Lord of the North as well.

III.
There's an Arm in the Isle of England, an Arm that is strong and grand,
It circles the world with a wealth of love outstretched from the Motherland.

'Tis the sword and shield of the children that over the oceans dwell-
'Tis the Arm of the King of England, but, 'tis the Arm of the East as well.

IV.
There's a man in the Isle of England, who holds in his kingly hand
The reins of a power, great and good, but those reins are a silken strand.
And the South, in its silken harness, will learn in his love to dwell,
For the man who is King of England is the Lord of the South as well.

V.
And we of the North, East, South and Westland, we'll battle, we'll dare, we'll do;
We will die for the King of England when the Empire wants us to.
Then cheer for the man in the British Isles till the ends of the earth shall ring,
For, as we fought for the Queen of England, we will fight for England's King.[17]

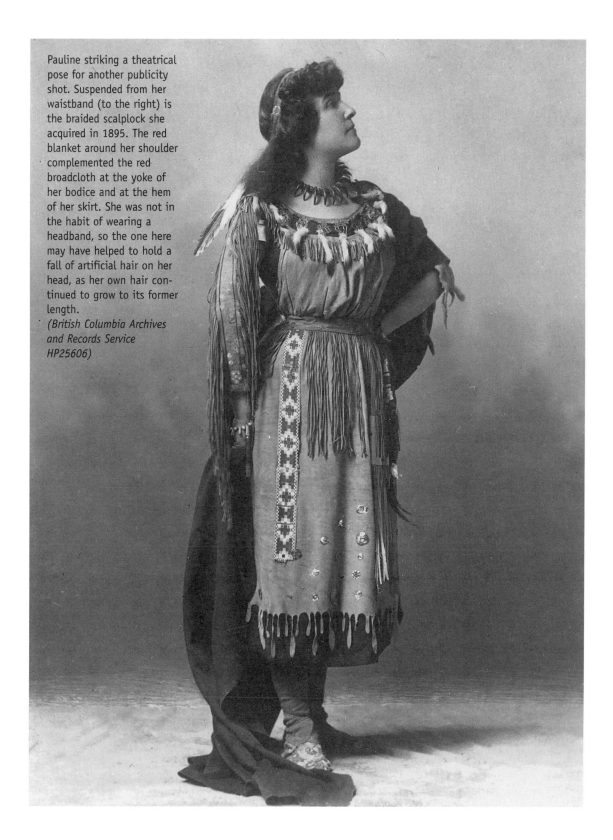

Pauline striking a theatrical pose for another publicity shot. Suspended from her waistband (to the right) is the braided scalplock she acquired in 1895. The red blanket around her shoulder complemented the red broadcloth at the yoke of her bodice and at the hem of her skirt. She was not in the habit of wearing a headband, so the one here may have helped to hold a fall of artificial hair on her head, as her own hair continued to grow to its former length.
(British Columbia Archives and Records Service HP25606)

pulled into Medicine Hat long after twilight and were informed by the porter that there was a washout ahead, and we were to be in the siding all night. The Americans aboard fired their last bunch of firecrackers, and the porter, after the manner of his kind, bundled us all into our berths, and the following morning the C.P.R. did a great and memorable thing. It pulled us one hundred and twenty-five miles west, then tied us up for forty-eight hours at Gleichen, in the heart of the Blackfoot Indian Reserve.

...We had not halted very long when the pride and delight of the true Canadian's heart, the Imperial Limited, roared up abaft, and in another twelve hours a second No. 1 stood in to harbor, and then we learned the truth-two bridges down, one east, one west, of Calgary...That criminal little Bow River has done what saint or satan, fiend or fairy, could never dare to do; it has brought the great panting transcontinental flyer to a standstill.

...At Gleichen what a holiday we had, and what a cosmopolitan gathering it was. Perhaps never in all the history of railroading has such a forty-eight hour community been established as we, the "Good Fellows of Gleichen"...More than six hundred of us were the guests of the C.P.R. for two days. At Calgary eight hundred, at Banff and at Field another five or six hundred-all treated like princes.

...The Indians made a good thing out of the C.P.R. mishaps, for the tourists hired horses from them at "a dollar a ride," and even the tenderfoot would vault into the Mexican saddle and ride away across the prairie. The sturdy shagginappi laying back his ears loped away with the long, clean, rocking motion never seen except in the prairie-bred animal. Only one lamentable accident occurred, in the evening, when we had baseball and horse races. In the latter a fine grey pony, the prop-erty of a splendidly handsome blanket and buckskin-clad Blackfoot, plunged into a badger hole, fell, and instantly expired with a broken neck.

And just here it is time to relate an aspersion frequently laid upon our wilder Indian tribes of the great west. The prejudiced white man will tell you that the Indians will eat anything animal that dies of disease, unclean portions of meat, etc. The detractors of the Redman, and there were plenty of them aboard, assured the crowd that "the Indians will have a great pow-wow, and the feast of the dead horse" over the unlucky animal that lay near the track. But the next morning and the next night, and yet another morning came and waned, and the horse lay where it had fallen, and the Blackfoot shook their heads when asked about a "feast." A goodly collection was taken up for the owner which reward he deserved, as his steed had expired in making "a white man's holiday."

This identical warrior exhibited great appreciation of class distinctions. A curious Chinaman came forth from his car, and a tourist asked the Blackfoot, "Is this your brother?" indicating the Mongolian. Such scorn and hauteur as the reply "No" expressed, such a lifting of the red chin, and indignant glance. It amazed some, but I was proud of my color cousin of the prairie, and of his fine old aristocratic red blood that has come down through the centuries to pulse in the conservative veins.

...We sighed a keen regret when the engineer sounded a long series of whistles to get us aboard, for word had been flashed from Calgary that the Bow River had been conquered and that our forty-eight-hour blockage was broken.[18]

Travels with Pauline

by Walter McRaye

Calgary was always a delight in its western breezy atmosphere. Usually there were a string of pintos tied outside the Ranchers Club. The Hotel Alberta was one of the best between Winnipeg and the coast; its landlord, Mr. Perley, was a perfect host; Teddy, the clerk, was genial and obliging, but the greatest asset the hotel had was its more than efficient porter, Fred Berney. This man knew everyone and every town, would check your luggage, buy your ticket and even lend you money to buy it. Travellers found this most convenient at times.

...I have seen Pauline Johnson in some strange surroundings. At Girard, B.C., a new town on Trout Lake, we were waiting for a boat to take us down the lake to Kaslo. Pauline was the only woman in town. The hotel was a shack, mostly a bar. We ate in a small room at a long table with oilcloth on it, and "Mobs," the proprietor, in his undershirt, cooking at the end of the room. Pauline sat among the miners and prospectors, told them stories, listened to theirs, no one taking any notice of the unusual occurrence. The old-time miner had an innate chivalry that was particularly his own.

...I remember one evening, while giving an entertainment in a small town, a shabby Englishman approached Pauline after the performance, and asked her if she would shake hands with him. When she extended her hand,

At the Glacier House, B. C.

This postcard shows the Rockies in British Columbia, with a passenger train in the foreground, surely a scene Pauline and Walter saw time and again on their travels.
(courtesy of Suzanne O'Halloran, Midland, Ontario)

Pauline posed for this formal portrait in an elaborate gown that showed off her shoulders and waistline, and enhanced her five-foot-four-inch figure.
(Brant Historical Society #1653)

the man, with tears in his eyes, told her it was the first time in years he had seen a woman in evening dress, and as his mother and sisters had always dressed for dinner the appearance of such a garb had made him homesick.[19]

Transportation By Any Means Available
by Walter McRaye

The only vehicle I could get to carry us to Fairview was a springboard wagon. This belonged to a cranky individual who wanted twenty-five dollars for the trip of twenty miles. On my trying to get him to do it for less, he laconically assured me, "Young man if you're calculatin' to go to Fairview that's what it will cost." He won and we jolted down the trail.[20]

No Opera House, No Community Hall, No Church Basement
by Walter McRaye

The stage took us on to Camp McKinney and stopped there. The camp was almost dead, but several of its citizens carried nail kegs and planks and fixed up an alfresco theatre and charged themselves a dollar each to sit on them.[21]

Pauline as a Visiting Celebrity
undated clipping

Miss E. Pauline Johnson, the poetess, who appeared at the Methodist church last evening, visited the Le Roi and other mines yesterday and was much interested in what she saw. Mr. C.C. Woodhouse, Jr. accompanied the lady and explained the difference between calcopyrites and gabbro to her. She seemed to be deeply interested in everything that she saw, although she looked puzzled sometimes when Mr. Woodhouse told her some of the scientific facts concerning mining in technical language.

For instance, Mr. Woodhouse said to the young lady: "In amorphous minerals there is no trace of crystalline form or special characteristics of structure due to individual crystals, although an intermittent deposition of the mass composing the mineral may have occasioned difference of color, hardness and texture..." To this the fair poetess smiled and remarked, "I guess so," and thus science, speculation and poetry walked hand in hand as it were through the dark galleries of the mines.[22]

That Injun Girl
by Isabel Ecclestone MacKay

Once she had been giving an entertainment to an audience composed largely of lumber jacks. They were terribly serious and the humorous part of the evening was sufficiently

painful. But next morning two of the audience were heard comparing notes in the bar. "Well, Bill," said one, "What'd you think of the show?" Bill took a drink and looked thoughtful. "Wall," he said, "It ain't my idea of a show. But that there Injun girl is right smart-considerin' what she sprung from."[23]

While on tour of the North-West in 1901, the two entertainers posed for this mid-winter photograph in Banff. The curious pose, of Walter reclining at the feet of the star, Pauline, defines their partnership.
(from Town Hall Tonight! *by Walter McRaye)*

Above the Tullameen
by E. Pauline Johnson

Did you ever "holiday" through the valley lands of the Dry Belt? Ever spend days and days in a swinging swaying coach, behind a four-in-hand, when 'Curly' or 'Nicola Ned' held the ribbons, and tooled his knowing little leaders and wheelers down those horrifying mountain-trails that wind russet skeins of cobweb through the heights and depths of the Okanagan, the Nicola and the Similkameen countries? If so, you have listened to the call of Skookum Chuck, as the Chinook speakers call the rollicking, tumbling streams that sing their way through the canyons with a music so dulcet, so insistent, that for many moons the echo of it lingers in your listening ears, and you will, through the years to come, hear the voices of those mountain rivers calling you to return.

But the most haunting of all the melodies is the warbling laughter of the Tulameen; its delicate note is far more powerful, more far-reaching than the throaty thunders of Niagara. That is why the Indians of the Nicola country still cling to their old-time story, that the Tullameen carries the spirit of a young girl enmeshed in the wonders of its winding course; a spirit that can never free itself from the canyons, to rise above the heights and follow its fellows to the Happy Hunting Grounds, but which is contented to entwine its sobs, its lonely whispers, its still lonelier call for companionship, with the wild music of the waters that sing for ever beneath the western stars.

As your horses plod up and up the almost perpendicular trail that leads out of the Nicola Valley to the summit, a paradise of beauty outspreads at your feet; the colour is indescribable in words, the atmosphere thrills you. Youth and the pulse of rioting blood are yours again, until, as you near the heights, you become strangely calmed by the voiceless silence of it all-a silence so holy that it seems the whole world about you is swinging its censer before an alter in some dim remote cathedral![24]

Our Hosts' Strident Sentiments
by E. Pauline Johnson

We halted for dinner at the "Badger," a neat little sod-covered shack kept by two American women of rather wide experience. We dined off exquisite Japanese china, for the West is a place of surprises and incongruities. Of the sixty thousand Americans that have settled in our North-West this year, there are two classes; those anxious to swear allegiance to the King and become good British subjects, and those, more numerous, alas!, who flaunt their hatred of us and yet come to us to earn a dollar they cannot get in their own country. Our hostesses evidently belonged to the latter class for during the meal hour one said to me:

"When next you come here you will see the Stars and Stripes flying over this shack." In jest I replied, "If I do I will empty a shot gun into it." She lifted her head proudly and said: "We can stand it, it won't be the first time the American flag has been shot at."

"No," I said, "nor the first time it has been shot at by an Indian. Did you ever hear of an Indian shooting at the Union Jack?" She turned the conversation. We left our Yankee hostess and her strident sentiments far behind us, our great Canadian prairie a sweeter thing to contemplate.[25]

OCTOBER IN CANADA

Afternoon of autumn lies a'tween me and
the hill,
Rising like a giant amethyst a mile away,
Dimmed by opal-tinted airs that intervene,
until
All looks like a cobweb mist of purple and
of grey.

Lying where the pebbles sprinkle all the
river sands,
I can dip my fingers in the water warm
and clear,
Watch the sunlight shimmer in the waves
above my hands,
Watch a snowy little sail that lazily floats
near.

Far beyond the flats where some are husk-
ing Indian corn,
I can see the oval, yellow stacks of straw
uplift,

Hear the hum of threshing; for since early
hours of morn,
'Round the barns a cloud of amber chaff
has been adrift.

Flocks of crows at random fly within the
upward air,
Ebon tufts that dot the clouds athwart a
pinkish sky;
Far away the stubble fields are stretching
dun and bare,
Edged with goldenrod and flecked with
leaves a-blowing by.

Night comes stealthily and thieves the
colour from the hill,
Naught she leaves upon its brown of
amethyst or blue;
Day will soon be over, and the twilight,
grey and still,
Whispers very gently that my dream-land
darkens too.[26]

The Call of the Old Qu'Appelle Valley

by E. Pauline Johnson

In the very heart of the great Province of Saskatchewan stretches the most wonderful valley in all the prairie country. Its early history, its present productiveness, its all-time beauty and romance are unequalled by any portion of the vast country that outrolls between the Red River and the Rockies. That magic name Qu'Appelle has lured men from overseas, from the far reaches of the Maritime Provinces, from the great country to the south of us, from the borders of our own beloved Pacific. The charm of its past, the promise of its future have beckoned with irresistible finger. When a man gets the name Qu'Appelle into his blood, it is like the enticement of the sea; to strive against it is useless, for it will get him eventually. It is the unexpected beauty that captivates, and as you drive along the level prairie trails you have no warning that a few rods before you Nature has opened her arms so silently that it seems like a transition into a dream world when at your feet there stretches a long peaceful chain of lakes margined with wolf willows and cottonwoods, and enclosed by a distant rim of russet-coloured heights whose summits are peakless and level, for from their topmost reaches the prairie again rolls out its limitless miles into the north. Only the artist in sepia understands how strangely beautiful a landscape can be painted in tints of brown alone. The valley is prodigal with its browns, and a score of shades blend into a harmony of russet I have never elsewhere seen, and in this cup of warmth and color sleeps the old Hudson's Bay trading post, Fort Qu'Appelle.[27]

Pauline Visits An Indian Industrial School
undated clipping

Miss Johnson was always interested in Indian work. Her visits to the Lebret Industrial School were always a great event. The young generation of Western red men always looked forward to a visit from one of the noblest of their race. And she, she was always beaming when she could tread the hills and ravines of the great and beautiful Qu'Appelle Valley…From her early visit to the valley, Miss Johnson often said herself that she had derived the best objective in her works. She loved the places where the Sioux and Cree fought their greatest fights. Of the reserves she visited she always spoke in tones of regret. She deplored the condition of her noble race in the great lone land. Her greatest interest when visiting the industrial school was in the musical attainment of the children. Miss Johnson was a singer of no mean ability and one of her best remembered performances at Lebret was the day she sang one of her own ballads set to music. The boys' band always attracted her. She

would ask for a repetition of various pieces of music every time she visited the school. She missed no opportunity of manifesting her interest in the education of the little Indians. To the writer she suggested many times certain ways of dealing with the characteristics of the children. She seemed to know all of them and would also remember their names.[28]

En tour, in Michigan
October, 1903

My Dear Harry [O'Brien]
How I would like to see you again, but I cannot tell when we will be East. We will however leave this state at the earliest possible moment, we dislike it so. The people are _very_ uncultured, very ignorant, very illiterate. Daily I grow to be more and more of a "Canuck" and Mr. McRaye is quite rabid as a Canadian patriot now. Through all this time that we have been associated he has been just the same unselfish, considerate boy you saw him to be in Ottawa. His management has indeed proved a great thing for me, and my freedom from business cares and anxieties has rejuvenated me beyond words. I was able to take a summer holiday this year for the first time in four years, and the rest was a sadly needed one.

Did you know I had got out another book of poems? [_Canadian Born_]. When I get "home" again I shall have one, but I brought only those across the line that were to go to American

The manufacturers of Brantford entertained the Canadian Manufacturers' Association at a Made-in-Canada banquet in 1903. They petitioned former resident, Pauline Johnson, for a poem suitable for the occasion:

MADE-IN-CANADA

What is the creed and the calling that we of the North uphold-
It is never the cry for power, it is never the greed for gold,
Let the east and south and west contend like wolves for a maverick's bone,
But Canada for the Canadians is the creed that we call our own.

Good wishes are at Kaiser Wilhelm's, good cakes are at Uncle Sam's,
And in dear old Britain's larders are the best of plums and jams,
But beef and bread and a blanket, a pipe, a mug and a fire,
Are the things that we have in Canada-what more can a man desire?

We don't need the marts of Europe, nor the trade of the Eastern Isles,
We don't need the Yankee's corn and wine, nor the Asiatic's smiles,
For what so good as our home-made cloth, and under the wide blue dome.
Will you tell me where you have tasted bread like the bread that is baked at home?

And we are the young and strong, and who so fit for fight as we?
With our hands of steel and our iron heel and our hearts like the oaken tree.
For we are home-made, home-fed, the pride of a princely land,
And the things that are made in Canada are the things that her sons demand.

So this is the creed and the calling that we of the North uphold,
It is never the cry for power, it is never the greed of gold,
Let the east and south and west contend like wolves for a maverick's bone,
But Canada for the Canadians is the creed that we call our own.[29]

authors. The book is small, but very dainty. *The Toronto Globe* and *Saturday Night* gave it a most scathing "roast." But the *News* and the *Montreal Star* gave me such splendid reviews. Lady Laurier wrote me such a kind letter about the book. And Sir Lawrence Alma-Tadema, whose art I have inscribed a poem to, has also written me very cordially. You know I met them and was entertained at their house several times while in England. The *Globe* says this poem on "The Art of Alma-Tadema" is the only good thing in my book. Poor book. And half the poems it contains were accepted by *Harper's* and brought me some excellent notice. Well, I must try a novel now, and get criticized.

What a long letter all about myself. I always do write of myself, do I not? Mr. McRaye sends his very kind regards. He so frequently expressed a wish this summer that you could have been out camping with us. This was echoed by Allen and myself.

Always your very sincere friend,
E. Pauline Johnson[30]

TRAVERSE BAY

Outside, a sweep of waves and winds that roar
Beneath storm-threatened skies,
But here, a harbour sheltered by a shore
That circles, crescent wise
Like some young moon that left its aerial lands
To shape and spill its silver on these sands.

I stand and watch the line of liquid blue
Where skies and waters meet,
The long green waves that crowd the nearer view
And break about my feet.
The waters lift and heave, then drop away
Beaten and breathless, sweeping up the bay.

All the wonder of the wind-swept sea
And its tempestuous sky
Its hidden past, its unknown history
Its centuries gone by-
Rise and proclaim the Infinite, until
The doubt within my heart grows hushed, then still.[31]

The Tale of Pauline's Poem "The Train Dogs"
by Walter McRaye

Pauline Johnson's poem "The Train Dogs," has a remarkable story. We were standing one late spring morning on Jasper Avenue, Edmonton; McDougall and Secord's store was across the way. With a "Yip-Yip!" down the street came a train of husky dogs dragging a sleigh loaded with skins. The snow had gone and the days were getting warmer. The Indian runner had come from the north in the night, travelling on the early morning frost. His dogs were skeletons, their ribs showing, and he himself weary and worn, but he cheerfully said, "Good dogs, we beat um."[32]

Pauline's poem "The Train Dogs," previously published in 1904 in *Rod and Gun*, was published again 1908 in *The Outing Magazine*, but this time attributed to one Mr. Owen E. McGillicuddy. Before long *The Outing Magazine* had printed a correction, citing Pauline Johnson as the true author of the poem, and Mr. McGillicuddy as the plagiarist. "The Train Dogs" can be found in *Flint and Feather*.

Brandon, Manitoba
February, 1904

My dear Sir Wilfrid

Your most kind letter of the 16th January with the enclosed letters of presentation to Lord Brassey and

Lord Strathcona, has been forwarded to me here. I beg to thank you very warmly for this kindness of yours, which will mean so much to me in England. I particularly wish to express my thanks for your previous mention of my father and your allusions to my Indian ancestor's loyalty. I can only add that I shall do my utmost to merit your letters and to worthily deserve them. For your good wishes for my English visit I am most grateful. You have given me the means of introduction, that will make my success very possible.

I am my dear Sir Wilfrid
Faithfully yours
E. Pauline Johnson Tekahionwake[33]

The Celebrated Bob Edwards Meets the Celebrated Pauline Johnson
by Walter McRaye

Sir Wilfrid Laurier (1841-1919), Liberal Prime Minister of Canada between 1896 and 1911. Pauline corresponded with Laurier on many occasions throughout the years, primarily seeking letters of introduction from him to distinguished persons. She received such letters from him in 1904 for an anticipated trip to England-a trip that she managed to make in 1906.
(National Archives of Canada, Ottawa, C1971)

We met the celebrated and notorious Bob Edwards. He had been in the West for years, running newspapers in Wetaskiwin, Leduc, Gleichen and High River. It was in the last town that we finally met up with him. He had for a partner a hotel keeper named Jerry Boyce. They were promoters; they would go to a settlement, Jerry would start a hotel, and Bob would start a paper, one of these usually called *Eye Openers*. There was just one room large enough for a crowd in High River at that time, the bar room of Jerry's hotel. So he fixed it up, built a stage, put in benches and took the money at the door. I think there was about seventy-five dollars in the house. Jerry handed it over, and told us it was worth more than that to have an entertainment in the "new burg." Bob Edwards wrote up the affair in his usually vigorous fashion, ending with "Come again Pauline and bring the genial Mac with you."[34]

A Rider of the Plains
by Mrs. W. Garland Foster

Once she was as far north in Alberta as Fort Saskatchewan. There Pauline made a pleasant visit with the Major and Mrs. Constantine. The major, a typical rider of the plains, had enough experience behind him to delight the heart of Pauline for many a day. He had served in both Rebellions, and was chosen for the pioneer police work in the Yukon rush. A man of great strength, sure judgement, he had spent four years in the Yukon. He was transferred to

Pauline in 1903, at age 42.
(City of Vancouver Archives, P.1633, N.957)

the prairie country. It was here that Pauline met him. It was his wife whom she delighted to especially honour; for "Mother o' the Men"* was Mrs. Constantine, the story of whose sacrifice and the efforts made to distract her attention from her trouble kept the good hearted force busy for days.[35]

* Pauline's short story, "Mother o' the Men," was included in the volume *The Moccasin Maker*, published in 1913.

Coaching on the Cariboo Trail
by E. Pauline Johnson

We left the train at Ashcroft, British Columbia, and even from the station platform, we could see, winding through the sand hills and sage brush, the renowned Cariboo Trail, which outreached four hundred miles to the gold-fields of Barkerville. Up this trail we were to "coach" for twenty glorious days, behind a four-in-hand driven by "Cariboo Billy," the best whip in all British Columbia. He was ready and waiting for us, a tall, sun-tanned Westerner with a cowboy hat, fringed gauntlets and knotted scarlet handkerchief at his throat; and the outfit he had consisted of four splendid roadsters hitched to a light, double-seated canopied surrey.

The thermometer registered 104 degrees in the shade, and the arid hills of the dry belt pulsed under a blistering sun. We two climbed languidly into the back seat. Cariboo Billy and the luggage occupied the front. There was a swinging hiss of a long blacksnake whip, and we were away, with two thousand feet of trail to climb before we reached the timber line and

Pauline is pictured in the front seat, right. The ladies in the cart, and the gentleman on the porch are unidentified. This was presumably taken at some point during her 1904 adventure on British Columbia's Cariboo Trail.
(Archives of Ontario, Toronto, S899)

the delight of breathing mountain air.

Every twenty miles up the entire trail are road-houses of rare excellence, and at each one the British Columbia Express Company provided us with relays of animals. Here, too, we got meals at any and all hours, for as we arrived the first thing seen was the sallow face of the Chinese chef peering from the back door. He always took it for granted that we were starving and would immediately prepare substantials that would satisfy the most exacting appetite.

When we rested at night the beds were like a mother's arm to us, the linen cool and fresh, and oh! the mornings, when the day broke in that vast far railroadless country, where the horse is king and you have shaken yourself loose from exacting conventions and

forgotten how to spell the word *care* – those glorious mornings when before sun-up Cariboo Billy would wake us with "Hello, pals! Hit the trail in one hour, got to do seventy miles to-day!"

Then the scramble up to a breakfast of picked food from the ranches!-broilers, cream, fresh eggs, or perhaps a venison steak. To see four splendid roadsters at the door, impatient to get away, and Cariboo Billy waiting, idly twirling his cowboy hat in one hand, while he rolled a cigarette with the other; to tuck ourselves away in the surrey for a long day's swing into the Northland-to hear the hearty "Good-bye and good luck" from host and hostess; then to hit the trail at a spanking gait, to feel the plunge of the leaders, the tug of the wheelers, and to dash out into the early morning, *with no one to boss, no one to obey*, and to feel that we *owned* Cariboo Billy and the outfit, and to feel that in all the world not a human being could command our whims or say us nay. That was a holiday kings might envy but never hope to have.[36]

Pauline Dances with Handsome Dick
by Mrs. W. Garland Foster

That year (1904) there was a by-election in Lillooet, and Premier McBride and Attorney-General Wilson were stumping the country. By some chance they arrived at Lac La Hache, the very night of the Pauline Johnson concert. Seeing the crowd, they asked what was going on, and being told that the concert was booked for the evening, asked to be allowed to speak at the end of the programme. From 8 to 10 the concert delighted the audience, and then till midnight, the politicians held the audience. After that the ball opened and held sway till daybreak. Anyone who knew either Pauline or "Handsome Dick" will realize with what delight they entered that first set of dancers, and the merriest of the merry kept up with the fun. Beside a silvery lake stood the old barn, which did duty for the three programmes of the evening and a motley crowd was there collected-miners, ranchers, cowboys, half-breeds, Indians, dressed in motley costumes. The centre of the fun, the Premier of B.C. in an old tweed suit with a handkerchief instead of a collar, and Pauline in a beautiful brocaded silk gown she had brought back from London, a little crumpled by the trip, and occasionally

shedding a few oats owning to the artist having dressed for her part the night before in an oat bin![37]

I Laughed Like a Child
by E. Pauline Johnson

We had done 80 miles that day, but we felt no fatigue; indeed, I cannot recall feeling wearied or "carriage stiff" during that entire drive of 860 miles in the wonderful mountain air. I slept like a baby, laughed like a child and ate like a lumberjack. Two days later we galloped into historic Barkerville, the nucleus of the Cariboo gold fields. A little out-of-the-world town, it is 400 miles from the railroad, with its whole-souled people, 400 times more hospitable to wandering rest-seeking strangers because of it. We stayed three days and said good-bye with faltering voices and misty eyes; for it is unlikely that we shall ever see Barkerville again. A holiday like that comes to a person but once in a lifetime.[38]

Pauline is Angered by Slum Conditions in England
by Jean Stevinson

Pauline loved England, especially London, and visited many famous cathedrals, but could not reconcile conditions as she saw them. "There was one," she told me, "a magnificent edifice, which employed thirteen curates, and all they did was to go around to pink teas. At the very back door of this great cathedral were the most terrible slums in the world ... I was sitting up (one night) writing in the pension where we were staying, and about twelve o'clock I heard steps pass and a knock at a door down the hall. An Anglican clergyman was living there, and he went out at all hours to visit the sick and the dying, so I thought nothing of it when I heard two men pass out. I was still at my article at two o'clock when I heard a man stagger in and down the hall. The steps paused at my door and there was a weak knock. As my manager was not far off I was brave enough to open the door, but was horrified to see the clergyman standing there and shaking as though he had the palsy while his face was the color of ashes. 'Why, what's happened?' I asked, making him come in and sit down.

'Brandy!' he gasped, and I gave him a little in a glass and saw the color creep back into his face. He buried his head in his hands.

'Oh, Miss Johnson,' he groaned, 'I don't know what I've done. At twelve a man came to see if I would go and baptize a dying child, and when I arrived at the address it was a dreadful room in the heart of the slums. Men and women were lying in a drunken sleep all over the bare floor, but standing near the wall with a young child in his arms was a man who was sober.'

'This child will be dead in an hour,' he said with stricken face, 'and I want it baptized; but it's only fair to tell you that the young woman lying drunk at my feet is its mother, and I am both its father and its grandfather.'

'In presence of death there I had to decide. A soul was waiting, and I said I would do it. It was against all the teachings of my church-that helpless child-soul was supposed to be damned-but I baptized the babe and sent it with a prayer to a greater Judge than I.

Perhaps I've perjured my soul, but I had to do it.' "

Pauline knit her brow as she looked at me, "with slums like this in the heart of London they'll dare to send missionaries to our Indians in Canada."[39]

The Poet Meets the Critic
by Theodore Watts-Dunton

In 1906 I met her during one of her tours. How well I remember it!...It was in Steinway Hall, and the audience was enthusiastic. When, after the performance, my wife and I went into the room behind the stage to congratulate her, I was quite affected by the warm and affec-

London's Steinway Hall in the 1920s. Pauline and Walter gave a concert at this location in the summer of 1906. The building no longer exists.
(courtesy of Steinway & Sons, London, England)

tionate greeting that I got from her. With moist eyes she told her friends that she owed her literary success mainly to me.

And now what does the reader suppose that I had done to win all these signs of gratitude? I had simply alluded-briefly alluded-in the London Athenaeum some years before, to her genius and her work. Never surely was a reviewer so royally overpaid. Her allusion was to a certain article of mine on Canadian poetry which was written in 1889, and which she had read so assiduously that she might be said to know it by heart: she seemed to remember every word of it.[40]

The *London Daily Express* Benefits Greatly from Pauline's Power of Observation
by Walter McRaye

At a dinner party, before the guests had gone in to dinner, a quiet middle-aged man approached her and asked her if she was not Miss Johnson. On her answering yes, he asked her to write something for his paper. She inquired his name and he answered simply, "Pearson-I have some papers in London." He had more than thirty of them, as it was the late Sir Arthur Pearson, owner of the *London Daily Express*. Pauline wrote a series of articles for his paper. They were written from the standpoint of an Indian's impression of London, and were much commented on by correspondents. "A Pagan in St. Paul's" is a typical example.[41]

"A Pagan in St. Paul's: Iroquois Poetess' Impressions in London's Cathedral"
by E. Pauline Johnson, *London Daily Express*, August, 1906

...the prairie sounds are slipping away, and my ears catch other voices that rise above the ceaseless throb about me-voices that are clear, high, and calling;...They are the voices of St. Paul's, calling, calling me, St. Paul's where the paleface worships the Great Spirit, and through whose portals he hopes to reach the happy hunting grounds.

As I entered its doorways...the music brooded everywhere. It beat in my ears like the far-off cadences of the Sault Ste. Marie rapids, that rise and leap and throb-like a storm hurling through the fir forest-like the distant rising of an Indian war-song; it swept up those mighty archways until the grey dome above me faded, and in its place the stars came out to look down not on these paleface kneeling worshippers, but on a band of stalwart, sinewy, copper-colored devotees, my own people in my own land, who also assembled to do honor to the Manitou of all nations.

The deep-throated organ and the boys' voices were gone; I heard instead the melancholy incantations of our own pagan religionists. The beautiful dignity of our great sacrificial rites seemed to settle about me, to enwrap me in its garment of solemnity and primitive stateliness.

The atmosphere pulsed with the beat of the Indian drum, the eerie penetrations of the

A portrait of an older, subdued Pauline.
(from The Moccasin Maker *by Pauline Johnson)*

turtle rattle that set the time of the dancers' feet. Dance? It is not a dance, that marvellously slow, serpentine-like figure with the soft swish, swish of moccasined feet, and the faint jingling of elks'-teeth bracelets, keeping rhythm with every footfall. It is not a dance, but an invocation of motion. Why may we not worship with the graceful movements of our feet?

The paleface worships by moving his lips and tongue; the difference is but slight. The altar-lights of St. Paul's glowed for me no more. In their place flared the camp fires of the Onondaga "Long House," and the resinous scent of the burning pine drifted across the fetid London air. I saw the tall, copper-skinned fire-keeper of the Iroquois council enter, the circle of light flung fitfully against the black surrounding woods. I have seen their white bishops, but none so regal, so august as he. His garb of fringed buckskin and ermine was no more grotesque than the vestments worn by the white preachers in high places;...again the hollow pulsing of the Indian drum, the purring, flexible step of cushioned feet. I lift my head, which has been bowed on the chair before me. It is St. Paul's after all-and the clear boy-voices rise above the rich echoes of the organ.[42]

How The Poem "The Trail to Lilloet" Came to be Written, Version #1
by Blanche E. Holt Murison

The first time I ever heard Pauline Johnson recite her own verses was at a luncheon given in her honor by the local branch of the

Pauline in buckskin, with her red blanket. Older, but still the sweet singer of Mohawk songs.
(from Town Hall Tonight! *by Walter McRaye)*

Canadian Women's Press Club. She chose the poem titled "The Trail to Lillooet" and told us the circumstances under which it had been written. She told on her last trip to London she had one day been overwhelmed with home-sickness. Outside of her hotel window were fog and mist, and the crowded noisy thoroughfares of the great metropolis. Filled with unutterable longing for the spacious silences, the trail-threaded forests, the snowy shouldered mountains, and the swiftly flowing waters of her own beloved land, she sat down and wrote these lines.[43]

THE TRAIL TO LILLOOET

Sob of fall, and song of forest, come you here on haunting quest,
Calling through the seas and silence, from God's country of the west.
Where the mountain pass is narrow, and the torrent white and strong,
Down its rocky-throated cañon, sings its golden-throated song.

You are singing there together through the God-begotten nights,
And the leaning stars are listening above the distant heights
That lift like points of opal in the crescent coronet
About whose golden setting sweeps the trail to Lillooet.

Trail that winds and trail that wanders, like a cob-web hanging high,
Just a hazy thread outlining mid-way of the stream and sky,
Where the Fraser River cañon yawns its pathway to the sea,
But half the world has shouldered up between its song and me.

Here, the placid English August, and the sea-encircled miles,
There-God's copper-coloured sunshine beating through the lonely aisles
Where the waterfalls and forest voice for ever their duet,
And call across the cañon on the trail to Lillooet.[44]

Flint and Feather

How "The Trail to Lillooet" Came to be Written, Version #2
by Walter McRaye

"The Trail to Lillooet" was written between the acts of Somerset Maugham's play, *The Land of Promise* at the Haymarket in London. The atmosphere of the play was anything but Canadian, as intended, and I remarked on it and asked Pauline how she would like to be in British Columbia on the old trail again. The little poem practically wrote itself during the intermission.[45]

Pauline Encounters Madame Flanders...and Wins
by Walter McRaye

At Stanstead, close by Rock Island, was a school sponsored by the Methodist Church, and at that time was under the direction of the Reverend Dr. Flanders and his wife. Madame Flanders was something of a martinet and ruled her girls with an iron hand. We once gave a programme for them. We arrived late and were soundly berated by Mrs. Flanders. The stage was in a jumble and Pauline asked that it be arranged differently. Madame spoke sharply to her and ordered her to get into her costume. Pauline again politely asked that the stage be set as she desired. Madame spoke even more sharply, when Pauline, losing her patience, exclaimed: "See here my good woman, you may address your pupils in that tone but kindly adopt a different one when you speak to me. I'll dress when this stage is properly arranged and not until then, and do it quickly, else there will be no programme given here tonight." It was done as she desired! The girls of the school had amusement in their faces as they witnessed the discomfiture of their lady principal.[46]

Eva Johnson. (a.k.a. Evelyn)
(The William Ready Division of Archives and Research Collections, McMaster University Library, Hamilton, Canada)

Sunday, December 30th 1906
Bridgewater, Nova Scotia

Dear Ev, Even this won't be a long letter to you as this is my "work" day, writing, mending, shampooing, etc. We are here a day or so idle, having had three recitals in Holiday Week, a great thing. I have never had so many enjoyments in the holidays since I started this business. The night we arrived here, and had just got unpacked, I discovered that the hotel was on fire. I was all alone in my room on the 2nd flat, when suddenly my electric light went out. I waited a spell for it to come on, then went into the hall where an open fireplace was, a spare sitting room hall it is. The place was full of smoke and up the second stair I heard crackling wood. I went to the foot of the stair and looking up the second stair I saw the whole top story was ablaze. I rushed to the bannister and yelled down, "Fire. The hotel is on fire." Being Holiday Time there are very few in the hotel. But Walter was the first to dash up, before the Clerk rushed up. He pulled the alarm for the Hose Co. I stood while they made their way up and they came tearing down again saying they could not get into the upstairs rooms which were all aflame. I flew to pack up my Indian things and all our good London clothes. I told Walter I would pack his small things and he said he would help the men. You never saw such a mess. I packed 2 trunks (the third was not unpacked), 3 valises and cleaned every bit of our stuff up by which time the fire brigade had arrived, and the townsfolk in scores-The fire still raged and when the water supply came that was the ruination. We got our trunks down, but then water came in tons right through the two flats, pouring down the furnace pipes, soaking plaster off everything, flooding the halls, carpets, beds-everything. Eventually it was put under control. My room somehow escaped and I am in it now. But Walter's room is soaked plaster, bed and all. We slept in another house that night, but as a number of rooms were saved, we returned here yesterday morning. About 20 bedrooms, the front stair and the sitting room upstairs are all burnt or water soaked. They are now closed off and we are most comfortable. When I discovered the fire it was 7:30 in the evening. I was the only person in each of the upper flats at the time. Had I been out undoubtedly the entire house would have gone. Luck and good fortune again. We would have lost everything we possessed...Think of the ruination to us, my costume, our papers, etc. I am so grateful. I tell you that every sign of snow having disappeared, the weather being glorious, springlike, sunny, warm we betook ourselves to the woods this morning. Great pine woods, that border the town on all sides. I did wish you could have been with us. The bluebirds are chirping and I am enclosing a sprig of the green spruce we used to decorate the old Tuscarora Church with at Christmas and a bit of Norway Spruce, like those the Governor planted north of the lawn years ago and a sprig of regular old fashioned pine, like the tree on the brow of the hill, to the west...A week ago it was 12 degrees below zero and glorious sleighing. Today the crows are cawing and I cannot bear my coat buttoned. What a time you must have had with your lady who was ill, poor creature. When you write tell me if the man was at least decent enough to "settle" in hard cash...Did I tell you I was pretty thin? lost pounds since I returned from England, but feel well outside eternal lassitude.

With love your affectionate Sis, Paul[47]

In this photograph from Pauline's own collection, she is seated centre, flanked by Mrs. Carter (left), Walter McRaye's cousin, and an unnamed woman (right), during a visit in Boulder, Colorado, 1907. Pauline and Walter were in the area during their time on the Chautauqua circuit.
(The William Ready Division of Archives and Research Collections, McMaster University Library, Hamilton, Canada)

TO FLORETTA MARACLE
(Pauline's sister-in-law)

They both live side by side, among
The wooded banks of endless song
Where wild birds carol all day long.

The iris grows beneath the ledge
Of bank, all overgrown with sedge
That creeps along the river's edge.

My little girl, so like that flower,
Strong in her purity of power,
Fidelity her richest dower.

Her sister trim, the iris blue,
With blossoms clothed in Heaven's hue,
So like her life, so tried and true.

They both live where they daily meet
Temptations, through their lives so sweet,
An undercurrent 'round their feet.

The streams of love and truth to blend,
A sweetness Heaven alone can send
The iris, and my little friend.[48]

Pauline (standing right) posing at the hollow tree, in Stanley Park, Vancouver with her friend Mrs. Edwards, Mrs. Edward's children, and the sister of Mrs. Edwards. Walter McRaye is perched upper right. This photograph was probably taken in the summer of 1908, during the time Pauline was making her decision to retire from the concert circuit and retire to Vancouver, a move she made in mid-1909.
(The William Ready Division of Archives and Research Collections, McMaster University Library, Hamilton, Canada)

The following excerpt is from an article written by Pauline, and intended for publication by one of the periodicals that regularly carried her prose. Whether this article was published or not is unknown.

The Stings of Civilization
by E. Pauline Johnson

In her untaught and primitive state one hundred years ago there was no happier woman in all the world than the Red Indian mother who queened it over her forest home and reared her children in the principles, manners, morals and strengths that for centuries had been approved and enjoyed by the men and womenkind of her world-old race. In other articles published in this magazine I have emphasized the fact that the North American Indian woman, and especially the mother-woman is most honoured and revered by the younger people and the men of her blood, notwithstanding all that has been said and written to the contrary. That she carries the burdens as well as the babies, that she does the hoeing of corn, drawing of water and chopping of firewood, is no argument that she is a beast of

Pauline (by Raymond R. Skye of the Six Nations) "I am an Indian. My pen and my life I devote to the memory of my own people. Forget that I was Pauline Johnson, but remember always that I was Tekahionwake, the Mohawk that humbly aspired to be the saga singer of her people, the bard of the noblest folk the world has ever seen, the sad historian of her own heroic race."[50]

burden, she is reared by her own mother in the teaching that all this is woman's work, and she accepts it with the cheeriness that the American and English woman in the same walk or strata of life accepts the fact that her birthright of labour is to wash, scrub, split wood, carry coal and bear children while doing it. I have seen, from railway carriage windows, white women pitching hay and driving harvest machines right in the state of Ohio. In the Canadian North-West I have seen Russian women, flaxen haired, creamy skinned, hitched to a plough in bands, like horses while the lordly husband, father or relation drove them-a pitiful sight blotting the freedom of God's virgin prairies. And some of these Russian plough-women were mothers! No Indian man ever asked or permitted his womankind to do such toil. He is exempt from the vice that prevails amongst the lower order of white men in the old world cities, who from unbridled temper or mere brutality beat their wives if immediate submission is not given them. An Indian man strikes a woman only when the white man's intoxicants have stolen his self-respect and enfeebled or enraged his brain. Thus, we revert to the opening lines of this article-the happiness and content of the Indian mother in her primitive state. With the onward march of civilization, and its accompaniments of Christianity and education in the ways of the alien whites, all her standards must be changed, standards of childbearing and childrearing that have been upheld for centuries as the acme of excellence in training the coming race. Her entire code of existence must be shattered, and the one that civilization insists must be set up in its place destroys her ideals, berefts her of her mother's traditions and frequently taxes her threads of faith...Her position is one that is difficult to define. It matters not whether one agrees or disagrees with her ideas of virtues and honours and manhood. The fact remains that her position as a mother demands that she instruct her children in things that she does not believe in herself, in customs of which she does not approve, in walks of life which she regards as detrimental to their honour and manhood. That she ignores her own convictions, stifles her own beliefs, the better to fit her child to face the world wherein the times and conditions have called him, only proves her to be one of the wisest and most unselfish of that great army that rings the whole world round, the army of mother-women.[49]

RECLAIMED LANDS

The long, flat lands out reach, field after
field,
    Low-lying at the hem
Of snarling seas that beat against the
shield
    Of dykes that shelter them.

No more the landward-lifting waves will
drown
    These shores with storm and tide;
The guardian earth they cannot battle
down;
    The sea is shut outside.

I hear the voices of the days long gone
    Clamor and call to me
O love, the shelter of your arms alone
    Shuts out the wolfish sea![51]

TO THE USE
AND ENJOYMENT
OF PEOPLE OF ALL COLOURS
CREEDS AND CUSTOMS
FOR ALL TIME
I NAME THEE
STANLEY PARK

Legends of
Vancouver

Vancouver Days

1909-1913

After an extraordinary stage career, Pauline walked away from the stage to establish a home in Vancouver. In an interview with the *Vancouver World* in 1908, she said: "There is no place in Canada that has a warmer spot in my heart than Vancouver."[1] Vancouver felt warmly about her, for "there was a tradition that Pauline Johnson always brought good weather to Vancouver."[2]

In 1909 she rented a two-bedroom apartment at 1117 Howe Street. For someone who acknowledged herself to be "homeless" during her career, this flat in a modern four-plex must have seemed like a dream. After her retirement she unpacked her cherished family heirlooms and personal belongings collected throughout her years of travel.

While Pauline adjusted to her new, stationary life, Walter was adjusting to married life. He had wed Lucy Webling in August of 1909. After the honeymoon, the McRayes began to tour Canada with their own show. The stage was where Walter truly wanted to be.

Pauline and Chief Joe Capilano met and walked together often, while he related the legends of his people. Pauline was entranced by the legends and let her friend speak uninterrupted, as she stored details of the beautiful stories in her memory. She believed the legends would make good short stories, and she began to make notes which soon grew into romantic retellings of Chief Joe's Squamish legends.

Besides submitting her stories to such popular periodicals of the day as *The Boys' World* and *Mother's Magazine*, Pauline thought that the *Vancouver Province* newspaper might be interested in publishing her versions of Chief Joe's legends. In February of 1910 she visited the newspaper's offices and was introduced to Lionel Makovski who was in charge of the *Province's* magazine. Mr. Makovski was familiar with Pauline's work and encouraged her to submit legends for publication. Pauline received $7 for each legend submitted. Through their working relationship Lionel became a good friend to Pauline. She began to refer to him as "dearest of all men."

Lucy Webling (1877-1952) whom Pauline introduced to Walter McRaye during a visit to the Webling's home in London, England, in 1906. At the age of seven, Lucy made her stage debut as Little Lord Fauntleroy, and toured the British Isles. She wed Walter in 1909 and together they toured Canada with their own show. J. Walter McRaye (born Walter Jackson McCrea, 1876-1946). While touring with Pauline, Walter's specialty was the Habitant poetry by Dr. William Drummond. These photos were kindly supplied by Walter and Lucy's son, Reverend Louis McRaye of England.

the aid of Lionel, who would take dictation of the legends as Pauline recited them.

During this trying time Pauline reacquainted herself with a young woman whom she had met in 1903 during a tour of Ontario. Jean Thompson was teaching in Vancouver, and she and Pauline grew close as they spent more and more time together.

"I never tired of hearing reminiscences of her work, as she was made up of lights and shadows, laughter and tears, she made us laugh with her and cry when she cried,"[3] recounted Jean in one of a series of newspaper articles she wrote about Pauline in the 1930s.

When well enough, Pauline walked from her apartment to Stanley Park. If she was feeling tired she would hire an open carriage to drive her around the park, but would stop from time to time to walk along the park's paths. One eyewitness to these solitary walks was a woman named Ethel Wilson. Years later she wrote: "I was taken one night, when I was about ten years old, to the plain small Methodist chapel in Homer Street, in Vancouver, to hear Pauline Johnson speak. What did we hear? Did she sing, did she recite? I do not remember. But I recall a buxom glowing woman with an eagle's feather in her hair and I remember, too, at the end of the evening, being propelled forward to shake hands. I heard the words 'You may come and see me if you like,' kindly spoken. 'Oh thank you,' I said in terror, floun-

At the same time, Pauline made an appointment with Dr. Thomas Ransom Biggar Nelles who diagnosed cancer of the right breast. The diagnosis was a death sentence, and the doctor could do nothing for Pauline but supervise the pain. Pauline's life was draining away.

After receiving news about her own health, Pauline faced the loss of her friend Chief Joe. Suffering from tuberculosis, he died in his sleep in March of 1910 at the age of 60. Pauline attended his funeral in North Vancouver and placed lilies on the coffin of the friend she had known for just four short years.

Shooting pains in her right arm forced Pauline to put down her pen throughout the spring and summer of 1910. During August and September she managed to produce work with

dering in a turmoil of doorbells, princesses, poets, eagle's feathers, escape and inadequacy (what would we talk about?, I feared, already sitting stiffly in a room). On the way home the sardonic goblin, who inhabits and bedevils and preserves shy people of all ages, laughed derisively. This he did daily, and I did not, could not, ring the princess's doorbell. Many years later I saw her in a crowded street. She was much, much older, yet she had a sad beauty; she was ill, walking very slowly and lost in sombre thought. Memory rushed in and, stricken, I watched her as though I had done it."[4]

Another witness recalls seeing her "leaning over the guard-rail near Siwash Rock while the tide was out, always alone, stoic and curiously dignified, watching the gulls."[5] Pauline herself believed: "It's the only way to chase the gloom away. Get out, no matter what the weather."

In October of 1910, Lucy McRaye returned to Vancouver to await the birth of her first child. Pauline and Lucy were great company for one another. The child born to the McRayes at Christmastime had a heart defect, and died early in the new year.

As 1911 advanced so did Pauline's cancer, and with it her need for income. She decided to sell some of her heirlooms, as the money she was receiving for her work was not enough to cover living and medical expenses. The Musson Book Company had expressed interest in republishing *The White Wampum* as part of their Canadian Masterpiece series, but Pauline sensed that this would bring few royalty cheques, and she rejected the offer.

It was at this low point that some of Pauline's friends stepped in to make her last two years bearable. Friendship had always been of the utmost importance to Pauline and it was a group of friends who now saw to her every need. In a story she wrote for *The Boys' World*

about the silvercraft of the Mohawks she said: "Stronger than his hate, stronger than death itself, is the friendship of a Red Indian... Friendship is the power of heat, of light, of strength. Without the sun of friendship the Mohawk holds that the heart of mankind would be the bleached, colourless, bloodless thing that a plant is when grown in the dark."[6]

Isabel McLean, a writer whom Pauline had met at the offices of the *Vancouver Province*, knew of Pauline's precarious financial position and prevented her from selling her precious personal possessions. She had an idea which would raise funds for Pauline. In September of 1911, Isabel arranged a meeting with representatives of the Canadian Women's Press Club, Lionel and the writer Bernard McEvoy.

They founded the Pauline Johnson Trust Fund to provide for the needs of the beloved poet. Former prime minister Sir Charles Tupper and Mr. McEvoy co-chaired the fund, under the auspices of the Imperial Order of the Daughters of the Empire. The goal of the Trust Fund was to collect the legends that Pauline had written, publish them in a volume and sell them. The proceeds would go to the author.

The original title of the book was *Indian Legends of the Coast*. According to Eva Johnson, it was Pauline's wish that the volume be entitled *Legends of the Capilano*, but members of the Trust Fund believed that with the title *Legends of Vancouver* the book would enjoy better sales. The book went on the market for $1.50. As the Author's Foreword, Pauline wrote: "These legends (with two or three exceptions) were told to me personally by my honoured friend, the late Chief Joe Capilano of Vancouver, whom I had the privilege of first meeting in London in 1906, when he visited England and was received at Buckingham Palace by their Majesties King Edward VII and

Queen Alexandra. To the fact that I was able to greet Chief Capilano in the Chinook tongue, while we were both many thousands of miles from home, I owe the friendship and the confidence which he so freely gave me when I came to reside on the Pacific coast. These legends he told me from time to time just as the mood possessed him, and he frequently remarked that they had never been revealed to any other English-speaking person save myself."[7]

By late 1911 the first edition of 500 copies of *Legends of Vancouver* sold out. Despite this, by the end of the year Pauline's expenses again exceeded her income, and she faced Christmas and the new year with no financial resources.

This is assumed to be the last photograph taken of Pauline (the spring of 1912). She perches on the steps of her home with Lucy McRaye (right). Her arms rest in her lap, and her face shows the ravages of cancer. Shortly after this photograph was taken, Pauline's doctor and friends arranged to have her stay permanently at Bute Street Hospital where she could receive the care she required.
(Brant Historical Society #249)

Mrs. Hardy, a friend in Brantford, forwarded $500 to Pauline. In a letter to Mrs. Hardy, Pauline had spoken about the hardship she was experiencing. Mrs. Hardy was moved to mount a door-to-door campaign and collected $500 from Brantford friends. In response to the unexpected gift Pauline sent Mrs. Hardy a copy of *Legends of Vancouver* and on the flyleaf she inscribed: "You have remembered me, fought for me, worked for me, even while I have drifted far from the old life, the old 'towns-folk' and today I am a grateful woman because of that other extreme womanhood, and fellowship which you have shown towards me. Pauline"[8]

In February of 1912, Pauline's health took a turn for the worse. The cancerous infection had weakened her and she suffered from severe bronchial attacks. As spring came to the west coast she rallied. However, having a day nurse and a night nurse at her Howe Street apartment was draining her finances. Her friends and doctor urged her to enter hospital and in May of 1912 arrangements were made to admit her to Bute Street Hospital, a private institution near her Howe Street home. Pauline's second floor room was small but private. Eva sent her sister $10 a month which enabled Pauline to install a telephone near her bed.

Shortly after entering hospital Pauline received a letter from Allen. He had enclosed a clipping from a newspaper describing Pauline's condition.

"November 22, 1911: Pauline Johnson, song bird of the red men, will sing no more. Every lover of Canadian literature hears with profoundest regret, that acute heart trouble [sic], with which she has been afflicted for some time has at last forced Miss Johnson into retirement. Her physicians state that the renowned Indian poetess will never lift a pen again. The daughter of the Five Nations [sic] lies out in the city of Vancouver a chronic invalid. And the pity of her illness is that she is in want. Poets are never celebrated for world riches. Canadian poets are no exception. Miss Johnson is as widely read as most Canadian poets. But she possesses no fortune to withstand the inroads of doctors' and nurses' bills."[9]

Pauline reacted angrily to Allen's letter and enclosure. Her indignation was such that she used her painful arm to personally autograph as many copies of *Legends of Vancouver*, by then in a third printing, as possible.

In the summer of 1912, Walter returned to Vancouver from his most recent tour and undertook a letter-writing campaign to sell her book of legends across the country. "I found her surrounded by friends and in her brave and cheerful frame of mind. The constant care and freedom from financial worry had improved her health. But, if this was to continue, something more must be done in the way of funds. I knew that many of her friends across Canada would be glad of an opportunity of assisting in the work of making happy the closing days of this great Canadian...Hardly anyone in Canada to whom I appealed failed to own and possess the author's signed copy of the book. The letters accompanying the cheque of two dollars each were a revelation to the poet. All of these expressed the honour it gave the purchaser to show their appreciation of her great work for Canada."[10]

As the spasms in Pauline's arm continued, Dr. Nelles increased the injections of morphine to help her manage the pain. Nurses at Bute Street Hospital took her for a walk or a drive while Walter and other hospital personnel pinned $2 cheques from the morning's mail on her bed and around her room where she would come across them later.

All this time Pauline was surrounded by a family of friends, with Allen and Floretta remaining in Ontario and Eva in the eastern United States. Thinking that Pauline would appreciate the company of her sister, Walter wrote to Eva inviting her to Vancouver. Shortly thereafter Eva did come to be with Pauline. The sisters had not seen one another for some years.

Eva and Pauline's relationship had been strained at times in the past, and it was put to the test during Pauline's painful last days. Their lives had followed very different paths since their Chiefswood days. Eva could not understand Pauline's flamboyance, while Pauline could not understand Eva's reserve. Eva's presence at her sick bed made Pauline fear that her remains would be shipped east for interment, something Pauline made clear to Lionel and other friends that she did not wish.

Legends of Vancouver created a renewed demand for Pauline's poems, so the Trust Fund decided that a collection of her poems would be the next project. The planned edition was entitled *Flint and Feather*. Pauline and her friends carefully chose the poems to be included, and by mid-1912 Pauline was able to proofread and correct the manuscript. *The Mail and Empire* newspaper in Toronto trumpeted the publication of this book, which became a Canadian classic, telling its readers: "All Canadians will be interested in the announcement of a new edition of the poems of our one Canadian Indian poet, Miss E. Pauline Johnson, shortly to be published under the provisions of the Pauline Johnson Trust Fund of Vancouver, B.C. Sympathy will be felt not only on account of the literary interest in the event, but because of a deeper feeling arising out of the fact that this writer, so picturesque and well known a figure on the recital stage from one end of Canada to the other, is now suffering from a malady which may prove fatal and has left its victim powerless to cope with a financial situation which has not been bright for some years...Only a woman of tremendous powers of endurance could have borne up under the hardships necessarily encountered in travelling through North-Western Canada in pioneer days as Miss Johnson did; and shortly after settling down in Vancouver the exposure and hardship

Prince Arthur William Patrick Albert (1850-1916, third son of Queen Victoria). He was named the Governor General of Canada on October 13, 1911, and remained in the position until his death. This photograph was taken in 1915. He crossed paths with Pauline on three separate occasions: 1866, 1894, and again in 1912 when he came to her sickbed.

(National Archives of Canada, C1004)

she had endured began to tell upon her, and her health completely broke down."[11]

In September, 1912, Pauline received a visit from Canada's Governor-General. Prince Arthur, the Duke of Connaught, was in Vancouver to open the Connaught Tunnel. He took thirty minutes from his busy schedule to have a private visit with Pauline Johnson. The red blanket, on which he had stood so many years ago when he was made an honorary chief of the Six Nations, had been strategically placed on a chair in Pauline's hospital room in honour of his visit. Eva Johnson remembers: "His Royal Highness recognized at once the photograph of her grandfather, Chief John Smoke Johnson, and said that he vividly recalled the time he was inducted by him in office as a chief of the Six Nations. His Royal Highness further declared that he had never forgotten that ceremony of more than forty years ago, and always considered the Six Nations had paid him a great honour."[12] What else the poet and the prince discussed remains a private matter.

Pauline dedicated *Flint and Feather* to:
His Royal Highness
The Duke of Connaught
Who Is Head Chief Of The Six Nations
Indians
I Inscribe This Book By His Own
Gracious Permission

For the foreword for her book she wrote: "This collection of verse I have named *Flint and Feather* because of the association of ideas. Flint suggests the Red man's weapon of war; it is the arrow tip, the heart-quality of mine own people; let it therefore apply to those poems that touch upon Indian life and love. The lyrical verse herein is as a 'Skyward floating feather, Sailing on summer air.' And yet that feather may be the eagle plume that crests the head of a warrior chief; so both flint and feather bear the hall-mark of my Mohawk blood."[13]

As her death drew nearer Pauline discussed her funeral with close friends. She was adamant about two issues: she would not allow her remains to be taken east, and she wished to be cremated, as she had had a life-long horror of being buried alive.

The *Vancouver Province* quoted Pauline as saying: "Some people tell me I've got to be burnt anyway, whether they bury me in a cemetery lot or not. Well, they can burn my body in this world so as to make certain of it. As for my spirit, that will be between the Great Tyee and myself. If they would scatter my ashes within sight and sound of the sea, near some great tree in Stanley Park, I would ask for nothing more from them."[14]

Until 1888, Stanley Park had been a military reserve, afterward being opened as a city park and leased to Vancouver for that purpose by the federal government. There are two versions of how permission was granted for Pauline's ashes to be interred in the park.

Lionel Makovski, writing in 1961 in *The Province*, remembered that after the Governor-General's visit with the poet, His Excellency asked if there was anything he could do for Miss Johnson. "I told him she wanted to be buried in Stanley Park by Siwash Rock," said Lionel. "Directly I get back to Ottawa I'll see what can be done. Please keep me in touch with the whole matter and let me know if there is anything I can do."[15] Lionel records that shortly after the Duke's return to the capital the necessary authority was given to make Stanley Park Pauline's last resting place.

Walter tells a different story: "When she knew that the end was near, she expressed a wish that she might be cremated and buried in

Vancouver, if possible near her beloved Siwash Rock. A telegram was sent to her old friend, A. Harry O'Brien, who was then in Ottawa, saying that Pauline had expressed a wish to the above effect, and asking him to see the Minister of Militia, who at that time was Sir Sam Hughes. Mr. O'Brien recounts the interview as follows: 'I showed Sir Sam the telegram, and said I was aware that it was ordnance, that is to say, mili-

Pauline's beloved landmark Siwash Rock, Stanley Park, Vancouver, B.C.. Pauline relates the legend of Siwash Rock in her book *Legends of Vancouver*. She writes: "Amongst all the wonders, the natural beauties that encircle Vancouver, the marvels of mountains shaped into crouching lions and brooding beavers, the yawning canyons, the stupendous forest firs and cedars, Siwash Rock stands as distinct, as individual, as if dropped from another sphere."
(courtesy of Suzanne O'Halloran, Midland, Ontario)

tary property. Sir Sam replied, "You need not say anything more. If Pauline Johnson wants to be buried in Stanley Park, she will be, and I will give instructions accordingly." He immediately rang for his secretary and dictated a telegram to the Vancouver authorities."[16]

Pauline made preparations for her funeral, including how she wished to be attired. During a visit with Elizabeth Rogers, a close friend, Pauline showed her a locket which she wore around her neck. Before opening the locket, she explained to Mrs. Rogers that she wished its contents to remain a secret. When Pauline opened the locket Mrs. Rogers saw a photograph of a man. She did not ask the identity of the man, nor did Pauline offer that information. The locket was mentioned in Pauline's will, drawn up a mere nine days before her death: "When dead, I desire to be dressed in my grey cloth evening cloak, with my small gold shield-shaped locket (containing the photograph of a young boy) fastened round my neck by my small gold chain."[17] Her wishes were carried out. The identity of the person in the locket, described by Mrs. Rogers as "a man" and by Pauline as "a young boy," is a mystery.

Another of Pauline's friends, Isabel Ecclestone MacKay, recalled an exchange between the poet and another visitor: 'It has been a varied life,' someone said to her near the end.

'But a good life!' she responded. 'Good friends, plenty of work, and not too much thought for the morrow. My great trouble now is that I cannot work. There are so many things that I want to do, my brain is full of them, but I'll never write again.'

'What an interesting life you have had,' another friend said during Pauline's last days.

'It is because I have followed Elbert Hubbard's advice. Don't you remember he says that to enjoy life one must look at it from the inside out? I have always regarded my life as an extreme privilege.' Pauline said."[18]

In March of 1913, Pauline's last shred of strength faded away. On the morning of Friday, March 7, a nurse attended her while Eva rested in a nearby room. At 11:30 a.m. Pauline drew her final breath.

The weekend of March 8 and 9 was filled with preparations for the funeral, to be held on the afternoon of Monday, March 10 – Pauline's 52nd birthday. All funeral expenses were covered from the coffers of the Pauline Johnson Trust Fund.

Although Pauline had wanted a closed casket, she was laid out in an open casket in the reception room of Bute Street Hospital throughout the weekend. Thousands of people who wished to see her one last time passed by. She had loved flowers, but Pauline wished that no flowers be sent for her funeral. However, friends, relatives, and local and national organizations did not know how else to express their sadness at her passing. All weekend the hospital accepted floral expressions of grief from across the country.

Sculptor Charles Sergison Marega, one of Pauline's Vancouver friends and admirers, came to the hospital to cast her death mask, which he used as the model for a marble portrait.

At 1:30 p.m. on Monday, Pauline's casket left the hospital and passed crowds of people who filled the streets. Others followed the funeral cortege the three or four blocks from the hospital to Christ Church. The spectators included many Natives from west coast First Nations. The church was banked with wreaths from, among others, Prime Minister Robert Borden and his cabinet, the Royal Society of Canada, Sir Wilfrid and Lady Laurier, and literary organizations.

The funeral service was conducted by Pauline's friend, Reverend Cecil C. Owen. Pauline had wanted Chopin's Death March played, but the organ did not work that day. It

A photograph of the deathmask of Pauline, made by the Vancouver sculptor, Charles Sergison Marega, a friend and admirer of Pauline's.
(City of Vancouver Archives, ADD, MSS. 678 Vol. 1)

was as if, with the passing of this singer of poems, the organ could not be persuaded to provide music of its own. Pauline's favourite hymn, "Peace, Perfect Peace" was sung by the congregation, the 90th Psalm and I Corinthians XV was read, a sermon was delivered and the anthem "Crossing the Bar" was sung.

The next morning *The Sun* newspaper wrote up the funeral: "Flags flew at half mast all day and a half gloom seemed to settle over the business and residential sections of the city. It was as if the rush and noise of the city had been stayed in respect to this gifted Indian woman. Very impressive was the funeral procession out of the church. The choristers led the way followed by the pall bearers...bearing the remains of the

great poetess. Mayor Baxter, prominent citizens and representatives of public organizations followed with bowed heads. Then came Chief Mathias, of the North Vancouver Tribe, and other members of Miss Johnson's race who have loved and respected their sister-poetess as one of marvellous gifts and super-human power."[19]

Her remains were taken to the Mountain View crematorium. According to Isabel Ecclestone MacKay: "It has been a long day and a sad one-although the simple service was beautiful and not oppressive, and one can't be sorry to think of Pauline happy and free. She suffered much at the last, and was conscious up till ten minutes of the end. If ever anyone bore suffering bravely she did, and it is good to know that she will sleep to-night."[20]

A newspaper article from Ontario said that: "While Canadians were honoring Pauline Johnson in Vancouver, it is not generally known that at the same hour of the funeral service in Vancouver, Rev. Robert A. Ashton conducted a simple memorial service in His Majesty's Chapel of the Mohawks, near Brantford, Ontario, attended by grey uniformed pupils of the neighboring Mohawk Institute and interested white people."[21]

Three days later Mrs. Rogers and Lionel Makovski were summoned to the crematory to view the ashes before they were placed in a makeshift urn, as proper urns were unobtainable in Vancouver in 1913, and sealed. According to Lionel, writing in 1961 for *The Native Voice* magazine: "Pauline Johnson's ashes are contained in an urn sealed in a cement baby's coffin, together with a copy of *The Legends of Vancouver* and *Flint and Feather*...The late Mrs. Jonathan Rogers and I received the ashes in the funeral parlor of Center and Hanna and signed the copies of the books."[22]

The next day the ashes were laid in their

final resting place in Stanley Park. Reverend Owen read a brief service, and Walter recited Pauline's poem "The Happy Hunting Grounds" as earth fell to cover the small coffin. Mrs. Rogers, representing the Women's Canadian Club, and Mrs. Alleyne Davidson, of the Imperial Order of the Daughters of the Empire, placed flowers on the tomb.

Sometime during the next week the contents of Pauline's last will were read. In it she requested: "I particularly desire that neither my sister nor my brother wear black nor what is termed 'mourning' for me, as I have always disliked such display of personal feeling."[23]

This confused Eva, and she wrote: "She did not want her relatives to go into black for her. Before I knew of this request, I had put on mourning, as had our brother Allen in Toronto. Since Pauline was so well known, people would have thought it odd if I did not wear black, particularly as she bore me a slight feeling of resentment. Allen took off his mourning when he learned of her wish, but I did not."[24]

After the very public funeral, but a painful and lonely time for Eva, it was her task to go through the contents of her sister's apartment. As she was doing so, a former friend from Brantford, Mr. T.S.H. Shearman, came by the apartment on Howe Street and found Eva tidying her late sister's papers and belongings. According to Mr. Shearman, Eva had burned some of Pauline's personal correspondence. During this task, Eva came upon the original manuscript of Pauline's poignant poem *And He Said, 'Fight On'* (first published in 1910). Eva took the original manuscript east with her and negotiated terms of sale for the use of the poem. It does not appear in the first edition of *Flint and Feather*, but in later editions it is the volume's last poem. It speaks of Pauline's defiance in the face of certain, prolonged and painful death.

The resting place of Pauline, at the foot of

A simple boulder marked the spot where Pauline's ashes were buried. This boulder remained the only marker of her resting place between 1913 and 1922, when it was replaced with a monument.
(Brant Historical Society #496)

a birch tree at Ferguson Point in Stanley Park, Vancouver, was marked for nine years by a single, simple boulder. Only her name "Pauline" was carved into the surface of the stone. Following the funeral, members of the Women's Canadian Club considered the idea of putting a monument at the spot where Pauline's ashes lay, something they achieved only years later, in May

GOOD-BYE

Sounds of the seas grow fainter,
Sounds of the sands have sped;
    The sweep of gales,
    The far white sails,
    Are silent, spent and dead.
Sounds of the days of summer
Murmur and die away
    And distance hides
    The long, low tides,
    As night shuts out the day.[26]

E. Pauline Johnson
Tekahionwake
Flint and Feather

of 1922.

In her will of February, 1913, Pauline wrote: "I desire that no tombstone or monument be raised in my memory, as I prefer to be remembered in the hearts of my people and my public."[25]

I First Met Pauline Johnson When...

by Lionel Makovski

I first met Pauline Johnson when Walter C. Nichol, owner of *The Province* [newspaper], summoned me to his office and there introduced me to "Princess Tekahionwake, whom perhaps you know as Pauline Johnson of the theatrical trails all across Canada...Miss Johnson has a story you might like to use for *The Weekly*."

...[Miss Johnson said,] "If you can use this story I can follow it up with others, all of which constitute something of the spirit or history of my people of the coast. The Londoner like you looks out on what you call The Lions because the name brings memories of Trafalgar Square. To the natives of the coast they are known as The Two Sisters. I have written their story here. My friend Chief Joe Capilano is an untapped reservoir of such legends which should be preserved."

She handed me the manuscript and with "I am living on Howe St. The number is there...very pleased to have met you," she walked out.

To illustrate the story I enlisted the aid of a photographer friend named Edwards. Thus *The Legends of Vancouver* first saw light in the pages of *The Weekly Province*. With a practical consideration for Miss Johnson's circumstances and with a sympathetic understanding of a woman's pride, Miss Isabel McLean [a contributor to *The Weekly Province*] began sowing the seeds which led to the flowering of The Pauline Johnson Chapter of the Daughters of the Empire, which played the vital part in the closing chapter of the author's life. For *The Legends of Vancouver* were for Pauline Johnson the last phase...Over and over again during those times when her health was rapidly deteriorating, I sat with her over a cup of tea and she "translated" some of Chief Joe's legends for me to transcribe. Not long before she died she said to me: "The history of the past raises monuments to the faith in the future. I would like to leave something of my faith to Vancouver."[27]

Vancouver's Coal Harbour Renamed Lost Lagoon

by E. Pauline Johnson

For many minutes we stood, silently leaning on the western rail of the bridge as we watched the sunset across that beautiful little basin of water known as Coal Harbour. I have always resented that jarring, unattractive name, for years ago, when I first plied paddle across the gunwale of a light little canoe, and idled about its margin, I named the sheltered little cove the Lost Lagoon. This was just to please my own fancy, for, as that perfect summer month drifted on, the ever-restless tides left the harbour devoid of water at my favorite canoeing hour, and my pet idling place was lost for many days-hence my fancy to call it the

Lost Lagoon. But the Chief [Joe], Indian-like, immediately adopted the name, at least when he spoke of the place to me, and, as we watched the sun slip behind the rim of firs he expressed the wish that his dug-out were here instead of lying beached at the farther side of the park.[28]

When a Great Chief Dies
by Jean Stevinson

It was a cruel blow to her when [Chief Joe Capilano] died. She was mistress of ceremonies at the funeral rites, and stood all day at the bereaved home in North Vancouver. "I can't eat," she told me, "I just drink strong, black tea all day long. Frozen fish is piled up like cordwood outside, but I can't stand it. The Indians who come like it, of course."...

On his death his son Billy (Mathias) became chief. He was a young man and the burden to him was overpowering. "It was awful, Tommy," Pauline said to me after the funeral. "When everything was over the young chief turned and went away alone. At the edge of the hill I saw him drop to his knees and lift his hands to the sky. 'Oh, my father, my father!' he cried. Never have I seen anything so dramatic in my life." She shuddered. "It takes me back to my father's death-that was the last time the death cry was sent down the Grand River. It is sent only when a great chief dies."[29]

Tillicum - Friend
by Lionel Makovski

Standing with her at the graveside of her "tillicum" (Chinook for "friend") Chief Joe Capilano, I heard her murmur, "I'm coming; I'm coming: I hear dem angels calling...poor old Joe!" When I turned to her she added quietly, "It is one thing of which we are certain, isn't it?"[30]

    "AND HE SAID 'FIGHT ON'"
        (Tennyson)

Time, and its Ally, Dark Disarmament
Have compassed me about,
Have massed their armies, and on battle bent
My forces put to rout,
But though I fight alone, and fall, and die,
Talk terms of Peace?-Not I.

They war upon my fortress, and their guns,
Are shattering its walls,
My army plays the cowards' part and runs
Pierced by a thousand balls,
They call for my surrender, I reply
"Give quarter now? Not I."

They've shot my flag to ribbons, but in rents
It floats above the height.
Their ensign shall not crown my battlements
While I can stand and fight.
I fling defiance at them, as I cry
"Capitulate? Not I."[31]

E. Pauline Johnson
Flint and Feather

𝕀 + 𝕀 + 𝕀 + 𝕀 + 𝕀 + 𝕀 𝕀 + 𝕀 + 𝕀 + 𝕀 + 𝕀 + 𝕀

Down in a Black Pit

by Jean Stevinson

It seemed now [after Joe Capilano's funeral] as though Pauline were in a pit of Stygian blackness, and for weeks gloom pressed her down. She was quite ill for a while, but when she felt better she asked me to call on a friend with her. We took the Robson car and I sat next to the window while she sat near the aisle.

"I have tickets, John," I told her. After five o'clock we used white tickets, which were cheaper than the regular issue, and I gave her the two white tickets. She held them out fan-wise in her fingers as the conductor was coming down the aisle. Suddenly I wondered. I had a collection of tickets – Detroit, Toronto, Winnipeg, etc. – and I looked in my purse again. Two white Winnipeg tickets were gone. Turning to Pauline I was about to tell her, but one look at her face was too much. There she sat, bored unconcern on her face, and in her fingers the two Winnipeg tickets spread out like a fan. I turned to the window, convulsed with suppressed laughter; the conductor reached us, the white tickets went into the slot; the conductor passed on.

"Those were Winnipeg tickets," I said, turning to Pauline. She took one look at me. Never will I forget the rapture which dawned slowly on her face.

"Oh, Tommy," she breathed gratefully, "you've pulled me out, you've pulled me out." She laughed and laughed. "You've pulled me out," she repeated. "I've been down in a black pit for weeks, and nothing could pull me out, but you've pulled me out, Tommy." She chuckled all the way to Mrs. C's home.[32]

Pauline's Priorities

by Jean Stevinson

"Do you know what I would do, Tommy," Pauline asked me once, "if I had only two dollars in the world and knew it would be my last? I'd spend half on my body and half on my soul. With one I would buy a wacking good meal and with the other a dozen cut carnations. Then I could die happy looking at my lovely flowers."[33]

June 21, 1910

My dear Tommy,

It is the longest day of the year, and a gloomy, grey one. What has become of our June? We really have only the roses to let us know the month is here...The poem I had, but thanks for sending it. The right name is "The Cattle Country," not "The Foothill Country.' Evidently the man who copied it into his paper thought he could improve on my titles. Well, I have left behind me the heaviest week's work I have ever done in seven consecutive days. Every morning up at 7:15; breakfast and doing up the rooms and I at work at nine o'clock. In all I did 12,500 words, 9,500 for the Elgin people at $6.00 per M, if it is all accepted the 3,000 for the Province, bringing me in about ten dollars. So, if everything is accepted, as I am pretty confident it will be, I shall net over sixty dollars for my week's work. My eyes and shoulder played out toward Friday, but I'm at it again this week...Today, for a change, I cut out a skirt for myself. I really must get some clothes made, so when my arm plays out I attack the dressmaking problem...Will you be over this week? Try and come or I won't see you, I suppose, before you go east. I am fair sick of a pen and the very sight of ink, but I am satisfied with what I accomplished last week.

P.S. I see a Sapperton man got *The World* contest prize, $250.00. I think I shall try the next one. I don't suppose he needed the money, do you?[34]

Down To Her Last Quarter
by Jean Stevinson

Once when I dropped into her apartment Pauline was ill in bed and the gas-man was reading the meter in the kitchen. The range worked on one of those diabolical quarter-in-the-slot contrivances, and though the apartments were supposed to be heated they were so cold that Pauline tried to get warm by putting extra quarters in the range and leaving the oven and grill doors open. This morning the gas-man took thirteen dollars and seventy-five cents from the range. I had discovered that a new sharp-edged quarter would last

Period postcard showing Hasting Street in Vancouver, B.C.
(courtesy of Suzanne O'Halloran, Midland, Ontario)

three times as long as a thin, worn quarter, so the new coins I got hold of I always laid on the shelf by the kitchen door, and though we never mentioned them I knew they were used as they always disappeared, but how needed they were I discovered this morning.

"Have you a quarter, Tommy?" she asked.

"Yes, John," I replied.

"Will you give it to the gas-man and get back the black quarter?"

I did so and handed her the retrieved money, which was covered with a coat of shoe polish. "It's the last money my mother ever gave me," she explained, then turned her face into the pillow and heaved with terrible sobs.[35]

Habits Formed While Young Are Habits Performed Forever
by E. Pauline Johnson

After years of life before the public, years of homelessness, of living in hotels, and drifting from ocean to ocean many times, I am sometimes amazed to feel the potent influence of my mother's teaching, astonished to find the habits she formed in me *still* habits, although my life is as different from hers, my present as opposite in every detail from my childhood's past, as midnight from high noon.[36]

Pauline Demonstrates Her Biting Wit
by Jean Stevinson

Her vitality was astounding. At times I feared she would not last a month, and the next time I called she would be out shopping. She dearly loved a sparring match of wits. Once she was talking to an important gentleman. "Nova Scotia has no big men," she remarked. The gentleman bristled. He had come from Nova Scotia himself. "Well," he said, "I don't know about that. Nova Scotia's turned out some of the best men in Canada."

"That's it," Pauline flashed back, "she's turned them out."[37]

There Would Have Been More Poems, But...
by Jean Stevinson

Memory goes back to many a social hour in Miss Johnson's apartment in the west end of Vancouver, when we enjoyed delectable dinners prepared by her in her little kitchenette. She was more genuinely pleased with a delighted remark over a grilled steak, a perfectly roasted chicken or a beautifully assembled salad than she was over a compliment paid to a new poem. It may have been at her girlhood home on the reserve at Brantford that she learned the art of cookery, for she told me more than once of her trials with poems and beefsteak. "Many a poem I lost," she said pensively. "I would be working at it and my little mother would come to the door and knock and say: 'Pauly, will you fry the beefsteak for me, please?' I would answer: 'Yes, mother,' and the poem would be gone. But I'm glad," she would conclude, "that I never refused her."[38]

which it was explained, were the proceeds of the concert she had missed. Tears filled the poet's eyes, and for some minutes she was not able to voice her gratitude. Always afterwards she spoke of Miss Hanwell by a pet name of her own designing.[39]

Pauline Reluctantly Cancels an Appointment
by Mrs. W. Garland Foster

On the last occasion on which she tried to give a concert [after officially retiring], she was billed for a recital at Hammond on the Fraser River [June, 1911]. A few days before the date she reluctantly sent word that she would be unable to keep the appointment. Hearing of this, two girl farmers of that district, Miss Ethel Hanwell and Miss Nellie Van Fleet, the latter of whom was a Brantford girl, decided that whether their farm suffered or not, they must see that the concert went through and that Pauline should have the money that she so much needed. They personally undertook to canvass the district, secured enough local talent to make the evening a success, and then sold all the tickets. The result was that everyone was pleased, and on the following morning Miss Hanwell arrived in Vancouver, and sought out a friend to go with her to deliver Pauline's share of the receipts. When they were received by Pauline, Miss Hanwell handed her a box of strawberries, saying that they were the first of the season, and that better berries would be found underneath. When Pauline examined the better ones she found on the bottom a layer of gold pieces,

Pauline Pays Her Bills-With Flare
by Jean Stevinson

"Now, Tommy," she said one day, "I've got some money in from the estate-Chiefswood, you know-and I'm going to pay my bills. Listen and you'll have some fun. I'm going to phone each merchant that I owe that I want to settle my bill, but am not well enough to go out. I'll thank them for their courtesy in waiting so long, and ask them if they will be kind enough to send their collector around this week. They'll all say it doesn't matter at all, that any time will do, but-every one will be here inside of an hour."

The phoning began, the grocery first. "Why, certainly, Miss Johnson," was the reply. "There's no hurry at all, but we have a man passing your corner this morning and he'll drop in." The meat shop next. "Certainly, Miss Johnson, if you're sure it's quite convenient. Our man is starting out now and we'll run and catch him."

So it went, and Pauline, chuckling with delight, stepped down from the phone and went for her file of bills.[40]

Fame, and What It's Worth

by Jean Stevinson

At this time her *Legends of Vancouver* were being published in the *Province* and hosts of new friends were rising, but it was the old

---

LA CROSSE
(Acrostic.)

Crown Prince born of the forest courts-
A child of the stealthy Redskin Race,
Now you are throned as the King of
Sports-
Acclaimed as ruler, while yet the trace
Dark and savage of Indian blood,
Arrows its way with a tiger's grace-
Surging your veins with its headlong
flood.

Nature has made you a virile thing-
Agile and lithe, that no time can tame,
Tawny your sire, but your mothering
Indian and Paleface, both may claim,
Owing your birth to the wilds remote-
National game of the robust North,
A panther, wrapped in a racehorse
coat-
Live with its blood you are forging
forth.

Sinew of deer in your woven net,
Pulse of the ash in your curving frame,
Obeying the master-hand firm set
Renews the birth, you can not forget
That crowns you Canada's kingly fame.
    E. Pauline Johnson,
    Tekahionwake. May 30, 1911

---

friends she cherished. "Fame is nothing, Tommy," she told me one day. "Remember, it's not worth that!" snapping her fingers in front of me. But she could not stem fame, which was to roll and billow around her.[41]

(This is to certify that the Acrostic Poem entitled "La Crosse" I have written exclusively for Mr. Bror Florman for his lacrosse tour of 1912. I give to Mr. Florman the exclusive rights of the use of the poem.)[42]

Pauline Attends My Wedding

by Jean Stevinson

In August, 1911, she gathered herself together and came over to Christ Church to [my] wedding, and bravely inscribed her name as one of the witnesses. "I've lost you, Tommy," she said grimly several weeks later. "I know you think things are the same and that you'll be true to me, but in six months your husband will know everything I've ever said to you." She was peculiarly alone at this time, and my heart ached for her. Her book of *Legends* was not yet off the press, and she did not know that she was to rise on the crest of a wave of fame that would be with her to the last. She was still keeping house. She was a splendid housekeeper, and kept things polished up beautifully when she was well. If she were having a bad spell and I went in she would say "Don't look at the dust on the carpet, Tommy. I'm going to plant potatoes on the floor in the spring."[43]

October 5th, 1912
The Bute Street Hospital, Vancouver

My Dear Mrs. Campbell:
Three weeks ago last Tuesday you came to pay me a most delightful visit ... and from all the Prairie towns there drifts in an almost daily evidence of the work you are doing for me. Orders for books and cheques also; I feel it is going to be difficult to find words to thank you for your interest and energy on my behalf. But my good friend I have the old Indian appreciation of a kindness just as strong within my being as if there were not a drop of "white" blood in my veins, and what you are doing sinks deeply within my heart, and some way or other I feel you know how grateful I am, even if my words cannot well express it all. I am to lose my dear old comrade of many years, Walter McRaye and his wife on Monday, as they start for the East and what I am to do without them here appals me to think of. It has meant so much to me all this beautiful summer to have them. Walter has made by his own unaided efforts such a splendid sale of my books, that I have been relieved from all anxiety through the past summer and consequently am much stronger and able to get about and yet enjoy life a little, when the pain is not too severe, which my good and skilful Doctor seldom allows it to be. Mr. McRaye hopes to see you, I think, when he reaches Winnipeg. He is the best friend I ever had and I owe much to his splendid management. And to you dear Mrs. Campbell, my sincerest and most loyal regard and gratitude.

Faithfully yours,
E. Pauline Johnson[44]

TO WALTER McRAYE

This to the friend I love, who up life's trail
Rode side by side with me through gallant days
And who yet journeys near, that I may hail
Him as he passes through the old byways.

This to the friend who loves me, who would fain
Halt me from mounting for my lonely ride,
Who would rive vast possessions to detail
Me on the range this side The Great Divide.

But I shall pledge you in this stirring cup
Before I ride into the far sunset-
I shall not fail you at The Great Round Up
O! friend of mine, who never failed me yet.[45]

"What Women Are Doing"
clipping, unidentified Calgary newspaper

As an expression of appreciation of the works of the beloved Indian poetess, Pauline Johnson, the Woman's Canadian Club of Calgary has sent an order for twenty-four copies of her recent book *Legends of Vancouver*.

Nearly every one who has heard of Pauline Johnson knows that she is an invalid in stringent financial circumstances. The Canadian Club hopes to dispose of these beautiful autographed volumes before Christmas, and thereby cheer the Canadian poetess in her lonely and dependent condition. It will be remembered that Pauline Johnson charmed thousands of Canadians on her annual concert tours of Canada a few years ago. It will be remembered also that it was this volume, *Legends of Vancouver,* which was presented to the Duchess of Connaught by the Canadian Club of Vancouver. In the following appreciative, yet pathetic letter to the corresponding secretary of the Woman's Canadian Club of Calgary she expresses her heartfelt pleasure:

November 29, 1912

My Dear Madame: How good you have been to secure such a splendid order for my books! I beg to acknowledge your cheque for twenty-four dollars for my legends, and am happy that today I am well enough to write and thank you for it all myself. I have taken unto myself the privilege of inscribing a few of these books especially for Christmas, writing a little message to the kindly unknown friend who purchases them. Yours is the second Woman's Canadian Club to respond to an appeal to advance the sale of my books. Canadian Clubs, both of men or women, have not interested themselves at all, and I have sometimes felt very hurt that notwithstanding what I have tried to do in literature for our beloved Canada, it has met with so little response from Canadian Clubs. The Daughters of the Empire and the Press clubs have done so much more in "standing by" me when I most need it, so

you may well know how much I appreciate loyal Calgary in interesting itself so liberally in my behalf...I have always loved Calgary, and how it is loving and loyal to me, and I am very, very grateful. I cannot always write letters to the gracious friends who send these cheques, but today is a "well" day, and so I mail greetings to you. Faithfully yours,

E. Pauline Johnson,
Bute Street Hospital, Vancouver[46]

Pauline Sees the New Year In
by Evelyn Johnson, 1914

I could not but recall a year ago as I sat with Paul at the hospital and we watched the New Year in and heard the rejoicing whistles and din which rolled up to us from downtown. I remained with Paul until 12:30 and as I passed the window and she leaned out to call goodnight and "New Year!" to me, and I called back to her "New Year! New Year!" I thought at the time how she must feel-knowing that it would be her last "New Year."[47]

Pauline's Friendship a Privilege
by Blanche E. Holt Murison

I t was my privilege to call her friend, and perhaps because of this I may be able to leave with you a more intimate impression of her personality than you might get from merely reading her poems. The last time I saw Pauline Johnson was not so very long before she passed the last frontier of all and reached the happy hunting grounds whither so many she loved had wandered before her. The meeting place was a little white bedroom in the Bute Street Hospital, a little room that somehow seemed all too small to hold this earth-loving, gracious-hearted woman. The bars which suffering and disease had built about her, had sadly circumscribed the activities of her fine physical forces; but they could not limit the liberty of her nature-loving spirit. Always there was some magic way by which she could escape. She knew there was one more unblazed trail to tread, and she knew that the journey might not be long delayed. She had trodden unblazed trails before, why should she be afraid of one more adventure-the greatest of all? The gay raillery of the once vibrant voice, though thinned to a tired tone, was still rich with the warmth of friendship and cheery greetings. I have never forgotten that last meeting of mine with Pauline Johnson. I never shall.[48]

...The Love I Have for This Great Country of Mine...

by E. Pauline Johnson

When we are born into a world of sorrow everyone rejoices; but when we die and go to the happy hunting grounds everyone mourns. Well, I don't want even my best friends to mourn for me. If now and again the people of Canada read some line of my work, which brings home to them the love I have for this great country of mine, then they may remem-

ber me as having done my best to share with them something that the Great Tyee had given to me. After all, if an Indian knows how to hate he also knows how to love, and the love of country is something that every Indian draws from his mother's breast. Nowadays they don't teach the real meaning of love of country, and that means sacrifices. I wish that there was but one of my poems that could set fire to the hearts of men, and thrill them with the glory of their nationhood.[49]

Canada's Best Beloved Vagabond

editorial, *The Daily Province*, March 8, 1913

By the death of Pauline Johnson Canada loses a great daughter of the flag. The inspiration of her genius was all Canadian. All she wrote betrayed her love of the country which had passed from the rule of her fathers into the hands of aliens. She inherited from her ancestors a real love for the race that developed the country, and just as they had fought consistently, and maybe savagely, for the British, she, their daughter, was an enthusiastic Imperialist and carried all the Mohawk tradition of loyalty.

Her personality influenced all who knew her. Her affection for her friends was one of the finest traits in her character. If she once gave her hand in friendship nothing that occurred after could ever alter her feelings. She invariably found their good points and insisted that these outweighed all their failures. Through a great many of her works there runs a thread of savagery that betrayed her origin.

In spite of her English mother she was Indian to the core. The trail and the forest, the mountains and the rivers were her home. Four walls could never imprison her Great Spirit. And when once she had come to the Pacific Coast she brought to the land of her adoption all the passionate love of nature which had already shown itself in so many of her verses in the East.

Her *Legends of Vancouver* are a magnificent illustration of her understanding and her genius. Through them all there runs that instinct for poetry which has found expression in "The Song My Paddle Sings" and many others of her poems. And on the fragmentary anecdotes of the Indians of the coast she built a saga that will live long after the generation that knew her has followed her across the Great Divide.

The keynote of her whole disposition was a generous charity towards everything and everybody with whom she came in contact. There was no trouble too great for her to take, no detail too small for her to neglect, when it was a matter of giving happiness to others. She was one of those great souls who would starve themselves on the trail, work unwearyingly for her companions, cheer them ever onwards through good times and bad, and rejoice with them when the goal was achieved. She loved life with a passionate devotion that was almost pathetic in its intensity. In spite of all her travelling, her experiences, which were by no means easy, Pauline Johnson never lost the capacity for getting the best out of life. She was absolutely natural and simple in her love of happiness. She disliked artifice of any kind.

The seasons as they came and went were in themselves a constant source of pleasure to her. She loved the Pacific Coast with its ever-changing colours, the sea and the deeply gashed mountains. The wind in the great firs and the roaring of the mountain torrents were music in her ears.

Last spring she fought for her life, nerved by the hope that she would spend one more summer in Vancouver, and the glory of last fall never faded from her mind.

With the passing of the winter passes also the soul of Pauline Johnson to the happy hunting grounds, there to find eternal freedom untrammelled by mortality. To all who knew her she was the "best beloved vagabond." It was always fine weather and good going on the trail of life when Pauline Johnson blazed the way.[50]

Mourners Crowd Christ Church for the Funeral

clipping, Vancouver's *New-Advertiser*, March 11, 1913

Christ Church, where the funeral service was held, was crowded long before the time set for the service. The gathering was representative of all classes and organizations of Vancouver's population, and a pathetic setting to the immense gathering was the large crowd of silent Red Men, who lined Georgia Street and who stood immobile all through the service and until the funeral cortege had passed on the way to the cemetery. The Capilano tribe, made famous in Miss Johnson's later writings, was officially represented at the funeral by Chief Mathias, who in full regalia, followed directly behind the cortege.[51]

I + I + I + I + I + I

Tekahionwake's Ashes

clipping, *Vancouver Sun*, March 14, 1913

Where the twining roadway branches into two at Ferguson Point, in Stanley Park, Vancouver, and near the Siwash Rock of which she sang, the ashes of the late Pauline Johnson, Canada's Indian poetess, were laid to rest yesterday afternoon in the place of her own choosing. The burial was private, and only the late Miss Johnson's closest friends were invited to be present at the time of the interment, but people walking in the park gathered to the graveside, and there were some fifty mourners when the last rites were being conducted by the Rev. C.C. Owen of Christ Church.

It was a typical March day, with a calm but overcast sky, and not a breath stirring the tall trees when the urn containing the ashes, which was encased in a concrete vault, which had been brought from Centre & Hanna's parlors, was placed in the ground just beside a fallen forest giant from whose dead trunk there sprouted and overhung fresh fir branches, symbolic, as it were, of life from the dead. A granite boulder was rolled over the grave, the ground was strewed with fir branches, so dear to the poetess in life, and the wreathes of friends placed around; a canoe with daffodils on the boulder itself, and prominently at the sides a wreath of oak leaves and an Indian brooch of double hearts-the tribal badge of the Mohawk Indians, of which the poetess was Princess Tekahionwake.[52]

A photograph showing the funeral of Pauline Johnson on a sunny, but chilly, March 10, 1913. The cortege is seen passing along Georgia Street, about to cross Granville Street, on its way to Mountain View Cemetery.
(City of Vancouver Archives, P.1422. N.742)

The grave of Pauline Johnson in Stanley Park, surrounded by a rude railing. This photograph was taken before 1922. A larger monument was erected to the memory of Pauline in 1922, at this site, by the Women's Canadian Club of Vancouver.
(Brant Historical Society #1658)

CHAPTER   8

Gone, But Not Forgotten
1913-1997

August, 1913:	Announcement of the publication of *The Moccasin Maker* and *The Shagganappi*, both collections of Pauline's short stories.
November, 1913:	Souvenir publication of the poem "And He Said 'Fight On'" issued. This souvenir was sent to cities and towns in the fall of 1914 and sold to raise funds for the war effort.
1914:	Pauline's poem "A Toast" was set to music and sung at a Vancouver, B.C., pageant.
1915:	A machine gun, named for Pauline, was sent to the Allies overseas for combat in WWI.
1915:	The Brantford General Hospital named one of its wards the "Pauline Johnson Ward" and erected a brass plaque to commemorate the occasion.
March, 1917:	The Brant Historical Society unveiled a brass plaque in memory of Pauline at the Conservatory of Music in Brantford, Ontario.
1921:	Pauline Johnson Confectionery Manufacturing Inc. founded, beginning with a candy store on Robson Street, Vancouver, B.C.
1922:	First printing of a new edition of *Legends of Vancouver*, by McClelland and Stewart, Limited, illustrated by J. E. H. MacDonald.
1922:	A monument in memory of Pauline was unveiled at the site of her resting place in Stanley Park, Vancouver, B.C., by the Women's Canadian Club of Vancouver. A feature of the monument was water running into a shallow basin.

1923:   Pauline Johnson School in West Vancouver, B.C., opened.

1929:   Pauline's poem "Canadian Born" set to music by Harry Livens (of Mitchell, Ontario).

1931:   Mrs. W. Garland Foster wrote *The Mohawk Princess: Being Some Account of the Life of Tekahionwake (E. Pauline Johnson)*, published by Lions' Gate Publishing Company, Vancouver, B.C..

1936:   *Legends of Vancouver* in its sixth McClelland and Stewart edition.

1937:   16th edition of *Flint and Feather* published.

March, 1945:   Pauline's monument in Stanley Park, Vancouver, was vandalized and all the bronze was stripped.

1947:   Walter McRaye's book *Pauline Johnson and Her Friends* was published by The Ryerson Press of Toronto.

1953:   Chiefswood was declared of national historic significance by the Historic Sites and Monuments Board of Canada (Ottawa).

1954:   Pauline Johnson Collegiate Institute opened in Brantford, Ontario.

1956:   The Historic Sites and Monuments Board of Canada reaffirmed the 1953 designation of the Chiefswood site and encouraged the development of Chiefswood as "Canada's first distinctly genuine literary shrine."

July, 1958:   The Province of Ontario erected a historical plaque on the grounds of Chiefswood.

January, 1961:   Canada Post announced plans to issue a Pauline Johnson commemorative stamp.

March 10, 1961:   Marking the 100th anniversary of Pauline's birth, a ceremony was held at the site of Pauline's monument in Stanley Park, Vancouver, B.C.

March 10, 1961:   Ontario Premier Leslie Frost paid tribute to Pauline in the Ontario Legislature.

March 10, 1961:   Canada Post issued its commemorative stamp. She was the first Canadian author, the first Canadian Native, and the third woman (other than a member of the Commonwealth's Royal Family) to have appeared on a Canadian stamp. Vancouver Mayor A.T. Alsbury and Brantford Mayor Robert Beckett exchanged greetings to mark the issuance of the stamp.

March 11, 1961:   Pauline Johnson Week began at schools on the Six Nations Reserve, Ontario.

March 11, 1961:   A banquet was held at the Ohsweken Community Hall, Six Nations Reserve, in honour of Pauline. Gilbert Monture (a onetime Canadian delegate to the United Nations) was the guest speaker. Ethel Brant Monture read from Pauline's works.

March 17, 1961:   A special commemorative program was held at Pauline Johnson Collegiate and Vocational School, Brantford, Ontario.

April, 1961:   McClelland and Stewart Limited issued a new edition of *Legends of Vancouver* with a cover design by Bob Reid and illustrations by Ben Lim. The publisher noted that since 1911 the *Legends* had been printed in book form twelve times in four separate editions.

May, 1961:   An exhibition of paintings designed to illustrate Pauline's poems was sponsored by the Indian Art Club of Ohsweken, Six Nations Reserve, Ontario.

July, 1961:   A ceremony at Chiefswood.

July, 1961:   A special, 40-page Pauline Johnson Centenary Edition of *The Native Voice* magazine was published in Vancouver.

July 8, 1961:   Six Nations members visited Vancouver to honour Pauline. After visiting the monument in Stanley Park the delegation visited Vancouver newspapers to draw attention to the fact that the base of the monument was swampy, because no drainage had been provided for the running water at the monument.

August, 1961:   Pauline's life story was related in drama at the Six Nations annual outdoor pageant.

September, 1961:   An exhibition based on the life and work of Pauline was shown at the Ohsweken Agricultural Fair.

October, 1961:   At the three-day International Iroquois Conference of Scholars, held at McMaster University, Hamilton, Ontario, delegates heard an address entitled: *The Place of Pauline Johnson in Canadiana.*

1961:   A petition circulated in Vancouver to re-name Vancouver's Little Theatre after Pauline Johnson. The bid failed.

1962:   The water intake at the Pauline Johnson Monument in Stanley Park was permanently disconnected, because the city's works department decided that it would be too expensive to repair it without tearing up the pool. The pool had originally been constructed without a drain, so water reaching it overflowed, creating a swamp around the base.

June, 1963:   Chiefswood was opened to the public.

1965:   Marcus Van Steen's book, *Pauline Johnson, Her Life and Work*, was published by Musson Book Co., of Toronto.

1968:   Pauline Johnson (elementary) School opened in Hamilton, Ontario.

1969:   Pauline Johnson (elementary) School opened in Scarborough, Ontario.

1975:	Pauline Carey's play, *Pauline Johnson*, was first performed.

1981:	After the closure of Chiefswood, the Chiefswood Restoration Committee was formed to fundraise and make plans for the re-opening of Chiefswood. The committee was created by the elected band council of the Six Nations Reserve, Ontario.

1981:	As part of its *Winners Series*, CBC TV produced a half-hour dramatization of Pauline's life. It starred Fern Henry as Pauline, and James B. Douglas as Walter McRaye.

1981:	Work was done on the Pauline Johnson Monument in Stanley Park. The original pool was torn out, new plumbing (including a proper drain) was installed, and the pool rebuilt.

1981:	Betty Keller's book *Pauline: A Biography of Pauline Johnson* was published by Douglas & McIntyre of Vancouver and Toronto.

1983:	Pauline was designated a person of national historic significance through the Historic Sites and Monuments Board of Canada (Ottawa).

1984:	On the exterior walls of a downtown building, the City of Brantford hung a series of large portraits of famous people who figured in the history of Brant County. One portrait (and the only woman among the others) featured Pauline Johnson in her buckskin outfit.

May, 1986:	A trilingual (Mohawk, English, French) plaque commemorating the achievements of Pauline was erected at Chiefswood.

October, 1986:	CBC Radio aired Erika Ritter's radio play, *Pauline Johnson: The Concert She Never Gave*, for the first of three times (December, 1986, and October, 1987). Linda Sorensen was Pauline, Charmion King was Emily Johnson, Stephen Ouimette was Walter McRaye, Barbara Gordon was Eva Johnson.

1987:	*The Moccasin Maker* by Pauline was re-issued by the University of Arizona Press, with introduction, annotation and bibliography by A. LaVonne Brown Ruoff.

1988:	*The Lost Island and Other Stories* was published in Russia by Detskaya Literature Publishing House; the edition, with tens of thousands of copies printed, was a combination of material from Pauline's *Legends of Vancouver*, *The Shagganappi* and *Flint and Feather*, translated by scholar Alexandr Vaschenko of the Gorky Institute of World Literature, Moscow, Russia. The full edition sold out within a couple of years-mostly to young readers. A second printing was necessary.

1989:	Artist Raymond R. Skye created a charcoal pencil drawing of Pauline, incorporating a 1903 image of her in "broadcloth," as well as an 1893 image of her in "buckskin."
1990:	Thomas A. Kostaluk of London, Ontario designed one side of a commemorative medallion, featuring Pauline, for the Brantford Numismatic Society, celebrating the club's 30th anniversary.
1991:	Poet Joan Crate of Alberta wrote a book entitled *Pale as Real Ladies* celebrating Pauline. Published by Brick Books of Ilderton, Ontario.
1991:	Six Nations artisan Mrs. Eva Williams recreated Pauline's buckskin outfit.
1992:	Artist Shelley Niro co-produced and co-directed an award-winning short film entitled *It Starts With a Whisper*, which featured a character inspired by Pauline.
1992:	Chiefswood was recognized by the National Parks and Monument Board of Canada as a National Historic Site. The Board's minutes of June, 1992 stated: Chiefswood is of national, architectural and historic significance and should be commemorated by means of a plaque.
August, 1993:	The Pauline Johnson Delegation travelled to Moscow Russia at the invitation of the Gorky Institute of World Literature (Alexandr Vaschenko), and made two presentations about Pauline's life and work. Delegates: Sheila Johnston (London, Ontario, speaker); Raymond R. Skye (Brantford, Ontario, artist); Simon Johnston (London, producer); and Wilma Skye (Brantford, tour co-ordinator).
1993:	The Classical Cabaret company of Toronto produced *Tekahionwake*, a piece featuring Pauline's prose and poetry, read by Gary Farmer, as well as original compositions of music by Larysa Kuzmenko.
1993:	The Maenad Theatre company of Calgary, Alberta produced *A Recital: E. Pauline Johnson, Proud Patriot and Poet* by Betty Donaldson. Robin Melting Tallow played Pauline.
1994:	The Pauline Johnson Delegation toured British Columbia, giving presentations to chapters of the Association of Canadian Clubs in Vancouver, Victoria and New Westminster. An additional presentation was given in Ganges, on Salt Spring Island, and another was given to the entire student body of the Pauline Johnson School in West Vancouver.
1995:	Sculptor David Halliwell, of Salt Spring Island, British Columbia, travelled to Ontario and presented his bas-relief of Pauline Johnson to the Chiefswood Restoration Committee. The artwork is being held at Brantford's Woodland Cultural Centre until it can go to the Chiefswood Museum on Six Nations.

1995:   Paula Whitlow of the Six Nations was appointed curator of Chiefswood.

August 20, 1996:   The Pauline Johnson Digital Project team demonstrated the McMaster University's Pauline Johnson Archives Project. The project, conducted by McMaster University Library and Humanities Computing, digitized the archives of Pauline Johnson for Industry Canada's SchoolNet. The team worked to complete the web site and a CD-ROM. The material is available to students world-wide through SchoolNet.

August 27, 1996:   The Chiefswood Board of Trustees hosted a "Preview" of Chiefswood, in anticipation of the re-opening of Chiefswood in 1997.

August 27, 1997:   Chiefswood Museum opened to the public.

In these ways, and in others yet to be, Pauline Johnson is indeed, remembered "in the hearts" of her people and her public.

Selected Bibliography

Books

Abbott, Elizabeth, editor-in-chief. *Chronicle of Canada*. Co-ordinated by Jacques Legrand. Montreal, PQ: Chronicle Publications, 1990.

Anonymous. *Canadian Singers and Their Songs*. Toronto: William Briggs, 1902.

Atwood, Margaret, editor. *The New Oxford Book of Canadian Verse in English*. Toronto: Oxford University Press, 1982.

Berger, Thomas R. *A Long and Terrible Shadow: White Values, Native Rights in the Americas 1492-1992*. Vancouver/Toronto: Douglas & McIntyre, 1991.

Brown, Craig, Editor. *The Illustrated History of Canada*. Toronto: Lester Publishing Limited, 1987.

Butler, Rick. *Vanishing Canada*. Toronto/Vancouver: Clarke, Irwin & Company Limited, 1980.

Charlesworth, Hector. *Candid Chronicles: Leaves from the Note Book of a Canadian Journalist*. Toronto: The Macmillan Company of Canada Limited, 1925.

Council Fire: A Resource Guide. Brantford, ON: Woodland Cultural Centre, 1989.

Crate, Joan. *Pale as Real Ladies: Poems for Pauline Johnson*. Coldstream: Brick Books, 1989.

de Visser, John. *Grand River Reflections*. Erin, Ontario: Boston Mills Press, 1989.

Dodds, Gordon and Roger Hall. *A Picture History of Ontario*. Edmonton: Hurtig Publishers, 1978.

Durant, Vincent. War Horse of Cumberland: *The Life and Times of Sir Charles Tupper*. Hantsport, N.S.: Lancelot Press, 1985.

Ferguson, Ted. *Kit Coleman: Queen of Hearts*. Toronto: Doubleday Canada Limited, 1978.

Flexner, James Thomas. *The Mohawk Baronet: A Biography of Sir William Johnson*. New York: Harper, 1959.

Foster, Mrs. W. Garland. *The Mohawk Princess (Tekahion/wake), Life of E. Pauline Johnson.* Vancouver: Lions' Gate Publishing Co., 1931.

Fowler, Marian. *Redney: A Life of Sara Jeannette Duncan.* Markham, Ontario: Penguin Books Ltd., 1983.

Francis, Daniel. *The Imaginary Indian: The Image of the Indian in Canadian Culture.* Vancouver: Arsenal Pulp Press, 1992.

Fraser, Mary M. *Joseph Brant Thayendanegea.* The Joseph Brant Museum, 1969.

Fredrickson, N. Jaye. *The Covenant Chain: Indian Ceremonial and Trade Silver.* Ottawa: National Museum of Man, National Museums of Canada, 1980.

Garvin, John W., editor. *Canadian Poets.* Toronto: McClelland, Goodchild & Stewart, 1916.

Graymont, Barbara. *Indians of North America: The Iroquois.* New York/Philadelphia: Chelsea House Publishers, 1988.

Gwyn, Sandra. *The Private Capital: Ambition and Love in the Age of Macdonald and Laurier.* Toronto: McClelland & Stewart Limited, 1984.

Hagan, William T. Longhouse Diplomacy and Frontier Warfare. Albany, N.Y.: New York State Education Department, 1974.

Hale, Horatio E. *The Iroquois Book of Rites.* Philadelphia, D.G. Brinton Library of Aboriginal American Literature, Number II, 1883.

Hamilton, Milton W. *Sir William Johnson and the Indians of New York.* Albany, N.Y.: The University of the State of New York, 1975.

Hartley, Lucie. *Pauline Johnson, The Story of an American Indian.* Minneapolis: Dillon Press, 1978.

Henry, Thomas R. *Wilderness Messiah: The Story of Hiawatha and the Iroquois.* New York: Bonanza Books, 1955.

Hungry Wolf, Adolf. *Traditional Dress: Knowledge and Methods of Old-Time Clothing.* Summertown TN.: Book Publishing Company, 1990.

Indian Act. Ottawa, ON: Canadian Government Publishing Centre. Supply and Services Canada, 1989.

Johansen, Bruce E. *Forgotten Founders: How the American Indian Helped Shape Democracy.* Boston, MA: The Harvard Common Press, 1982.

Johnson, Emily Pauline – Tekahionwake. *The White Wampum.* London, England: John Lane, 1895.

Johnson, Emily Pauline – Tekahionwake. *Canadian Born.* Toronto: George N. Morang & Co., Limited, 1903

Johnson, Emily Pauline – Tekahionwake. *When George Was King, and Other Poems.* The Brockville Times, Brockville, Ontario, 1908.

Johnson, Emily Pauline – Tekahionwake. *Legends of Vancouver.* Vancouver: Privately Printed, 1911.

Johnson, Emily Pauline – Tekahionwake. *Flint and Feather.* Toronto: The Musson Book Company Limited, 1912.

Johnson, Emily Pauline – Tekahionwake. *The Moccasin Maker.* Toronto: William Briggs, 1913.

Johnson, Emily Pauline – Tekahionwake. *The Shagganappi.* Toronto: The Ryerson Press, 1913.

Johnson, Evelyn H.C. *The Martin Settlement.* New York, February 2, 1911.

Johnson, Evelyn H.C. *Grandfather and Father of E. Pauline Johnson.* Toronto: Archaeological Report, 1928.

Johnson, Evelyn H.C. *Chiefswood.* With assistance from Mrs. Dorothy Johnston and Martha McKeon. Manuscript, Archives of Ontario, Toronto, Ontario, 1936.

Johnson, Linda Wikene. *Showcase Animals.* Victoria/Toronto: Press Porcepic, 1986.

Keller, Betty. *Pauline: A Biography of Pauline Johnson.* Vancouver/Toronto: Douglas & McIntyre, 1981.

Lighthall, William Douw, editor. *Songs of the Great Dominion: Voices from the Forests and Waters, the Settlements and Cities of Canada.* London, England: Walter Scott, 1889.

Lochhead, Douglas, and Raymond Souster. *100 Poems of the Nineteenth Century.* Toronto: MacMillan of Canada, 1974.

Logan, Dr. H.D. *Highways of Canadian Literature.* Toronto: MacLelland & Stewart, 1924.

Lurie, Nancy Oestreich. *North American Indian Lives*. Milwaukee: Milwaukee Public Museum, 1985.

Lutz, Hartmut. *Contemporary Challenges: Conversations with Canadian Native Authors*. Saskatoon, SK: Fifth House Publisher, 1991.

MacEwan, Grant. *Eye Opener Bob*. Edmonton: Institute of Applied Art, 1957.

Maracle, Brian. *Back on the Rez, Finding the Way Home*. Toronto: Viking, 1996.

March, J.M., Editor-in-Chief. *The Canadian Encyclopedia*. Edmonton: Hurtig Publishers Ltd., 1985.

McClung, Nellie L. *The Stream Runs Fast*. Toronto: Thomas Allen Ltd., 1946.

McLellan, Catherine Mae. *Rambling Round Stanley Park*. Toronto, ON: The Ryerson Press, 1935.

McRaye, Walter. *Town Hall Tonight*. Toronto: The Ryerson Press, 1929.

McRaye, Walter. *Pauline Johnson and Her Friends*. Toronto: The Ryerson Press, 1947.

Miller, Muriel. Bliss Carman: *Quest and Revolt*. Newfoundland: Jesperson Press, 1985.

Myers, Jay. *Canadian Facts and Dates*. Toronto: Fitzhenry & Whiteside, 1986.

The Native Voice. "Special Pauline Johnson Centenary Edition," Vol. XV, No. 7. Vancouver: Native Voice Publishing Co., 1961.

Newman, Peter C. *Canada - 1892: Portrait of a Promised Land*. Toronto: Penguin Books Canada Limited, 1992.

Percival, W. P. *Leading Canadian Poets*. Toronto: The Ryerson Press, 1948.

Petrone, Penny. *Native Literature in Canada: From the Oral Tradition to the Present*. Toronto: Oxford University Press, 1990.

Reville, F. Douglas. *History of the County of Brant*. Brantford, 1920. Reprinted, Brantford, ON: The Hurley Printing Co. Ltd., 1967.

Robertson, Heather. *More Than A Rose: Prime Ministers, Wives and Other Women*. Toronto: McClelland-Bantam, Inc., 1991.

Rogers, Edward S., and Smith, Donald B. *Aboriginal Ontario, Historical Perspectives on the First Nations.* Toronto, ON: Dundurn Press, 1994.

Saddlemyer, Ann. *Early Stages: Theatre in Ontario 1800-1914.* Toronto: University of Toronto Press, 1990.

Sears & Russell, Consultants. "Chiefswood Museum Restoration Project Final Report." Toronto, January 1992.

Speck, Frank Gouldsmith. *The Iroquois.* Bloomfield Hills, MI: Cranbrook Institute of Science, 1945.

Stevenson, O.J. *A People's Best.* Toronto, ON: The Musson Book Co. Ltd., 1927.

Van Kirk, Sylvia. *Many Tender Ties: Women in Fur-Trade Society, 1670-1870.* University of Oklahoma Press, 1980.

Van Steen, Marcus. *Pauline Johnson and Her Life and Work.* Toronto: Musson Book Co., 1965.

Waldie, Jean. *Brant County: The Story of Its People,* Volume I (1984) and Volume II (1985). Brantford, ON: Brant Historical Publication.

Webling, Peggy. *Peggy: The Story of One Score Years and Ten.* London, England: Hutchinson and Co., 1924.

Wright, Ronald. *Stolen Continents: The "New World" Through Indian Eyes Since 1492.* New York, NY: Viking Penguin, 1992.

Articles

Brown Ruoff, A. LaVonne. "Justice for Indians and Women: The Protest Fiction of Alice Callahan and Pauline Johnson". *World Literature Today,* 66:2 (Spring, 1992).

Chalmers, John W. "Tekahionwake". *Alberta Historical Review,* Vol. 22:3. Calgary, AB.: Historical Society of Alberta, 1974.

De Jong, James. "Agenda Paper: Chiefswood, Six Nations Grand River Reserve, Ontario". Ottawa, ON: Historic Sites and Monuments Board of Canada, 1992.

Hale, Horatio E. "Chief G.H.M. Johnson, Onwanonsyshon: His Life and Work Among the Indians." *The Magazine of American History,* New York, February, 1885.

Ingram Kidd, Darlene. "Pauline Johnson Took Her Poems to Her People." *Western People*, Saskatoon, SK, October, 1982.

Lee, David. "Agenda Paper: Pauline Johnson (1861-1913)." Ottawa, ON: Historic Sites and Monuments Board of Canada, 1983.

Loosley, Elizabeth. "Pauline Johnson 1861-1913". in *The Clear Spirit: Twenty Canadian Women and Their Times*, Mary Quale Innis, ed., Toronto: University of Toronto Press, 1966.

Lyon, George W. "Pauline Johnson: A Reconsideration". *Studies in Canadian Literature*, Vol. 15:2, 1990.

MacKay, Isabel Ecclestone. "Pauline Johnson: A Memory and An Appreciation". British Columbia Archives, Victoria, B.C. ADD MSS 2367 File 10. No date.

McRaye, Walter. "East and West with Pauline Johnson." *The Canadian Magazine*, Toronto, 1923.

Scott, Jack. "The Passionate Princess". *Maclean's Magazine*, Toronto, April, 1952.

Shrive, Norman. "What Happened to Pauline?" *Canadian Literature*, The University of B.C., Vancouver, B.C., Number 13, 1962.

Stringer, Arthur. "Wild Poets I've Known - Pauline Johnson." *Saturday Night Magazine*, Toronto, ON, October 1941.

Waldie, Jean. "The Iroquois Poetess, Pauline Johnson." *Ontario Historical Society*, Volume XL, Toronto, 1948.

Endnotes:

Chapter 1

1. Isabel Ecclestone MacKay, "Pauline Johnson: A Memory and An Appreciation."

2. E. Pauline Johnson, "The Six Nations", *The Brantford Expositor*, Souvenir Number, Brantford, Ontario, 1895.

3. Evelyn H.C. Johnson, "The Martin Settlement."

4. Ibid.

5. Ibid.

6. Ibid.

7. E. Pauline Johnson, "My Mother," *The Moccasin Maker*.

8. F. Douglas Reville, *History of the County of Brant*.

9. E. Pauline Johnson, "My Mother," *The Moccasin Maker*.

10. Ibid.

11. Ibid.

12. Ibid.

13. Ibid.

14. Ibid.

15. Ibid.

16. Ibid.

17. Ibid.

18. Ibid.

Chapter 2.

1. E. Pauline Johnson, *Legends of Vancouver*.

2. F. Douglas Reville, *History of the County of Brant*.

3. E. Pauline Johnson, "My Mother," *The Moccasin Maker*.

4. Horatio Hale, "Chief G.H.M. Johnson, Onwanonsyshon: His Life and Work Among the Indians." *The Magazine of American History*.

5. Evelyn H.C. Johnson, "Chiefswood," Archives of Ontario.

6. Horatio Hale, "Chief G.H.M. Johnson, Onwanonsyshon: His Life and Work Among the Indians." *The Magazine of American History*.

7. Evelyn H.C. Johnson, "Chiefswood."

8. Ibid.

9. Horatio Hale, "Chief G.H.M. Johnson, Onwanonsyshon: His Life and Work Among the Indians." *The Magazine of American History*.

10. E. Pauline Johnson, "My Mother," *The Moccasin Maker*.

11. Clipping, The Hamilton Spectator, Ontario, February, 1878.

12. Horatio Hale, "Chief G.H.M. Johnson, Onwanonsyshon: His Life and Work Among the Indians." *The Magazine of American History*.

13. Evelyn H.C. Johnson, "Chiefswood."

14. Jean H. Waldie, "The Iroquois Poetess, Pauline Johnson" *Ontario History* Vol. XL.

15. Evelyn H.C. Johnson, "Chiefswood."
16. E. Pauline Johnson, "My Mother," *The Moccasin Maker*.
17. Hand-written document from the hand of either Eva Johnson or Pauline Johnson; University Archives, Trent University, Peterborough, Ontario.
18. E. Pauline Johnson, "A'bram", *The Brantford Expositor*, Ontario, Christmas Number, 1891.
19. Evelyn H.C. Johnson, "Chiefswood."
20. Ibid.
21. E. Pauline Johnson, "My Mother," *The Moccasin Maker*.
22. Evelyn H.C. Johnson, "Chiefswood."
23. E. Pauline Johnson, "The Story of the First Telephone," *The Boy's World*, October 22, 1910.
24. E. Pauline Johnson, "Forty-Five Miles on the Grand," *The Brantford Expositor*, December, 1892.
25. Jean H. Waldie, "The Iroquois Poetess, Pauline Johnson", *Ontario History* Vol. XL.
26. St. Marys Museum, St. Marys, Ontario.
27. Evelyn H.C. Johnson, "Chiefswood."
28. Ibid.
29. University Archives, Trent University, Peterborough, Ontario.
30. Evelyn H.C. Johnson, "Chiefswood."
31. E. Pauline Johnson, "From a Child's Viewpoint," Chapter 1. *Mother's Magazine*, Elgin, Illinois, May, 1910.
32. Ibid.
33. Marcus Van Steen, *Pauline Johnson and Her Life and Work*.
34. Mrs. W. Garland Foster, *The Mohawk Princess (Tekahion/wake) Life of E. Pauline Johnson*.
35. The William Ready Division of Archives and Research Collections, McMaster University Library, Hamilton, Canada.
36. Horatio Hale, "Chief G.H.M. Johnson, Onwanonsyshon: His Life and Work Among the Indians." *The Magazine of American History*.
37. Ibid.
38. E. Pauline Johnson, "My Mother," *The Moccasin Maker*.
39. William Douw Lighthall, *Songs of the Great Dominion: Voices from the Forests and Waters, the Settlements and Cities of Canada*.
40. Obsequies of Red Jacket at Buffalo, *Buffalo Historical Society*, Volume III October 9th, 1884.

Chapter 3.

1. Evelyn H.C. Johnson, "Chiefswood."
2. Trent University Archives, Peterborough, Ontario.
3. Clipping, *The Brantford Expositor*, August, 1886.
4. Clipping, *The Brantford Expositor*, 1886.
5. Marcus Van Steen, *Pauline Johnson and Her Life and Work*.
6. Clipping, *The Toronto Globe*, October, 1886.
7. Mrs. W. Garland Foster, *The Mohawk Princess (Tekahion/wake) Life of E. Pauline Johnson*.
8. Clipping, *The Brantford Expositor*, January, 1891.
9. Clipping, *The Brantford Expositor*, November, 1891.

10. Evelyn H.C. Johnson, "Chiefswood."

11. Mrs. W. Garland Foster *The Mohawk Princess (Tekahion/wake) Life of E. Pauline Johnson.*

12. Marcus Van Steen, *Pauline Johnson and Her Life and Work.*

13. Madge Robertson, "Prominent Canadian Women", clipping, The Institute of Iroquoian Studies.

14. Clipping, *The Week,* Vol. III November 18, 1886.

15. Jean H. Waldie, "The Iroquois Poetess, Pauline Johnson" *Ontario History* Vol. XL.

16. Johnson family papers, Woodland Cultural Centre, Brantford, Ontario.

17. Ibid.

18. Evelyn H.C. Johnson, "Chiefswood."

19. Johnson family papers, Woodland Cultural Centre, Brantford, Ontario.

20. Evelyn H.C. Johnson, "Chiefswood."

21. Johnson family papers, Woodland Cultural Centre, Brantford, Ontario.

22. Evelyn H.C. Johnson, "Chiefswood."

23. Johnson family papers, Woodland Cultural Centre, Brantford, Ontario.

24. Evelyn H.C. Johnson, "Chiefswood."

25. Johnson family papers, Woodland Cultural Centre, Brantford, Ontario.

26. Evelyn H.C. Johnson, "Chiefswood."

27. Johnson family papers, Woodland Cultural Centre, Brantford, Ontario.

28. Theodore Watts-Dunton, Introduction, *Flint and Feather* 3rd edition, by E. Pauline Johnson.

29. E. Pauline Johnson, *The White Wampum.*

30. The William Ready Division of Archives and Research Collections, McMaster University Library, Hamilton, Canada.

31. Peggy Webling, *Peggy: The Story of One Score Years and Ten.*

32. Trent University Archives, Peterborough, Ontario.

33. Jean H. Waldie, "The Iroquois Poetess, Pauline Johnson" *Ontario History* Vol. XL.

34. Mrs. W. Garland Foster, *The Mohawk Princess (Tekahion/wake) Life of E. Pauline Johnson.*

35. Clipping, *Kitchener-Waterloo Record,* Kitchener, Ontario, undated.

36. Johnson family papers, Woodland Cultural Centre, Brantford, Ontario.

37. Ibid.

Chapter 4.

1. Evelyn H.C. Johnson, "Chiefswood."

2. Walter McRaye, Town Hall Tonight!

3. Mrs. W. Garland Foster, *The Mohawk Princess (Tekahion/wake) Life of E. Pauline Johnson.*

4. *Statistical Year-Book of Canada,* 1892.

5. E. Pauline Johnson, "A Red Girl's Reasoning", *The Moccasin Maker.*

6. Unidentified newspaper clipping, August 16, 1893.

7. Hector Charlesworth, *Candid Chronicles: Leaves from the Note Book of a Canadian Journalist.*

8. E. Pauline Johnson, *The White Wampum.*

9. Clipping, unidentified Montreal newspaper, March 23, 1927.

10. E. Pauline Johnson, *The White Wampum.*

11. Clipping, unidentified Montreal newspaper, March 23, 1927.

12. Clipping, *20th Century Review*, New York, 189-.

13. E. Pauline Johnson, *The White Wampum.*

14. Clipping, unidentified Toronto newspaper, February 21, 1892.

15. E. Pauline Johnson, "Forty-Five Miles on the Grand," *The Brantford Expositor*, December, 1892.

16. E. Pauline Johnson, "A Strong Race Opinion on the Indian Girl in Modern Fiction," *The Dominion Illustrated Magazine*, February, 1893.

17. Trent University Archives, Peterborough, Ontario.

18. The collection of Marcus Van Steen, Brantford, Ontario; donated to the author.

19. *Canadian Courier*, December, 1913, Erin, Ontario; quoted in Mrs. W. Garland Foster, The Mohawk Princess (Tekaion/wake) Life of E. Pauline Johnson.

20. Trent University Archives, Peterborough, Ontario.

21. Evelyn H.C. Johnson, "Chiefswood."

22. Jean Stevinson, *Edmonton Journal*, 1933.

23. Clipping, *The Toronto Globe*, November 19, 1892.

24. Trent University Archives, Peterborough, Ontario.

25. Clipping, *The Boston Herald*, 1893.

26. Trent University Archives, Peterborough, Ontario.

27. Marcus Van Steen, *Pauline Johnson and Her Life and Work.*

28. Arthur Stringer, "Wild Poets I've Known-Pauline Johnson," *Saturday Night Magazine.*

29. Queen's University Archives, Kingston, Ontario.

30. Evelyn H.C. Johnson, "Chiefswood."

31. Clipping, *The Brantford Courier*, April 27, 1894.

32. Clipping, *Ottawa Daily Free Press*, June, 1894, reprinted from The Gazette, London, England.

33. McMaster University Monthly, 1904, Vol. XIV; as quoted in Mrs. W. Garland Foster, *The Mohawk Princess (Tekahion/wake) Life of E. Pauline Johnson.*

34. Walter McRaye, *Pauline Johnson and Her Friends.*

35. Clipping, *M.A.P. (Mostly About People)* (British Magazine), May, 1906.

36. Queens University Archives, Kingston, Ontario.

37. Ernest Thompson Seton, "Tekahionwake (Pauline Johnson)," unidentified source.

38. Unidentified newspaper clipping, The William Ready Division of Archives and Research Collections, McMaster University Library, Hamilton, Canada.

39. Queens University Archives, Kingston, Ontario.

40. The collection of Marcus Van Steen of Brantford, Ontario; donated to the author.

41. Unidentified clipping from Vancouver, B.C., The William Ready Division of Archives and Research Collections, McMaster University Library, Hamilton, Canada.

42. E. Pauline Johnson, *Canadian Born.*

43. Mrs. W. Garland Foster, *The Mohawk Princess (Tekahion/wake) Life of E. Pauline Johnson.*

44. The collection of Marcus Van Steen of Brantford, Ontario; donated to the author.

45. E. Pauline Johnson & Owen Smiley, "There and Back," *The Toronto Globe*, December 15, 1894.

46. Peggy Webling, *Peggy: The Story of One Score Years and Ten.*

47. Queen's University Archives, Kingston, Ontario.

48. Clipping, Year Book, Johnson family papers, Woodland Cultural Centre, Brantford, Ontario.

49. Unidentified clipping from England, The William Ready Division of Archives and Research Collections, McMaster University Library, Hamilton, Canada.

50. Clipping, *The Sketch*, July 24, 1895, England.

51. Horatio Hale, "The Critic," June 4, 1895; quoted in Mrs. W. Garland Foster, *The Mohawk Princess (Tekahion/wake) Life of E. Pauline Johnson*.

52. Mrs. W. Garland Foster, *The Mohawk Princess (Tekahion/wake) Life of E. Pauline Johnson*.

53. E. Pauline Johnson, "Trails of the Old Tillicums," *Daily Province Magazine*, Vancouver, B.C., December 31, 1910.

54. Hector Charlesworth, "Miss Pauline Johnson's Poems," *Canadian Magazine*, 1895.

55. Johnson family papers, Woodland Cultural Centre, Brantford, Ontario.

56. Clipping, *The Toronto Mail*, The William Ready Division of Archives and Research Collections, McMaster University Library, Hamilton, Canada.

57. Walter McRaye, *Pauline Johnson and Her Friends*.

58. Mrs. W. Garland Foster, *The Mohawk Princess (Tekahion/wake) Life of E. Pauline Johnson*.

59. Ibid.

60. Clipping, *The Express*, Terre Haute, Indiana, December 5, 1896.

61. Evelyn H.C. Johnson, "Chiefswood."

62. Evelyn H.C. Johnson, "Chiefswood."

63. E. Pauline Johnson, *The Mail and Empire*, June 4, 1896.

64. Clipping, *The Magnet Magazine*, January 6, 1897.

65. Saskatchewan Archives Board, Regina, Saskatchewan.

66. Clipping, Winnipeg Free Press, December, 1897.

Chapter 5.

1. Clipping, *The Brantford Expositor*, January 26, 1898.

2. Clipping, *The Brantford Courier*, January 27, 1898.

3. *Halifax Herald*, Nova Scotia, June 2, 1900.

4. The William Ready Division of Archives and Research Collections, McMaster University Library, Hamilton, Canada.

5. Isabel Eccelstone MacKay, "A Reminiscence," *Canadian Magazine*, July, 1913.

6. Gertrude O'Hara Papers, Public Archives of Canada, Ottawa, Ontario.

7. The William Ready Division of Archives and Research Collections, McMaster University Library, Hamilton, Ontario.

8. Clipping, *The Brantford Courier*, February 25, 1898.

9. Clipping, *The Brantford Courier*, July 30, 1898.

10. E. Pauline Johnson, quoted in Mrs. W. Garland Foster, *The Mohawk Princess (Tekahion/wake) Life of E. Pauline Johnson*.

11. Ibid.

12. Sifton Papers, Public Archives of Canada, Ottawa, Ontario.

13. Mrs. W. Garland Foster, *The Mohawk Princess (Tekahion/wake) Life of E. Pauline Johnson*.

14. Clipping, *M.A.P.* (*Mostly About People*) (British Magazine), May, 1906.

15. Public Archives of Canada, Ottawa, Ontario.

16. E. Pauline Johnson, "The Unfailing Lamp," *The Vancouver Province*, March 20, 1912.

17. Mrs. W. Garland Foster, *The Mohawk Princess (Tekahion/wake) Life of E. Pauline Johnson.*

Chapter 6.

1. *The Mail and Empire*, Toronto, May 30, 1902.

2. Walter McRaye, *Town Hall Tonight!*

3. Walter McRaye, *Pauline Johnson and Her Friends.*

4. E. Pauline Johnson, *Canadian Born.*

5. Walter McRaye, *Town Hall Tonight!*

6. Evelyn H.C. Johnson, "Chiefswood."

7. Walter McRaye, *Pauline Johnson and Her Friends.*

8. Evelyn H.C. Johnson, "Chiefswood."

9. Mrs. W. Garland Foster, *The Mohawk Princess (Tekahion/wake) Life of E. Pauline Johnson.*

10. E. Pauline Johnson, "When George Was King and Other Poems," *The Brockville Times*, Ontario, 1908.

11. The William Ready Division of Archives and Research Collections, McMaster University Library, Hamilton, Canada.

12. Walter McRaye, *Pauline Johnson and Her Friends.*

13. The William Ready Division of Archives and Research Collections, McMaster University Library, Hamilton, Canada.

14. *William Henry Drummond, Johnnie Courteau and Other Poems*, New York and London: G.P. Putman's Sons, 1907.

15. *The Telegram*, Winnipeg, Manitoba, June 6, 1902.

16. Walter McRaye, *Pauline Johnson and Her Friends.*

17. Huronia Museum, Midland, Ontario.

18. E. Pauline Johnson, "Among the Blackfoots: Interesting Results of Blockade on the C.P.R.," *The Toronto Globe*, August 2, 1902.

19. Walter McRaye, *Pauline Johnson and Her Friends.*

20. Walter McRaye, "Tragedy and Comedy in Pauline Johnson's Tours of BC," *The Vancouver Province*, B.C., 1927.

21. Walter McRaye, *Pauline Johnson and Her Friends.*

22. The William Ready Division of Archives and Research Collections, McMaster University Library, Hamilton, Ontario.

23. Isabel Ecclestone MacKay, "Pauline Johnson - A Memory and an Appreciation."

24. E. Pauline Johnson, "Above the Tullameen," *The Vancouver Province*, B.C., December 17, 1910.

25. E. Pauline Johnson, "Coaching on the Cariboo Trail," *Canadian Magazine*, February, 1914.

26. Harriet Irving Library, University of New Brunswick, Fredericton, N.B.

27. E. Pauline Johnson, "The Call of the Old Qu'Appelle Valley," *The Daily Province Magazine*, Vancouver, British Columbia, November 19, 1910.

28. "An Appreciation of Miss Pauline Johnson (By One Who Visited Qu'Appelle Lakes With Her)," unidentified clipping, The William Ready Division of Archives and Research Collections, McMaster University Library, Hamilton, Canada.

29. Brant Historical Society, Brant Count Museum, Brantford, Ontario.

30. Queen's University Archives, Kingston, Ontario.

31. The collection of Marcus Van Steen of Brantford, Ontario; donated to the author.

32. Walter McRaye, *Pauline Johnson and Her Friends.*

33. Ibid.

34. Ibid.

35. Mrs. W. Garland Foster, *The Mohawk Princess (Tekahion/wake) Life of E. Pauline Johnson.*

36. E. Pauline Johnson, "Coaching on the Cariboo Trail," *Canadian Magazine*, February, 1914.

37. Mrs. W. Garland Foster, *The Mohawk Princess (Tekahion/wake) Life of E. Pauline Johnson.*

38. E. Pauline Johnson, "Coaching on the Cariboo Trail," *Canadian Magazine*, February, 1914.

39. Jean Stevinson, *Edmonton Journal*, March 7, 1933.

40. Theodore Watts-Dunton, "Introduction," in E. Pauline Johnson, *Flint and Feather.*

41. Walter McRaye, *Pauline Johnson and Her Friends.*

42. E. Pauline Johnson, *London Express*, August 3, 1906.

43. Blanche E. Holt Murison, *The Native Voice*, The Native Voice Publishing Co. Ltd., Vancouver, July, 1961, Vol. XV, No. 7.

44. E. Pauline Johnson, *Flint and Feather.*

45. Walter McRaye, *Town Hall Tonight!*

46. Walter McRaye, *Pauline Johnson and Her Friends.*

47. Trent University, Peterborough, Ontario.

48. Marcus Van Steen, *Pauline Johnson and Her Life and Work.*

49. City of Vancouver Museum, Vancouver, B.C.

50. E. Pauline Johnson, *The Shaggganappi*, Introduction by Ernest Thompson Seton.

51. Harriet Irving Library, University of New Brunswick, Fredericton, N.B.

Chapter 7.

1. Clipping, *Vancouver World*, June, 1908.

2. Mrs. W. Garland Foster, *The Mohawk Princess (Tekahion/wake) Life of E. Pauline Johnson.*

3. Jean Stevinson, *Edmonton Journal*, March, 1933.

4. Ethel Wilson, clipping, The William Ready Division of Archives and Research Collections, McMaster University Library, Hamilton, Canada.

5. Jack Scott, "The Passionate Princess," *Maclean's Magazine*, April 1, 1952.

6. E. Pauline Johnson, "Silvercraft of the Mohawks," *The Boy's World*, May, 1910.

7. E. Pauline Johnson, *Legends of Vancouver.*

8. Jean Waldie, "The Iroquois Poetess, Pauline Johnson," *Ontario History* Vol. XL.

9. Clipping, *Jarvis Record*, Jarvis, Ontario, November 22, 1911.

10. Walter McRaye, *Pauline Johnson and Her Friends.*

11. Clipping, *The Mail and Empire*, Toronto, 1912.

12. Evelyn H.C. Johnson, "Chiefswood."

13. E. Pauline Johnson, *Flint and Feather.*

14. *Vancouver Province*, March 7, 1913; quoted in Mrs. W. Garland Foster, *The Mohawk Princess (Tekahion/wake) Life of E. Pauline Johnson.*

15. *Vancouver Province*, B.C., 1961.

16. Walter McRaye, *Pauline Johnson and Her Friends.*

17. *The Native Voice*, The Native Voice Publishing Co. Ltd., Vancouver, B.C., July, 1961.

18. Clipping, unidentified Vancouver newspaper.

19. *The Sun*, Vancouver, B.C., March 11, 1913.

20. Isabel Ecclestone MacKay, clipping, Vancouver, B.C.

21. Walter McRaye, *Pauline Johnson and Her Friends.*

22. L. Makovski, *The Native Voice*, The Native Voice Publishing Co. Ltd., Vancouver, B.C., July, 1961.

23. Ibid.

24. Evelyn H.C. Johnson, "Chiefswood."

25. *The Native Voice*, The Native Voice Publishing Co. Ltd., Vancouver, B.C., July, 1961.

26. E. Pauline Johnson, *Canadian Born.*

27. Lionel W. Makovski, *Vancouver Province*, B.C., March 10, 1961.

28. Mrs. W. Garland Foster, *The Mohawk Princess (Tekahion/wake) Life of E. Pauline Johnson.*

29. Jean Stevinson, *Calgary Herald*, 1930s clipping.

30. Lionel Makovski, *Vancouver Province*, B.C., 1961.

31. E. Pauline Johnson, Souvenir Programme, (Toronto: Musson Company, 1913).

32. Jean Stevinson, *Calgary Herald*, 1931.

33. Jean Stevinson, *Calgary Herald*, 1932.

34. Jean Stevinson, *The Edmonton Journal*, March 7, 1933.

35. Jean Stevinson, *Calgary Herald*, 1931.

36. E. Pauline Johnson, "From the Child's Viewpoint," Chapter One, *Mother's Magazine*, Elgin, Illinois, May, 1910.

37. Jean Stevinson, *Calgary Herald*, 1931.

38. Jean Stevinson, clipping, *Lethbridge Herald*, Alberta, March 21, 1931.

39. Mrs. W. Garland Foster, *The Mohawk Princess (Tekahion/wake) Life of E. Pauline Johnson.*

40. Jean Stevinson, *Calgary Herald*, 1931.

41. Jean Stevinson, *Calgary Herald*, 1932.

42. E. Pauline Johnson, The William Ready Division of Archives and Research Collections, McMaster University, Hamilton, Canada.

43. Jean Stevinson, *Calgary Herald*, 1931.

44. The William Ready Division of Archives and Research Collections, McMaster University Library, Hamilton, Canada.

45. Walter McRaye, *Town Hall Tonight!*

46. Clipping, late 1912, The William Ready Division of Archives and Research Collections, McMaster University Library, Hamilton, Canada.

47. Evelyn H.C. Johnson, Trent University, Peterborough, Ontario.

48. *The Native Voice*, The Native Voice Publishing Company, Vancouver, B.C., July, 1961.

49. Clipping, *The Daily Province*, Vancouver, B.C., March 8, 1913.

50. Editorial, *The Daily Province*, March 8, 1913, quoted in Walter McRaye, *Pauline Johnson and Her Friends.*

51. *New-Advertiser*, Vancouver, B.C., March 11, 1913.

52. Clipping, *Vancouver Sun*, March 14, 1913.

Index

About the Author
Sheila Johnston

Sheila M.F. Johnston grew up in Stratford, Ontario. While at high school she worked in the Stratford Festival Theatre and developed a deep interest in theatre. As a graduate of the English Department of the University of Western Ontario (London), she found work in the communications departments of theatres in Ontario, Saskatchewan and England. In 1988, when she realized that Mohawk poet/performer E. Pauline Johnson-Tekahionwake's theatrical accomplishments had been largely overlooked, Sheila set out to learn all she could about this extraordinary Canadian woman. Sheila's journey of discovery took her across the country and to England, researching the intrepid life of Pauline Johnson. Along the way Sheila and Raymond R. Skye gave many presentations about the life of Pauline Johnson to audiences in Ontario, Alberta, British Columbia and Moscow, Russia.

The odyssey that began in 1988 has culminated in this book, the first illustrated biography celebrating a true pioneer of Canadian theatre. Her next book will explore a theme in Canadian theatre history. Sheila Johnston lives in London with her husband, playwright Simon Johnston.

About the Illustrator
Raymond Skye
Six Nations Artist

A Tuscarora Indian and resident of the Six Nations Reserve in Southern Ontario, Raymond Skye has worked diligently to distinguish himself as an artist of talent and ability. Self-taught and self-disciplined, he has chosen the drawing media techniques with which to express his fascination for the real image. His appreciation of wildlife, portraiture, architecture and still life has given him a tremendous range of imagery. He juxtaposes and blends reality and illusion to present views of his passion and romance for history. Much of Raymond's earlier works are reminiscent of the very disciplined developmental period in which he limited himself to pencil and charcoal to conquer line and tone.

Using pastel and watercolour, Raymond enjoys the challenges that art brings him. He readily admits his largest challenge is to find the time to paint as much as he would like to.

David M. General
Artist/sculptor and
friend of the illustrator

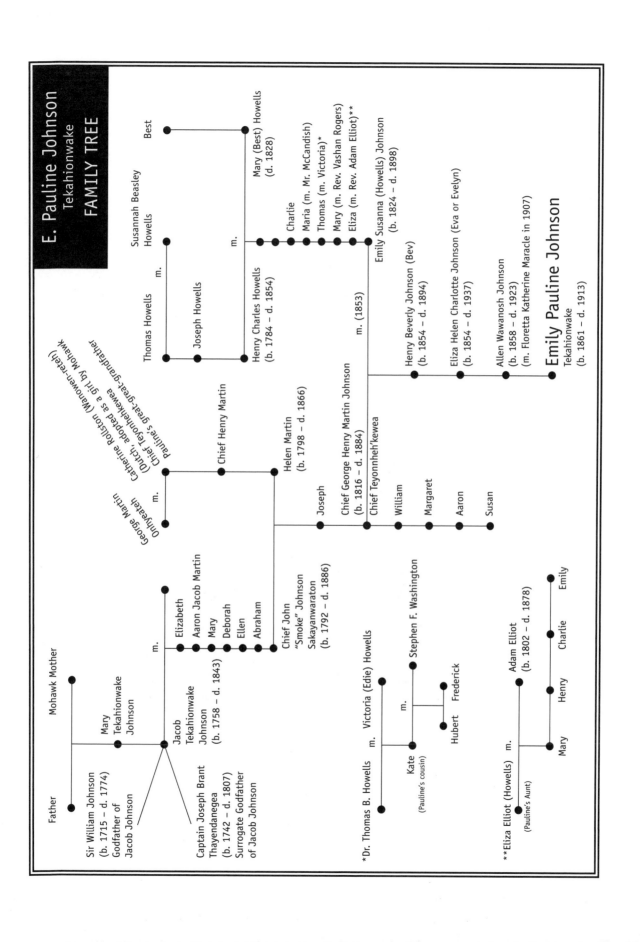

E. Pauline Johnson
Tekahionwake
FAMILY TREE